Adulthood, Morality, and the Fully Human

Adulthood, Morality, and the Fully Human

A Mosaic of Peace

John J. Shea

LEXINGTON BOOKS
Lanham • Boulder • New York • London

Published by Lexington Books
An imprint of The Rowman & Littlefield Publishing Group, Inc.
4501 Forbes Boulevard, Suite 200, Lanham, Maryland 20706
www.rowman.com

Unit A, Whitacre Mews, 26-34 Stannary Street, London SE11 4AB, United Kingdom

British Library Cataloguing in Publication Information Available

Library of Congress Cataloging-in-Publication Data

Names: Shea, John J., 1940- author.
Title: Adulthood, morality, and the fully human : a mosaic of peace / John J. Shea.
Description: Lanham : Lexington Books, 2018. | Includes bibliographical references and index.
Identifiers: LCCN 2018009894 (print) | LCCN 2018013930 (ebook) | ISBN 9781498574778 (Electronic) | ISBN 9781498574761 (cloth : alk. paper)
Subjects: LCSH: Philosophical anthropology. | Theological anthropology. | Self-actualization (Psychology) | Conduct of life.
Classification: LCC BD450 (ebook) | LCC BD450 .S43545 2018 (print) | DDC 128--dc23
LC record available at https://lccn.loc.gov/2018009894

∞ ™ The paper used in this publication meets the minimum requirements of American National Standard for Information Sciences Permanence of Paper for Printed Library Materials, ANSI/NISO Z39.48-1992.

Printed in the United States of America

Contents

Acknowledgments vii

Introduction ix

Part I 1

1 Integrity and Mutuality: Structure of the Fully Human 3

2 The Six Characteristics: The Fully Human as Mosaic 35

3 Care and Justice: The Fully Human in Action 75

4 Violence and Peace: Dialectic of the Fully Human 107

Part II 143

5 Education and the Fully Human 145

6 Psychotherapy and the Fully Human 185

7 Spirituality and the Fully Human 219

Conclusion 251

Appendix 255

Bibliography 261

Index 283

About the Author 295

Acknowledgments

I am very grateful to all who helped me in various ways with this book, especially:

—for guidance and support along the way: Tony Antin, Catherine Bernard, Michael De Gregorio, Tom Groome, Jim McCartney, Neil McGettigan, Therese Ratliff, John Schwab, and Jim Shea;

—for reading and feedback on different parts of the book: Maryanne Confoy, John Falcone, Rich Gula, Chris Kowalcky, Christa Morse, Beverly Musgrave, and Jerry and Ruth Starratt.

Introduction

THE HUMAN NEEDING ATTENTION

In a time when civility is less and less the norm, when differences in gender, race, ethnicity, world view, and belief turn oppositional, when rigid ideologies make dialogue impossible, when terrorism is a brutal fact of life, when the politics of "us" versus "them" is normalized, when authoritarian regimes deny the rights and freedoms of their citizens, and when violence is often the first response to conflict, we need a paradigm of the fully human if we are going to survive. The present understanding of the human in the globalized world—relying so heavily on autonomy, disembodied rationality, and the belief that there is a subject-object dichotomy framing reality—is incomplete, immature, and inadequate. Although advancing the culture in any number of exceptional and lifesaving ways—especially in the sciences and technologies—this present understanding cannot speak to relationality.

A paradigm of the fully human ought to include empathy and connection. It ought to prize relatedness as well as individuality. It ought to honor care as well as justice. It ought to respect the body as well as the mind. And without question, it ought to take violence and peace seriously into account. If violence describes the human in its negation of development, can peace—an "at-oneness" within and without—not describe the human in its developmental fullness? Is peace not only the missing hallmark of the fully human but actually the one thing necessary to bring us and the culture safely into the future?

Traditionally, full humanness is thought to be described in terms of being an adult or of being a moral person. We might ask then: "Do the notions of being adult and being moral give us some idea of the fully human and is there a structure, or a process, or an active way of being that both notions have in common?" Unfortunately, it can be hard to find good definitions of either adulthood or morality—aside from the fact that there is one notion they both share: being a responsible person. Otherwise, their cultural meanings are so varied as to be lost in vagueness and so impoverished that any human fullness they might point to remains hard to see.

Talking about adulthood is problematic because there is something judgmental in even considering it. Moreover, there is no forum for discussing what the criteria for being an adult might be. Perhaps we point to biological maturity: "Adults are those who bear children." Or we accept a conventional, chronological, and legal definition of maturity: "Adults are those who are sixteen, or eighteen, or twenty-one years old." Or we may automatically think of adulthood as a later stage in life rather than as something to be achieved or striven for.

Talking about morality is just as problematic. One reason is that shame, guilt, and morality go together so early in life that they easily define each other. A second reason is that morality is seen as something imposed or controlling, as a number of rules, for example, that are external to the self. Confirming this externality, a third reason is that, in a subject-object dichotomy of reality, morality is made to be objective and apparently not dependent on who we are as subjects. A fourth reason is that moralistic thinking, social pressure, and conformity are often conflated with morality. A fifth reason is that for some of us morality and religion can be so intertwined that being moral is a function of religious belief.

Thankfully, the culture—powerfully hegemonic as it is—does not have the last word. Sometimes it needs to be stood on its head. Two foundational notions—integrity and mutuality—characterize the dynamic core of being adult and of being moral. These two notions are the dynamic core of being fully human as well. Becoming a person who is whole enough and mutual enough—together as one—depicts not a superhero or a utopian ideal but someone who is authentic, someone about whom we might say: "This person is a real human being." Are care and justice part of this picture? They could not be more central. Being caring and acting justly—together as one—is the power of our integrity and the practice of our mutuality. They tutor each other as we make our way toward being mature and moral, toward being fully human.

An adult self, a moral self, a fully human self is revealed as an integral self-in-mutuality. Simple yet profound, this self is a dynamic process. It is a self that is reasonably whole, that relates in empathy to the other as the other is, that cares for genuine need, and that strives for justice. Acting in care and justice, this integral and mutual self—which we could also call a mutual self-in-integrity—is pursuing peace. As it becomes mutual and whole, this fully human self wants to live and needs to live in harmony with itself, with the other, and with the global community that would claim all of us as citizens.

This book does not focus on human development in the usual stages from womb to tomb. Fortunately, there are many books written from a number of different perspectives that do that very well. Rather, it is about what human development is in its fullness. This book is a phenomenology of the fully human—a phenomenology that would seem to be critically important for understanding who we are and yet a phenomenology that gets little or no attention at all. This book takes human development seriously because it takes seriously what that development is when it is all that it can be.

Part I depicts an integral and mutual self as the structure of the fully human, and it offers six defining characteristics of this self. It shows that being caring and just is how we act as fully human. It describes violence as the rejection of care and justice, and it describes peace as what only care and justice together are able to provide. Part I reveals the fully human as a three-in-one, as a vibrant mosaic or a living triptych: integrity and mutuality together beget care and justice, and care and justice together beget peace.

Chapter 1 details an integral and mutual self as the hallmark of a self that is both adult and moral. This chapter makes the case that integrity and mutuality—together as one—is the foundation, the structure, the process, the touchstone, the *sine qua non*, and the pinnacle of the fully human.

Chapter 2 expands and deepens the meaning of being an integral and mutual self by showing its six essential characteristics. It is a body-self, a feeling self, a self of inner depth, a self with clear boundaries, an intimate self, and a responsible self. These characteristics detail the mosaic of the fully human even as they stand as a serious critique of the disconnections and partial pictures of the human that being adult and being moral suffer from in the culture and in academia.

Chapter 3 describes care and justice—together as one—as an integral and mutual self in action. Coming directly from the first two chapters, this chapter is a major reconstruction of these two notions. In the culture and in academia, the meanings of care and justice—usually seen in separation—are often seriously skewed and quite dysfunctional. Defined in maturity, however, care and justice emerge rehabilitated and recognizable, involving and complementing each other. Being caring and acting justly is a foundational understanding of how we act as when we are adult, when we are moral, when we are fully human.

Chapter 4 describes violence and peace—arguably the two most urgent concerns we have as members of the human race—as the two major trajectories of human development. By negating care and justice, violence negates human development. By embodying care and justice, peace stands as the actual meaning of that development. The mosaic of the fully human is peace prevailing over violence. Peace is the measure of human development in its fullness.

Part II draws directly from the mosaic of the fully human to consider the practice of three of our most life-giving, life-enhancing activities. It asks the question: if integrity and mutuality is the structure of being adult and moral, if being caring and just is how we implement this structure, and if peace is the pinnacle of this structure, then what are the consequences of this three-in-one of the fully human for education, for psychotherapy, and for spirituality?

Chapter 5 focuses on the implications for education of becoming a self that is fully human. After considering a few focus questions, this chapter elaborates a pedagogy of connection that has empathy at its core. It describes empathy in some detail, offering examples of teaching empathy, teaching care and justice, and teaching peace. The chapter ends with a brief look at four profoundly human educators who foster a pedagogy of connection: Nel Noddings, Jerry Starratt, Paulo Freire, and Parker Palmer.

Chapter 6 considers psychotherapy as being in service of becoming fully human. With help from Sigmund Freud and J. B. Watson, it distinguishes preadult and adult morality, and it understands psychotherapy in light of the latter. In the thinking of Andras Angyal, Carl Rogers, and Eugene Gendlin, it offers a snapshot of psychotherapy from one tradition of human development. It concludes by looking at what the psychotherapy of trauma has to say about being fully human.

Chapter 7 sees spirituality—religious or not—as fostering, supporting, and challenging the fully human. This chapter distinguishes preadult and adult spirituality. It shows spirituality opening up the possibilities of the fully human and the fully human returning the favor by providing boundaries for the spiritual. It compares the compassion of the world religions with a spirituality that is fully adult, fully moral, and fully human. This chapter ends by seeing the unique relationship between spirituality and the trauma that comes from personal violence.

It should be noted that, as a help for processing the content and meaning of each of the chapters, there are "Practical Questions for Reflection and Dialogue" to be found in the appendix.

As this book begins, four questions invoking human development in a broader context may be in order. The first question is about early development. The second question is about motivation. The third question is about the role of religion in being a moral person. The last question is about the reality of evil. While it is not possible to talk about the fully human without theorizing, we need to respond to these questions—and to all the questions considered in this book—as descriptively as possible, appealing to a number of gifted thinkers along the way yet appealing ultimately to our own experience of what it is like to grow up as human beings.

The first question: How important is childhood for later life? An immediate answer to this question is that the early years of life are vitally important for the later years. Probably, there are many of us who can point to painful things that happened in childhood that have had a profound influence on who we are today. And yet, the formative years, even if they were problematic, need not be a lifelong sentence. If it is not unusual to have had a difficult time growing up, it is also not unusual to find the nurturance, the personal strength, and the sources of courage we need to change and grow. Developing as a human being is always the goal, even if the journey toward that goal is anything but smooth or fair. Although not focusing on human development in the typical way, this book is about the ultimate goal of that development, about becoming a reasonably whole and mutual human being, and about becoming fully human.

The second question: Why be moral? We are looking, I believe, for something powerful and persuasive enough to guarantee moral behavior, in ourselves and in others. To make ourselves behave in a moral way we invoke moral reasoning, universal rules, objective moral principles, religious teachings, and accepted moral norms. We appeal to a sense of duty, a sense of utility, the laws of society, persons in authority, exemplary role models, and various kinds of social pressure. All these things help us say what we ascribe to morally. Because, however, they are mainly an external approach to moral motivation and because they are often in conflict with each other, over time they can become less and less persuasive. Ultimately, if we are to become fully human, the motivation for morality must move from competing sources outside of us to a centered place within. This place within is at the heart of this book.

The third question: Isn't morality the function of religion? On the one hand, it is true that religion is a strong motivating factor for many of us to be moral. On the other hand, it is true that a person can be moral without being religious at all. Because morality is inherent in human interaction, it is central to human development whether or not that development includes religion. Furthermore, if religion can be understood by some as helping them to interact with incredible moral courage, it can be used by others to justify acts of the most horrible violence. The measure of mature morality is not whether or not a person is religious but whether or not a person is adult. This book is about how being an adult and being a moral person go together in being fully human.

The fourth question: How can we explain human evil? It is hard to understand, for example, the incredibly horrendous history of the twentieth century without some concept of evil. One arresting finding in this book is that, in part at least, evil is a developmental issue. If an adult-moral self is an integral and mutual self and if this self acts in caring and justice—the two pillars of this book—then coming to full humanness is a process of prevailing over evil. However we explain evil and however much we want others to fix this terrible blight on our humanity, becoming an adult-moral person, a person who is fully human, is an amazingly powerful response—and perhaps the only response we have—to evil's dehumanizing presence in the world.

Not only are these questions about human and moral development ever-present and provocative, but for many of us they also may be deeply personal. Our concerns about human development and about evil seem to be central to being human; our understandings of the motivations that allow us to be moral always seem to emerge as well. Still, no matter what understandings of morality we consciously appeal to, in the end the source of motivation that actually fosters moral maturity is being an adult. If we ask someone who is fully adult and moral: "What motivates you to be caring and just?" the answer—an answer coming from within—turns out to be: "I am caring and just because I am a human being. To act otherwise would violate my integrity, my sense of who I am. I would not be myself. I would not be fully human."

Part I

"self-in-relation" in
fem theory?

Chapter One

Integrity and Mutuality

Structure of the Fully Human

In the movie, *The Bourne Identity*, a trained assassin, Jason Bourne, is trying to kill a Nigerian political figure who is a thorn in the side of the United States government. Late one night on the politician's yacht, just as Jason is about to shoot him, the man and his children wake up. Jason freezes; he can't pull the trigger. In fleeing, he is shot leaping off the yacht into the ocean. Later, when found by local fishermen, he is suffering from amnesia. The rest of the movie is about Jason trying to find out who he is. He meets Marie and the two of them travel together, soon falling in love. At its best, the movie is about the development of character. As Jason is working out a new identity and struggling to come to some sense of inner coherence, he finds himself needing to respect and keep safe those whom he gets to know along the way. As his own wholeness is forming, his need to care for others in their unique circumstances is also forming. In this movie, integrity and mutuality are gradually developing together, not only for Jason but for Marie as well.[1]

This chapter describes integrity and mutuality as the foundation of the fully human. As a living paradox, an integral self-in-mutuality is fully itself even as it is fully mutual with the other. This living paradox is what human development leads to as well as what it flows from; it is what human development is for as well as what makes it possible. An integral self-in-mutuality is a developmental dialectic at the heart of our humanness.[2] Ultimately, integrity and mutuality—together as one—is the bond of trust between us when that bond is most developed, most authentic, and most resilient. In becoming ourselves and constructing our future, integrity and mutuality provide the essential foundation for a culture that is fully human.[3]

Two things are important to draw attention to as this chapter unfolds. First, being integral and being mutual gradually emerge as the meaning of being adult and of being moral. As we become mature and moral, we find ourselves functioning more and more as our own unique whole and we relate more and more to the other in a mutual way. In other words—countercultural as this may be—*an adult self is a moral self.* Second, what emerges as unique about this self is that its *integrity and mutuality cannot exist in disconnection.* As an interacting and developing self, the more whole we are becoming, the more mutual we are, and conversely, the more mutual we are becoming, the more whole we are.[4] This developing and connected self is in marked contrast to the disconnected, separate, static, subject-object self prized in the culture and in academia as "autonomy," "freedom," or "rationality."

In beginning to describe a self that is both adult and moral, we can observe that this self is developing in ways that are not only paradoxical but also fundamentally human. On the one hand, it is a self that is grown enough to claim the different "pieces" that make it whole. It is coherent enough "to stand on its own two feet," "to be its own person," "to have its own voice," and "to own its own soul."[5] Its locus of valuing has moved from significant others who say how I should be to a place inside, to a place where I know for myself how to be. In becoming adult and moral, *we become our own cohesive, felt-from-within, self-reflective, self-authoring whole.*[6] On the other hand—and this inescapably paradoxical part of our human development often is not grasped either in the culture or in academia—*we relate in mutuality to whomever or whatever is other, having genuine respect and care for the other's unique character, particular history, and special needs.* In relating to the other in mutuality—be it lover, family member, friends, groups, communities, events, institutions, animals, or the environment—we take the other's idiosyncratic circumstances into account.

As we go about realizing integrity and mutuality, we can see that they actually do define each other. They evoke each other; they require each other; they ensure each other; and they further each other. Integrity und mutuality is a living dialectic that would take us forward. In his own way, the Brazilian educator, Paulo Freire, captures the paradox of these two notions when he says: "No one can be authentically human while he prevents others from being so."[7] Not surprisingly, however, this living dialectic can be anything but automatic. It can occasion tremendous tension; it can leave us caught in a cauldron of terrible conflict; it can call for significant amounts of trial, of struggle, of patience, and of courage.

Negotiating our own need for wholeness while respecting the other's needs can be one of the most difficult things we do. Often, it is the central drama of life, stopping us in our tracks or setting us back until we can find a way to move forward again. Still, challenging as the dialectic of being integral and mutual may be at times, it does not collapse. The paradox that defines this self, the dialectic that this self essentially *is*, still holds. As inherently correlative, an integral and mutual self stands in sharp contrast, for example, to the less-than-fully human "evolutionary self" of the last century—a separate, non-dialogical, particle, or atomistic self—that is characterized so often in terms of aggression and selfishness.

At the outset, it is important to avoid two possible misunderstandings of this self we are describing. First, this self is a real person; it is not just some lofty, unobtainable ideal, not a category so wonderful that there is no one actually in it. *Being adult, moral, and fully human does not mean being perfect.* An integral self is not without unfinished pieces, shortcomings, and blind spots. But if not a perfect whole, this self is, in Erik Erikson's phrase, a "reasonably coherent whole."[8] Most importantly, it is developed enough to be its own whole, a whole with a sufficiently comfortable sense of self-possession, confidence, and agency. Likewise, the mutuality that goes hand in hand with this wholeness is also imperfect or somewhat ragged at the edges. D. W. Winnicott speaks of the mother who is "good enough" in caring for her young child.[9] Similarly, we are talking about integrity and mutuality that are good enough. None of us is perfect; none of us relates to the other perfectly. Fullness of development is not perfection.

Second, it is also important to see that adulthood, and especially adult morality, is not "above the law." In becoming adult, if the locus of valuing moves from the other to "a place that is within the self," it can look as if the other, including society and the culture, does not count anymore; it can look as if we become individualistic if not rather narcissistic. If adults decide for themselves how they will be, if they are a "self-reflective, self-authoring whole," it can look like adult morality is purely subjective. In adulthood, however—where paradox is so often the rule—what appears to be and what is are often very different things. As I become adult and moral, I find my own voice and accept responsibility for my own actions. At the same time "the other"—be that another person, an institution, the law, or the living planet—now acquires its rightful status as who or what I take seriously into account.

AN INTEGRAL SELF-IN-MUTUALITY

Becoming adult and moral—the forming of what it means to be fully human—can be clearly and accurately described, then, as an integral self-in-mutuality.[10] Not only do integrity and mutuality develop together, but we only seriously know what they mean as we find them forming and working together within us. Integrity and mutuality cannot be what they are in separation; they are found and only have their meaning in connection. "Integrity," observes John Beebe, "involves a willing sensitivity to the needs of the whole, an ethic that combines caring for others in the world with a sense of justice in insisting that others treat us and we treat them as we would like to be treated."[11] An integral self-in-mutuality is a relational self, an interactive self, a caring and just self. It is, in fact, a wholing and connecting self that is its own living and ongoing process of development.

Unfortunately, different cultural and intellectual traditions do not always help us to see integrity and mutuality together as a unified dynamic of growth. If we define ourselves—as some cultures encourage and as some of our moral theories suggest—as essentially stand-alone, disconnected, particle selves, we may fail to see that the things that are so inherently and so simply human—a community of others, trust and hope, love and care, justice and peace—are essential to who we are. If such precious human aspirations as autonomy and freedom can only be had by a self that is "self-contained, self-sufficient, self-defining and completely self-determined," we will never fully understand what it means to be part of a larger whole.[12] If "to give to the other is to take from the self," then life choices are like a seesaw, favoring either the self or the other.[13] In growing up, reality may appear in such an "either-or" dichotomy, but in full humanness this dichotomy gives way to paradox. Only as a paradox, where integrity and mutuality exist inseparably in creative tension, can adulthood and adult morality be understood.[14]

Conversely, if we define ourselves—as some cultures encourage and as some of our moral theories suggest—as only socially constituted, as being of value only because we are members of a group, we may fail to give attention to our own deepest values and concerns. If collective decision making and solidarity with the family can only be had at the expense of individuality, then individuality may appear to be selfish and disruptive. If we can only be ourselves when we meet the expectations of those with whom we belong, we may feel part of the larger whole, but we may never know an inner sense of depth or the voice of personal conscience. If we can only see the other as our group sees the other, we may miss the unique particularity and wholeness the other has. Again, while we are growing up, reality may appear in this "either-or" dichotomy. In the fully human, however, this dichotomy is transformed into a liberating paradox in which integrity and mutuality are no longer opposites but go hand-in-hand.

While cultures tend to rely on "either-or" dichotomies for shaping and clarifying identity, becoming an integral self-in-mutuality, even if it involves significant conflicts and trying tensions along the way, is a shared journey that cannot be split. The paradox of the fully human is that *integrity requires mutuality.* Integrity and mutuality together is a moral imperative—not an imperative that comes from philosophy but one that arises primarily from our own experience over time. Why this moral imperative? Why this motivation surfacing from within? The paradox at the heart of being fully human is that there is no integral self that does not need to relate mutually. Conversely, there is no full relating of a mutual self that does not involve the forming of integrity. Integrity and mutuality cannot exist in *disconnection.* They simply cannot go forward in separation. As I realize the one, I realize the other.

AN INTEGRAL SELF

We describe first the "integral self" in enough detail to get a clear picture of what this foundational co-touchstone of the human is. What does this part of "an integral self-in-mutuality" actually mean? How can we understand the integrity that, along with mutuality, characterizes the adult self as a moral self?

There is, of course, any number of ways of defining integrity. For many, integrity is understood as "honesty and fairness, sincerity and steadfast reliability."[15] Some see it as the ability "to keep one's self intact."[16] Some see it as "lying neither about nor to oneself."[17] Some see integrity as a synonym for morality or ethics.[18] Some see it as "a description of the overall person rather than a constitutive element."[19] Some see it as one of a number of other moral virtues that go to define an upright person.[20] Some see it as "perhaps the first virtue among virtues that go to make a good character."[21] Some see it as a "master virtue."[22] And some see it as "the content-free substratum of all virtue."[23]

A foundational definition of integrity is offered by Robert Grudin in *The Grace of Great Things*.

> Integrity is
>
> 1. an inner psychological harmony, or wholeness;
> 2. a conformity of personal expression with psychological reality—of act with desire, of word with thought, of face with mind, of the outer with the inner self; and;
> 3. an extension of wholeness and conformity in time, through thick and thin. Though integrity can be, and must be, expressed in individual actions, it is not fully realized except in terms of continuity.[24]

Grudin concludes this beautifully crafted three-fold definition by saying: "Thus understood, integrity may be defined as psychological and ethical wholeness, sustained in time."[25] In other words, distinctive of human wholeness are "the psychological" and "the ethical" as coextensive and progressing together. Confirming this understanding, Christina Becker says: "as we connect to our wholeness, we also connect to our inner morality and values."[26]

If we reflect on Grudin's description of integrity, we can begin to see the central importance this notion has for understanding the fully human.

1. To define integrity as "an inner psychological harmony or wholeness" is to capture its *primary* and *essential* meaning for being adult and moral. An integral self is a self in which all the inner "pieces"—whether thought of as aspects, or components, or elements, or parts—function together as a whole. Integrity is our ability "to combine all the disparate elements into a harmonious entity."[27] An adult and moral self, a fully human self, with all its experience, is not made up of pieces that remain disconnected, or isolated, or sequestered, or disowned. In a whole self, all the inner pieces—however different or difficult they may be—are intimately connected, coming together with enough internal consistency to allow them to function as a whole. *Integrity means that the self owns all of its pieces—the loved and the unloved, the comfortable and the uncomfortable, the good and the bad.* It is only in appropriating enough of this kind of integrity—an integrity that includes vulnerability and confronts the "undigested lumps of life"—that we are able to be an integral self-in-mutuality.[28]

It must be said immediately, however, that this "inner psychological harmony or wholeness" is something that may be very hard for us to realize. It would seem that with "normal" development, that is, with the appropriate blend of nature, nurture, and personal striving, we should come to adult integrity almost as a matter of course. There may be a few of us who come to this fullness of selfhood without a great deal of stress and strain, but unfortunately, and as we may suspect, "normal" development is not really the norm. Most of us—and for any number of reasons—suffer some deficiency in nature, nurture, and/or personal striving. There are problematic "pieces" of our experience that make it hard for us to act in an integral way. We may find, for example, that we suffer from prejudice, poor choices, failure, deprivation, rejection, addiction, illness, loss, laziness, fear, anxiety, egoism, deception, disability, isolation, stubbornness, shame, or trauma. A full measure of integrity—in which "all the parts are felt to make us a whole"—is the goal of human-moral becoming, but it may only be possible, at least for some of us, after heroic struggles in the face of serious inner and outer obstacles.[29]

2. Integrity as "conformity of personal expression with psychological reality" and "conformity of the outer with the inner self" are *secondary* and *derivative* characteristics of integrity, ones that flow from its primary meaning. Unfortunately, these definitions of integrity are how this notion is usually understood in the culture, and they are the meanings of integrity that often first spring to mind. To have integrity in this secondary sense, the "outer" must be in harmony with the "inner." In judging character—our own or another's—we look for honesty, truthfulness, sincerity, or authenticity. We say to ourselves or to the other: "Are you really who you say you are?" For ourselves, usually we want to have some measure of integrity and, to the extent that we do not, we often want to appear to have it. For others, especially for those on whom we rely, we hope that they have it, even when we may suspect that they have less of it than meets the eye. The "inner" of integrity is all-important, and we evaluate its "outer" signs as best we can.

While we look for integrity within the individual in terms of honesty or sincerity or authenticity, it is important to notice that the significance of these qualities is always relational. Integrity is not just that the "outer" reveals the "inner." If it were, then people who profess no respect for others and then proceed to lie, and steal, and cheat would serve as good examples. The conformity of "the outer with the inner," or "word with thought," or "face with mind" are integrity only if first there is an inner wholeness that makes for mutuality. Integrity, says Colin Rayner, necessarily "steers the individual to behave with truth, humanity, fairness or responsibility when dealing with issues that impact on other people."[30] A person who has integrity "respects the rights of others."[31] A person of integrity relates with "spontaneous empathy and compassion."[32] Genuine integrity, attests Marie-Hélène Parizeau, always "provides the basis for reliance, trust, friendship and love."[33] To be clear—and this could not be more critical to notice—*integrity is always about relating to the other in mutuality.*[34]

3. To see integrity as "an extension of wholeness and conformity in time, through thick and thin" and to see that "it is not fully realized except in terms of continuity" completes the definition. The self is what Andras Angyal calls a "time gestalt," that is, a living, ongoing whole that composes itself in and through time.[35] It is over time that all the different "pieces" of the self must be owned and kept connected. It is over time that the "outer" must be in harmony with the "inner." The challenge of integrity is to "stand for something and remain steadfast when confronted with adversity or temptation."[36] "Acting morally," says Gil Noam, "involves taking a stand, often an unpopular one. Not conforming to one's group or giving up the protection of the prevalent culture is always, even in little ways, an act of courage."[37] "Individual isolation," as Grudin points out, "may be a consequence of integrity, but would not be so if integrity had not motives more urgent than social acceptance."[38] In other words, standing on our own two feet in the face of adversity measures our integrity.

Important as it is, however, that integrity be "sustained in time," it is always a work in progress, challenged by personal loyalties, conflicting obligations, social pressures, and paths of least resistance. "Integrity cannot survive without an attitude of vigilance," John Beebe says, "and we are always, in effect, restoring our integrity from some attempt at compromise."[39] "A man of integrity can have moral lapses or deceive himself at times," says Raghavan Iyer in talking about Mahatma Gandhi, "but he will freely admit to lapses which he recognizes and he will do what he can to mitigate or avoid self-deception by ruthless self-examination."[40] Many of us come to know failure, brokenness, and a lack of caring and justice for self and other. "It is always the job of integrity to embrace the limitations of character."[41] If integrity is not the same as being perfect, neither is it the same as being righteous. As a quest that often unfolds in powerful personal drama, integrity only lives in paradox, its "is" and "is not" in intimate struggle within the "time gestalt" that is the self.[42]

THREE EXAMPLES OF INTEGRITY

If Grudin's definition of integrity as "psychological and ethical wholeness, sustained in time" is, along with mutuality, an excellent foundational co-touchstone of the human, there are three thinkers who exemplify this co-touchstone in very illuminating ways.

Parker Palmer

Parker Palmer, an educator and spiritual writer, talks about a "divided self." In *A Hidden Wholeness*, he admits what, I suspect, many of us know is true: "I yearn to be whole," he says, "but dividedness often seems to be the easier choice. A 'small, still voice' speaks the truth about me, my work, or the world. I hear it and yet I act as if I did not."[43] He continues: "I keep silent on an issue I should address or actively break faith with one of my own convictions. I deny my inner darkness, giving it more power over me, or I project it onto other people, creating 'enemies' where none exist."[44] For Palmer, there is no split between who we are as persons and the quality of our moral response. Being whole and being moral go together. As he says: "The divided life, at bottom, is not a failure of ethics. It is a failure of human wholeness."[45] The divided life is at once a "personal pathology" and the breaking of a bond with the other.

Palmer finds "an inner call to wholeness" at the core of who we are. When we fail to listen to this call, the self and the other are both affected.

> I pay a steep price when I live a divided life—feeling fraudulent, anxious about being found out, and depressed by the fact that I am denying my own selfhood. The people around me pay a price as well, for now they walk on ground made unstable by my dividedness. How can I affirm another's identity when I deny my own? How can I trust another's integrity when I defy my own? A fault line runs down the middle of my life, and whenever it cracks open—divorcing my words and actions from the truth I hold within—things around me get shaky and start to fall apart.[46]

Erik Erikson

Erik Erikson, a psychoanalyst and theorist of human development, has an eight-stage understanding of the issues that the self needs to negotiate from birth until death. His pivotal fifth stage, *Identity versus identity diffusion*, is a time to be oneself, and it ushers in the period of adulthood." The four stages leading up to adulthood are characterized by dependence on others, as issues of trust, autonomy, initiative, and industry are negotiated.[47] For Erikson, coming to the interdependence of adulthood is an inherently therapeutic time in which experiences of mistrust, shame and doubt, guilt, inferiority, and identity diffusion must be addressed. These are some of the "pieces" of the self that are hard to integrate, the negative residues that remain from negotiating the earlier stages. They need to be reworked, enough at least, for the self to become a "reasonably coherent whole." Adulthood, including personal, sexual, and social identity, respects the wholeness of the self, even as it respects the other in mutuality.

In Erikson's thinking, the human and the ethical go together. This is most clearly evident at three pivotal levels of moral development: (1) *childhood morality*, in which the values and prohibitions of the parents are internalized, often with an ample measure of shame and guilt; (2) *youthful ideology*, which relies on a system of ideas influenced by "totalistic logic and utopian conviction"[48] and is susceptible to "an alternation of impulsive judgment and odd rationalization;"[49] and (3) *adult ethics*, which is a relational ethics of mature conscience coming from an inner sense of identity. This adult ethics is one of values consciously chosen "with insight and foresight";[50] it is committed to "intimate relationships and work associations" and continues to deepen in the subsequent stages of life.[51] In the virtues Erikson describes in his last three stages of adult development—love, care, and wisdom—the fullness of our moral humanness is revealed. These virtues are ethical strengths that sustain the self, even as they sustain the other.

Gil Noam

Gil Noam, a psychoanalyst and a theorist of moral development, wants "to understand moral action in light of a developmental theory of the self."[52] He sees that a "strong self" and "moral action" work together, but he also sees that "the strong and healthy self is not the norm."[53] He finds not only that the "social and relational situations in which children grow and adults continue to develop are full of strife, loneliness, and alienation"[54] but also that these experiences can actually be "represented in the structure of the self."[55] If we are concerned about how the self and morality are related, then it is important to pay attention to "the vulnerabilities of the self."[56] He describes two such vulnerabilities, the "vacillating self" and the "alienated self," in some detail. These vulnerabilities are meant to correlate with a number of the psychopathologies listed in commonly used *Diagnostic and Statistical Manual of Mental Disorders*.[57]

The "vacillating self" is a self that can never quite trust its own abilities and has a hard time finding a sense of wholeness. This self has "a great need for guidance, tendencies toward submission, and a loss of mutuality."[58] It is "so preoccupied with its own survival and cohesion that the energy to think of others, a hallmark of morality, is quite diminished."[59] In fact, in "continuously questioning itself and its integrity," this self can "abandon any moral impulses." Described in contrast, the "alienated self" is a self that experiences others as untrustworthy and feels "very much alone."[60] Often an early recipient of "severe rejection" on the part of adults,[61] this self tightens up; it wants to be "in charge of everything"; it has boundaries that do not let others in. Appearing to be of "moral integrity and unity," in reality this self is rigid and quite controlling, having "little empathy either for itself or for others."[62] In both of these descriptions, Noam is quite clear: vulnerabilities of the self, if not effectively worked with, make moral maturity impossible. In other words, psychological deficits are moral deficits as well.

Our description of integrity, along with the examples of Palmer, Erikson, and Noam, let us understand that the way the notion is defined—quite different from how it is often taken in the culture and in academia—is crucial for seeing it in connection with mutuality. To see integrity as honesty, or sincerity, or authenticity only partially captures what it is. To see integrity as "conformity of the outer with the inner self" only partially defines it. At the core of the meaning of integrity—integrity as it is in actuality—is the wholeness of the self finding the wholeness of the other. An integral self, an adult self, a moral self, a fully human self, a self that "owns all of its pieces," is a self that finds the other in all of its unique pieces. In its fullness, *integrity actually means an integral self-in-mutuality*.

A MUTUAL SELF

Next, we need to describe "mutuality" in enough detail to get a clear picture of what this foundational co-touchstone of the human is. What does this correlative part of "an integral self-in-mutuality" actually mean? How can we understand the mutuality that, along with integrity, characterizes the adult self as a moral self?

In their article, "Naturalistic Conceptions of Moral Maturity," Lawrence Walker and Russell Pitts find two overall characteristics people use to describe the mature moral person. On the one hand, "the highly moral person has a range of strongly held values and principles" that are "joined by a strong sense of self or personal agency." On the other hand, this person has "notions of communion" and an "other-oriented compassion and care that entails helpful, thoughtful and considerate action and the nurturing of relationships through faithfulness and reliability."[63] Walker and Pitts are reporting that, in our everyday understanding, being mutual naturally goes together with being integral.

Normally, mutuality means a basic respect and appreciation of one for the other, a back-and-forth, an empowering exchange, a dialectic that tends to further the other even as it furthers the self. "Mutuality," says James Olthuis, "is attunement of expression, recognition, and desire, a dance in which the differing gifts and needs of each person are simultaneously honored, recognized, and often met."[64] He adds: "We recognize each other, seek each other's good, identify with each other—in the process loving the other as we love ourselves."[65]

In describing a "self-in-relation," Margaret Huff puts interpersonal mutuality at the heart of human growth and development. "The basic premise of self-in-relation," she observes, "is that persons in a mutual, empathic relationship evolve in the context of that relationship, and that complete selves can evolve *only* in such growth-enhancing relationships; further, the relationship itself is an integral part of the selves involved."[66] Similarly, Dawn Nothwehr says that "mutuality is *the sharing of 'power with' by and among all parties in a relationship in a way that recognizes the wholeness and particular experience of each participant toward the end of optimum human flourishing*."[67] Both Huff and Nothwehr see mutuality—hand-in-hand with integrity—as fostering the fully human.

If an accurate-enough picture of integrity is essential for understanding someone as adult and moral, an accurate-enough picture of mutuality is equally essential. Five aspects of mutuality need to be taken into account if we are to understand its foundational nature. The first two are about the wholeness of the other and about the needs, rights, and freedoms that have to be addressed for that wholeness to be realized. The second two are being caring and acting justly; they describe mutuality as it is lived by an integral self-in-mutuality. The last aspect is that mutuality is an *invitation* that an integral self extends to the other. Although an integral self relates to the other in mutuality, that mutuality may remain asymmetrical. An equal back-and-forth reciprocation is neither forced nor guaranteed. Often, for example, between a parent and a child, it may not even be possible. In other words, "mutuality refers to a commonality and sharing that may be quite different in form, quantity, or degree for each party."[68]

Mutuality Honors the Unique Wholeness of the Other

Finding the unique wholeness of the other is, as we have seen, at the core of adult mutuality. In mutuality we relate to a particular other. It is "this" actually existing person, or "this" actual institution, or "this" particular aspect of the environment.[69] Mutuality is about interacting with an actual unique other that is a whole in the making or part of a larger whole.[70] When we relate in mutuality, three things are happening. First, we are sensitive to the immediate particulars of the other. Second, we sense, or at least we try to sense, the nature or quality of the other's wholeness-in-the-making. For example, we ask ourselves: "Who is this other person becoming?" or "What is the nature of this organization?" or "What are the needs of our environment for its health and aliveness?" Third, in relating to the other's wholeness, we sense as best we can the other's social and cultural context. We ask as best we can: "Who or what does this person, or society, or culture, or planet need to maintain its humaneness and hospitality?"

If we are relating to another person in mutuality, then usually we find ourselves considering the "inner" of that person. We do this, again as best we can, because without attending to the inner of the other we really have little knowledge of the person in his or her unique, situated wholeness. "Crucial to a mature sense of mutuality," observes Judith Jordan, "is an appreciation of the wholeness of the other person, with a special awareness of the other's subjective experience."[71] We pay attention to the other if we want to know the nature, or purpose, or needs that other has. We listen with empathy to the "inner" of other persons to know and honor their integrity. In ways we will describe in the next chapter, we have to be open to the feeling and the inner depth of other persons if we want to relate to them in a mutuality that is considerate and real. In the same way, we need to be attentive to the "inner" or the spiritual identity of groups and institutions.

This first aspect of mutuality is easily seen, for example, in how we relate to those we are closest to. In marriage, we are "sensitive to the uniqueness" of our spouse and to "the details of the relationship."[72] In relating to our children, the uniqueness of each child is considered, along with that child's particular needs.[73] As Herbert Anderson says, "When each person in the family is regarded as 'unique and worthy of respect,' then 'family members flourish.'"[74] Then, if I am a reasonably coherent whole, I relate in mutuality, as appropriate, to other "others"—the local school system, the situation of global warming, the fund for cancer research, or a country that is facing genocide. I relate in a way that recognizes the other's uniqueness and that fosters whatever inchoate wholeness and mutuality may need to emerge and unfold. The whole-enough self honors the unique wholeness that the other is becoming.

Mutuality Is Concerned for the Needs, Rights, and Freedoms the Other Has in Realizing Wholeness

Everything and everyone has needs that have to be met in order to realize integrity and mutuality. This is true for plants and animals and for the ecosystem as a whole. It is also true for human beings in their social and cultural contexts. Without respect, care, and nurturance, living things cannot realize their integrity and live in mutuality. This also holds true for human institutions such as governments, schools, hospitals, shelters, economic groups, social groups, civic groups, religious groups, or political groups; it is their responsibility to foster growth and connectedness. And this holds true for all human beings: family, friends, and neighbors of course, but also immigrants, those living in other countries, and especially those who have urgent needs that must be met if they are to survive. In adulthood, mutuality attends to the needs, rights, and freedoms the other has for full becoming.

Abraham Maslow has a hierarchy of needs, what he calls "instinctoid needs," that seem to be basically true for all persons, no matter the different characteristics of their culture. First, and most basically, there are the *physiological needs*: food, water, air, sleep, and sex. As these are sufficiently satisfied, the *safety needs* become prominent: security, stability, protection, structure, order, and freedom from fear and anxiety. When these needs are sufficiently satisfied, we experience the *belonging and love needs*: the need to have friends and to be part of a group and the need to love to be loved by others. Finally as we approach adulthood, we have *esteem needs*: the need for deserved respect and recognition of our worth and competence coming from others along with the need we have for self-respect and a sense of self-worth as unique individuals. Maslow calls these basic human needs "becoming needs" because they are the needs we must realize in order to become a whole person.[75] Mutuality lies in addressing the needs of the self and the other on the way to realizing integrity.

Complementing the importance of needs for human becoming is an appreciation of the rights and freedoms that more recently are seen as necessary for realizing wholeness. In the middle of the last century, the United Nations published *The Universal Declaration of Human Rights*, based on the belief that "the recognition of the inherent dignity and of the equal and inalienable rights of all members of the human family is the foundation of freedom, justice and peace in the world."[76] Human rights, detailing as they do the need we all have for care and justice, usually include freedom of speech, of assembly, and of religion. They include freedom from persecution, unlawful imprisonment, slavery, feminicide, and genocide. They include the right to life, to potable water, to proper nutrition, to decent housing, and to basic education, along with the right to marry and raise a family, to earn a living wage, and to have adequate physical and mental health care. They include the right to own property and to have a voice in government.[77]

Mutuality Is Loving Care for the Other

"Becoming accomplished in the mutuality of love," says Paul Wadell, "is the indispensable key to becoming human."[78] And what is love? "Love is the thoughtful and deliberate practice of attending to the needs, concerns, and well-being of others."[79] All of us are in need of this kind of loving care that flows from the wholeness of an adult self. It is this kind of loving care that is "essential for moral development and personality integration."[80] Receiving love and care, especially in the early years of life, allows for gradual growth in human and moral maturity.

> Parents are children's most important teachers. It is the experience of the early years, mediated by parenting, that sets the child on a trajectory of either success or failure. A child's confidence, her concept of self, her readiness to launch herself into fearless learning and healthy relationships is dependent on and intricate-

> ly bound up in the quality of nurturing she receives from a loving adult.[81]

In caring, both the self and the other are able to grow and further their own wholeness. The fullness of life revolves around the loving care that the integral self provides. In loving care, the wholeness of the self supports the wholeness of the other.

Caring "*strengthens the doer even as it strengthens the other*."[82] Milton Meyeroff observes: "In helping the other grow I do not impose my own direction." He continues, saying: "I allow the direction of the other's growth to guide what I do, to help determine how I am to respond and what is relevant to such response."[83] Caring "appreciates the independent existence of the other, that the other is *other*."[84] Caring is always concrete. It is "responsible to the growth of *this* other."[85] It "involves continuous learning about the other: there is always something more to learn."[86] "If I do not basically experience the other as someone or something in its own right, then," says Meyeroff, "whatever else I may be doing, I am *not* caring."[87]

Mutuality Insists on Justice for the Other

Mutuality is often a code word for justice. The word itself suggests, as Susan Ross points out, "the principles of responsiveness and justice in relationship."[88] It is mutuality, then, that impels us to respond to the other in ways that are just. Frequently, this justice is framed in terms of what is owed to the other, as for example, in human rights, or animal rights, or conservation rights. The *Declaration on a Culture of Peace* of the United Nations insists on respect for the "equal rights of and opportunities for women and men," and it calls for promotion of the "rights of everyone to freedom of expression, opinion, and information."[89]

Justice is also frequently understood in terms of the law. Law is meant to be the instrument of justice. Mutuality means that in the eyes of the law we are all to be treated equally. No one, because of birth, race, class, ethnicity, political power, or connections, is more or less entitled than anyone else to rights, opportunities, and freedom of expression. Justice implies mutuality in that all persons are seen to be equal under the law. In the United States in the middle of the last century, there was an acute awareness of the civil rights that all citizens, black or white, were entitled to. In South Africa toward the end of the last century, there was a similar concern for human rights for all citizens, black, white, or colored. In both countries, there was a cry for justice by those who were oppressed, a cry that was a demand for the kind of mutuality that others in the country enjoyed.

Yet, paradoxically, relating in mutuality does not mean applying abstract principles of justice to others, as if everyone were the same. If we are all quite equal, we are also all quite unique. In many circumstances, I cannot relate justly to the other if I do not know who the other is. If I do not get close enough to the other to know enough of his or her particularities, how can I know what justice entails? If an "awareness of the other's subjective experience" is not important, how can I have "an appreciation of the wholeness of the other?"[90] There is an understanding of justice for which a principle of equality, although vitally important, is not enough. Jack Dominian reflects this when he says: "A great deal of our integrity relies on how well we can listen to others, for an accurate and sensitive interpretation of what they are saying is due to them in justice and love."[91] Mutuality means that paying attention to the "inner" of the other is an essential part of justice. As we will see in chapter 3, if there are times when justice calls for blind equality, there are also times, when justice calls for empathy and loving care. In justice, the wholeness of the self discovers and responds to the wholeness of the other.

Mutuality Does Not Demand Mutuality in Return

In adulthood, mutuality is offered to the other. The wholeness of the other can be nurtured, but it cannot be forced. A mutual response can be asked for and even be expected, but it cannot be coerced. The key in mutuality is our respect for the unique inner of the other and therefore the key is the quality of our own integrity. In other words, the mature mutuality we are describing as flowing from integrity is, in a very necessary way, a unilateral approach to full mutuality. It does not necessarily bring about "an empowering exchange" nor does it necessarily introduce "a dialectic that furthers the self, even as it furthers the other." A mutually empathic relationship is self and other initiating and responding together. This fullness of mature relating may be fervently wished for, but it is always a dance. In adulthood, loving care and justice allow us to do our part, whether or not the other is able to respond.

Our openness to the other, our welcoming attitude, our solicitude, our non-defensiveness, and perhaps our ability to take a risk are important for mature mutuality. At times, our vulnerability and our willingness to sacrifice are helpful.[92] Gabriel Marcel talks about being a "presence" to the other and about "*disponibilité*," a way of being available or of being of service.[93] Faithfulness and honoring commitments over time are also important for mature mutuality. Also, an abiding sense of hospitality fosters mutuality, especially in cultures that so often see the other as "the stranger" or "the alien," especially in cultures that turn concerns for safety into a security-industrial complex. As Grudin says with uncommon wisdom, "the only thing that is truly our own is what we truly share."[94] Generativity—the capacity and the willingness to nurture others—is at the heart of mutuality. The question we ask is: "How can growth-enhancing relationships be fostered?" The answer—the only answer that we have—is: these relationships can be fostered through the caring of a reasonably coherent self who relates to the other in love and justice.

THREE EXAMPLES OF MUTUALITY

Three authors talk about mutuality in ways that show how central this relational way of being is to an adult-moral self, a fully human self.

Judith Jordan

Judith Jordan, a feminist developmental thinker and psychotherapist, believes that interpersonal relating, understood as "mutual intersubjectivity," is the "central organizing dynamic of people's lives."[95] She finds that "the deepest sense of one's being is continuously formed in connection with others and is inextricably tied to relational development." Mutuality lies, then, at the heart of human development and for her what make mutuality possible is empathy. "When one feels empathy for the other person, it provides a palpable sense that one influences and emotionally touches the other person. In empathy I am present, vulnerable, open, responsive, and concerned."[96] In empathy, which "is receptive to the impact of the other" there is, on the one hand, a "relaxation of the sense of separateness," while on the other hand, the other's well-being becomes "as important as one's own." Empathy is *the way* of mutuality. Through mutual empathy, each person develops as his or her own unique self.[97]

What makes "mutual intersubjectivity" mature is that there is "cognitive-emotional awareness of and responsiveness to the subjectivity of the other person through empathy." For each of the persons relating, there is an "ability to reveal one's own inner states," "to share one's thoughts and feelings," and "to make one's needs known."[98] There may, however, be major impediments to our relating in mutuality. One member of the dyad may be inaccessible or disconnected, unable to be "emotionally present or available." The narcissistic person may end up in a "grandiose state of self-sufficiency and encapsulation," unable to see the other as "a whole person."[99] The person who is depressed may also have difficulty realizing mutuality. "Depressed people suffer from a diminished interest in the inner world of the other and little ability to attend to, let alone minister to, the needs of others."[100] For Jordan, full mutuality, the essence of adult-moral relating, is developmental, and its key lies in mutual empathy.

Dawn Nothwehr

For Dawn Nothwehr, a feminist thinker and moral theologian, mutuality means three things: first, "the common recognition of the full personhood of the other"; second, "the concomitant valuing of the other"; and third, "a common regard marked by trust, respect, and affection."[101] In mutuality, "the wholeness and the particular experience" of the self and the other is held in a creative tension that holds for the common good of all parties. "Mutuality moves the *starting point for ethical reflection* to a radically inclusive place, where literally everyone and everything is included."[102] Great "courage and strength" are required of each person to act, not out of self-interest but for "the flourishing of all involved."[103] Love is essential to mutuality: "Mutuality requires that all love, including sacrificial love, be mutual in so far as greater and more complete mutuality is its goal."[104] Justice is also essential: "Mutuality requires that justice be established with the full participation of all involved, with full dignity and integrity."[105]

Nothwehr is particularly concerned about "formal norms" in religious ethics. Formal norms are ways of describing who we are as moral persons. For her, these norms are foundational; they describe how we should always be, no matter what the specific situation we are facing. Traditionally, love and justice are these two foundational ways of being, but, says Nothwehr: "More than the norms of love and justice, mutuality places humans in a perspective with the whole of creation."[106] It is important to see that "just as one ought to act lovingly and justly, so one ought to act mutually" in order to insure that there is nothing that is not considered. In other words, *mutuality is the quintessential norm in religious ethics*. "When only love and justice are considered, some of the conditions for optimum human flourishing remain obscured."[107] Good examples of this are the tolerance of slavery, the privileging of men over women in society, and the failure to be concerned about our ecosystem. "When mutuality is added to the equation, the conditions for optimum human flourishing are more adequately revealed and measured."[108]

Harold Oliver

Harold Oliver, a philosopher and theologian, believes "that experience consists exhaustively of *relating*" and "that *mutuality* is the prime feature of being."[109] Experience *is* mutual relating with the other. We have to talk about a "relational self," an alternative to "the individualistic, egocentric view of selfhood that prevails in the West."[110] "Western Society," he holds, "has no legacy of a proper 'social' view of the self upon which to draw in addressing current pressing psychological and ecological issues."[111] It fails to see that: "The true self is to be understood relationally, that is, in terms of a relational metaphysics according to which only relation, relating, is real."[112] In other words, *relating* is the actual experience that we have. What we call "the self" and "the other" are only "coderivitives" of our experience that surface upon reflection. [113] If we mistake these "coderivitives" as the primary reality, we think of the other as "nonmutual" because we mean by the other the "non-I."[114] Our mistake—morally and psychologically as well as metaphysically—is not to see that in reality "the deepest sense of the self" is only found in mutuality.

In his metaphysics of the relational self, Oliver makes three foundational claims: first, "experience is a unity"; second, "mutuality is reality"; and third, "distinctions within this unity are rational constructs, that is, abstractions."[115] According to this relational metaphysics, *the essence of the human and the moral lies in the immediacy of mutual relating*. "The 'I' emerges with its 'Thou' in the same creative act."[116] Whether a person or a thing, the "experiential other" is there for us not in disconnection but in mutuality.[117] If we give primacy, however, not to mutuality but to "the self" and "the other," our way of understanding adulthood and adult morality moves from being a living relationship to a focus on a separate self trying to relate to a separate other. The human and the moral are seriously misunderstood from the beginning. Left in our *disconnection* from the other, we enlist whatever abstract rational constructs we can muster in an effort to define what mature relating ought to be. Oliver's relational metaphysics is very clear at the start: our human reality is first revealed as mutuality.[118]

Our description of mutuality, along with the examples of Jordan, Nothwehr, and Oliver, lets us understand that the way the notion is defined—quite different from how it is usually taken in the culture and in academia—is crucial for seeing it in connection with integrity. To see mutuality as "the primary reality" out of which the self and the other are differentiated and to see that love and empathy are at its heart is very clarifying. To see mutuality in terms of authoring wholeness, to see that it is the existential foundation of care and justice, and to see that it is often asymmetrical are all critically important. At the core of mutuality—what mutuality is in actuality—is the living relational matrix, the developmental matrix, the experiential matrix out of which integrity comes. In its fullness, *mutuality actually means a mutual self-in-integrity*.

NOTES

1. *The Bourne Identity*, DVD, directed by Paul Greengrass (2002; Universal City, CA: Universal Pictures Home Entertainment, 2016).

2. Michael Basseches, *Dialectical Thinking and Adult Development* (Norwood, NJ: Ablex Publishing Corporation, 1984), 22, defines dialectic as "*developmental transformation*" occurring "*via constitutive and interactive relationships.*"

3. For those philosophically inclined, integrity and mutuality can be thought of as a practical ontology, as an ontology (a study of being) of full human development in theory and in practice.

4. Stephen Mitchell observes: "Personal autonomy is not something that antedates interaction with others, but an emergent property of interactive processes, not something than can be sheltered from influence, but something that grows through influence." See Stephen A. Mitchell, *Influence and Autonomy in Psychoanalysis* (Hillsdale, NJ: The Analytic Press, 1997), 21. Lewis Aron mentions "the misleading opposition between autonomy and connection to others that so pervades our culture." Lewis Aron, *A Meeting of Minds: Mutuality in Psychoanalysis* (Hillsdale, NJ: The Analytic Press, 1996), 151. From an existential perspective, Viktor Frankl makes the case that freedom and responsibility are always connected. Viktor E. Frankl, "Dynamics, Existence and Values," *Journal of Existential Psychiatry*, 2 (1961): 5–16.

5. See Henry Krystal, *Integration and Self-Healing* (Hillsdale, NJ: Analytic Press, 1988). For an understanding of "voice" that is as helpful for men as it is for women, see Mary F. Belenky et al., *Women's Ways of Knowing: The Development of Self, Voice, and Mind* (New York: Basic Books, 1986).

6. See Lewis Aron, "The Clinical Body and the Reflexive Mind," in *Relational Perspectives on the Body*, ed. Lewis Aron and Frances S. Anderson (Hillsdale, NJ: Analytic Press, 1998), 3–37.

7. Paulo Freire, *Pedagogy of the Oppressed*, 30th Anniversary Edition (New York: Continuum, 2009), 85.

8. Erik H. Erikson, *Identity: Youth and Crisis* (New York: Norton, 1968), 87.

9. D. W. Winnicott, *Through Paediatrics to Psycho-Analysis* (New York: Basic Books, 1975), 302.

10. Three influences on the notion of *an integral self-in-mutuality* can be mentioned. The first influence is from Erik Erikson who sees the identity of young adulthood going hand-in-hand with mutuality. See Erik H. Erikson, *Insight and Responsibility: Lectures on the Ethical Implications of Psychoanalytic Insight* (New York: Norton, 1964), 231–33. The second influence is Andras Angyal who sees all living things developing in two tendencies that always go together: *autonomy* (the need of every organism to grow as itself in the environment) and *homonomy* (the need of every organism to be with others like itself). Andras Angyal, *Foundations for a Science of Personality* (New York: Viking Press, 1972). The third influence is a review article of Shan Guisinger and Sidney J. Blatt, "Individuality and Relatedness: Evolution of a Fundamental Dialectic," *American Psychologist* 49, no. 2 (February 1994): 104–11.

11. John Beebe, "The Place of Integrity in Spirituality," in *The Psychology of Mature Spirituality: Integrity, Wisdom, Transcendence*, ed. Polly Young-Eisendrath and Melvin E. Miller (London: Routledge, 2000), 12.

12. Roberta S. Loewy, *Integrity and Personhood: Looking at Patients from a Bio/Psycho/Social Perspective* (Boston: Kluwer Academic, 2000), 53.

13. Andras Angyal, *Neurosis and Treatment: A Holistic Theory*, ed. Eugenia Hanfmann and Richard M. Jones (New York: Viking Compass, 1965), 22. See also Tod Sloan, *Life Choices: Understanding Dilemmas and Decisions* (Boulder, CO: Westview Press, 1996).

14. John Shea observes: "Paradox in adulthood basically means that the dichotomies, the contradictions, and the differences in the self and its way of relating are able to exist together. Paradox means that the 'is' and the 'is not' of the self can live in harmony—the one not negating the other—in an ongoing process of creative tension." John J. Shea, "The Adult Self: Process and Paradox," *Journal of Adult Development* 10, no. 1 (January 2003): 24

15. See, for example, Amelie O. Rorty, "Integrity: Political, Not Psychological," in *Integrity in the Public and Private Domains*, ed. Alan Montefiore and David Vines (New York: Routledge, 1999), 108–9. See also John Rawls, *A Theory of Justice,* rev. ed. (Cambridge, MA: Harvard University Press, 1999), 455.

16. Gabrielle Taylor, "Integrity," *Proceedings of the Aristotelian Society*, Supplementary Volumes 55 (1981): 152.

17. Marie-Hélène Parizeau, "Scientific Integrity," in *Integrity in the Public and Private Domains*, ed. Alan Montefiore and David Vines (New York: Routledge, 1999), 164.

18. Patricia H. Werhane, "Competing with Integrity: Richard De George and the Ethics of Global Business," *Journal of Business Ethics*, 127, no. 4 (April 2015): 737–42.

19. Michael Palanski and Francis J. Yammarino, "Integrity and Leadership: Clearing the Conceptual Confusion," *European Management Journal* 25, no. 3 (2007): 174.

20. See, for example, Augusto Blasi, "Moral Character: A Psychological Approach," in *Character Psychology and Character Education,* ed. Daniel K. Lapsley and F. Clark Power (Notre Dame, IN: University of Notre Dame Press, 2005), 67–100.

21. Stephen L. Carter, *Integrity* (New York: HarperCollins, 1996), 7.

22. Cheshire Calhoun, "Standing for Something," *The Journal of Philosophy* 92, no.5 (May 1995): 260. Calhoun goes on to suggest that integrity is "less a virtue in its own right than a pressing into service of a host of other virtues—self-knowledge, a strength of will, courage, honesty, loyalty, humility, civility, respect, and self-respect."

23. Tom Kitwood, *Concern for Others: A New Psychology of Conscience and Morality* (London: Routledge, 1990), 210.

24. Robert Grudin, *The Grace of Great Things: Creativity and Innovation* (New York: Ticknor & Fields, 1990), 73–74.

25. Ibid., 74.

26. Christina Becker, *The Heart of the Matter: Individuation as an Ethical Process* (Wilmette, IL: Chiron Publications, 2004), 13.

27. David H. Rosen, "Foreword," in John Beebe, *Integrity in Depth* (College Station: Texas A&M University Press, 1992), xi.

28. See John Beebe, "Integrity in the Analytic Situation," *The Psychoanalytic Review* 86 (1999): 607–25. See Marina McCoy who makes the point that "vulnerability is a necessary component of living a rich and authentic human life in community." Marina B. McCoy, *Wounded Heroes: Vulnerability as a Virtue in Ancient Greek Literature and Philosophy* (New York: Oxford University Press, 2013), ix, doi:10.1093/acprof:oso/9780199672783.001.0001. The "undigested lumps of life" is a phrase of William P. Mahedy, *Out of the Night* (New York: Ballantine Books, 1986), 48.

29. Katya Bloom, *The Embodied Self: Movement and Psychoanalysis* (London, Karnac, 2006), 62.

30. Colin Rayner, "Integrity in Surgical Life: What Happens If It Is Missing?" in *Integrity in the Public and Private Domains*, ed. Alan Montefiore and David Vines (New York: Routledge, 1999), 193.

31. Ibid.

32. Daryl Koehn, "Integrity as a Business Asset," *Journal of Business Ethics* 58 (2005): 126.

33. Parizeau, "Scientific Integrity," 165.

34. For a thinker who makes the case for integrity being a social as well as a personal virtue, see Calhoun, "Standing for Something."

35. Andras Angyal, "Personality as a Time Gestalt," in *Neurosis and Treatment: A Holistic Theory*, ed. Eugenia Hanfmann and Richard M. Jones (New York: Viking, 1965), 62–68.

36. L. S. Paine, "Integrity," *The Blackwell Encyclopedia of Management: Business Ethics*, 2nd ed., ed. P. H. Werhane and R. E. Freeman (Malden, MA: Blackwell Publishing, 2005), 248.

37. Gil G. Noam, "'Normative Vulnerabilities' of Self and Their Transformations," in *The Moral Self*, ed. Gil G. Noam and Thomas E. Wren (Cambridge, MA: MIT Press, 1993), 219.

38. Grudin, *Grace of Great Things*, 85.

39. Beebe, *Integrity in Depth*, 40.

40. Raghavan N. Iyer, *The Moral and Political Thought of Mahatma Gandhi* (New York: Oxford University Press, 2000), 9.

41. John Beebe, "Integrity in the Analytic Situation," 624.

42. Again, see Shea, "The Adult Self," 23–30.

43. Parker J. Palmer, *A Hidden Wholeness: The Journey Toward an Undivided Life* (San Francisco: Jossey-Bass, 2004), 4.

44. Ibid.

45. Ibid., 7.

46. Ibid., 5.

47. See Erik H. Erikson, "Eight Ages of Man," *Childhood and Society*, 2nd ed. (New York: Norton, 1963), 247–74.

48. Erik H. Erikson, "Reflections on the Dissent of Contemporary Youth," *Daedalus* 99, no. 1 (Winter 1970): 164.

49. Erik H. Erikson, *Insight and Responsibility: Lectures on the Ethical Implications of Psychoanalytic Insight* (New York: Norton, 1964), 225.

50. Erik H. Erikson, "Reflections on the Dissent," 164.
51. Erikson, *Insight and Responsibility*, 226.
52. Noam, "'Normative Vulnerabilities,'" 211.
53. Ibid., 216.
54. Ibid., 215.
55. Ibid.
56. Ibid., 222.
57. American Psychiatric Association, *Diagnostic and Statistical Manual of Mental Disorders* (DSM-5) (Washington, DC: American Psychiatric Association, 2013).
58. Noam, "'Normative Vulnerabilities,'" 227.
59. Ibid., 228.
60. Ibid., 230.
61. Ibid., 231.
62. Ibid., 232.
63. Lawrence J. Walker and Russell C. Pitts, "Naturalistic Conceptions of Moral Maturity," *Developmental Psychology* 34, no. 3 (1998): 414–15.
64. James H. Olthuis, "Face-to-Face: Ethical Asymmetry of the Symmetry of Mutuality," in *Knowing Other-wise: Philosophy at the Threshold of Spirituality,* ed. James H. Olthuis (New York: Fordham University Press, 1997), 147.
65. Ibid.
66. Margaret Craddock Huff, "The Interdependent Self: An Integrated Concept from Feminist Theology and Feminist Psychology," *Philosophy and Theology* 2, no. 2 (Winter 1987): 161.
67. Dawn M. Nothwehr, *Mutuality: A Formal Norm for Christian Ethics* (San Francisco: Catholic Scholars Press, 1998), 233.
68. Aron, *A Meeting of Minds*, xi.
69. See Selya Benhabib, "The Generalized and the Concrete Other: The Kohlberg-Gilligan Controversy and Feminist Theory," in *Feminism as Critique: On the Politics of Gender*, ed. Selya Benhabib and Drucilla Cornell (Minneapolis: University of Minnesota Press, 1987), 77–93.
70. Lawrence A. Blum, "Gilligan and Kohlberg: Implications for Moral Theory," *Ethics* 98 (April 1988): 474–75.
71. Judith V. Jordan, "The Meaning of Mutuality," in *Women's Growth in Connection: Writings From the Stone Center*, ed. Judith V. Jordan, Alexandra G. Kaplan, Jean Baker Miller, Irene P. Stiver, and Janet L. Surrey (New York: Guilford, 1991), 82.
72. Pauline Kleingeld, "Just Love? Marriage and the Question of Justice," in *Mutuality Matters: Family, Faith, and Just Love*, ed. Herbert Anderson, Edward Foley, Bonnie Miller-McLemore, and Robert Schreiter (Lanham, MD: Rowman & Littlefield, 2004), 36.
73. See Robert Selman, *The Growth of Interpersonal Understanding: Developmental and Clinical Analyses* (New York: Academic Press, 1980).
74. Herbert Anderson, et al., "Introduction," in *Mutuality Matters*, 1.

75. See Abraham H. Maslow, "A Theory of Human Motivation," *Motivation and Personality*, 2nd ed. (New York: Harper & Row, 1970), 35–58.

76. United Nations General Assembly, *Universal Declaration of Human Rights* (New York: United Nations, 1948).

77. For a globally comprehensive listing of human rights, see Richard Falk, "Comparative Protection of Human Rights in Capitalist and Socialist Third World Countries, *Universal Human Rights* 1, no. 2 (April–June 1979): 3–29. For a helpful discussion of human rights from the perspective of the East as well as the West, see Jacqueline Langwith, ed. *Human Rights* (New York: Greenhaven Press, 2008).

78. Paul J. Wadell, "The Family as a Crucible of Grace: Finding God in the Mutuality of Love," in Anderson, et al., *Mutuality Matters*, 12.

79. Ibid., 14.

80. Mufid James Hannush, *Becoming Good Parents: An Existential Journey* (Albany: State University of New York Press, 2002), 2.

81. Mary Gordon, *Roots of Empathy: Changing the World Child by Child* (Toronto: Thomas Allen, 2005), 17.

82. Erikson, *Insight and Responsibility*, 233.

83. Milton Mayeroff, *On Caring* (New York: HarperPerennial, 1972), 9.

84. Ibid., 27.

85. Ibid., 29.

86. Ibid.

87. Ibid., 49.

88. Susan A. Ross, "Evil and Hope: Foundational Moral Perspectives," in *Proceedings of the Catholic Theological Society of America*, ed. Paul Crowley (Santa Clara, CA: Santa Clara University, 1995), 46–63.

89. United Nations General Assembly, *Declaration on a Culture of Peace*, Fifty-Third Session, Resolution 53/243 (New York: September 13, 1999).

90. Jordan, "The Meaning of Mutuality," 82.

91. Jack Dominian, *The Capacity to Love* (London: Darton Longman & Todd, 1985), 37.

92. See McCoy, *Wounded Heroes*.

93. See Gabriel Marcel, *Homo Viator: Introduction to a Metaphysic of Hope*, trans. Emma Caufurd (Chicago: Henry Regnery, 1951), 23.

94. Grudin, *Grace of Great Things*, 126.

95. Judith V. Jordan, "Relational Development Through Mutual Empathy," in *Empathy Reconsidered: New Directions in Psychotherapy*, ed. Arthur C. Bohart and Leslie S. Greenberg (Washington, DC: American Psychological Association, 1997), 343.

96. Ibid., 343–44.

97. Jordan, "The Meaning of Mutuality," 82.

98. Ibid., 83.

99. Ibid., 91.

100. Ibid.

101. Dawn W. Nothwehr, "Mutuality and Mission: A No 'Other' Way," in *Mission Studies* 21, no. 2 (2004): 250.
102. Ibid., 262.
103. Ibid., 264.
104. Ibid., 267.
105. Ibid.
106. Nothwehr, *Mutuality: A Formal Norm*, 250.
107. Ibid., 15.
108. Ibid.
109. Harold Oliver, *Metaphysics, Theology, and Self: Relational Essays* (Macon, GA: Mercer University Press, 2006), 92.
110. Ibid., 95.
111. Ibid., 97.
112. Ibid., 102.
113. Ibid.
114. Ibid., 103.
115. Harold H. Oliver, *Relatedness: Essays in Metaphysics and Theology* (Macon, GA: Mercer University Press, 1984), 162.
116. Ibid.
117. Ibid.
118. Ibid.

Chapter Two

The Six Characteristics

The Fully Human as Mosaic

In *To Kill a Mockingbird*, a movie set in the rural south of the United States in the first part of the last century, Atticus Finch, a white lawyer and a nonviolent man, has been asked to defend a Negro man, Tom Robinson. Tom has been accused of raping a white woman whose house he used to pass every day on his way to work in the fields. The whole town is abuzz about the coming trial. On her first day at school, Atticus's daughter, Scout, gets into a fight with a local boy who is taunting her and saying terrible things about her father. After the second fight she has with this boy, Atticus sits down with his young daughter on their front porch to talk things over. He says to Scout: "You never really understand a person until you consider things from his point of view, till you climb inside of his skin and walk around in it." Atticus talks with his daughter about the fights she is having with this boy by talking to her about empathy. Empathy, of course, was the one thing tragically missing in how most of the white citizens of the town were relating to the Negro citizens.[1]

In this chapter, we describe the particular characteristics that are at the heart of being adult and moral, of being fully human. If integrity and mutuality—together as one—is the foundation and the essential structure of being fully human, it is helpful to show in enough specificity the characteristics that are intrinsic to this foundational structure and that give it context, meaning, and depth. We may, for example, like the notion of being a "whole person" but rarely do we spell out the specific characteristics that are unique to someone who embodies reasonably full humanness. This chapter describes six such developmental characteristics, detailing a living mosaic of an adult-moral self as integral and mutual, a mosaic that allows us to witness the distinctness of character, the embodied genuineness, and the reliable maturity found in us when we are reasonably full human beings.

The first three characteristics of an integral and mutual self are: it is a *body-self*, that is, a self that owns its own body; it is *a feeling self*, that is, a self that relates inwardly and outwardly through empathy; and it is *a self of inner depth*, that is, a self that is its own within as it relates to the other. Its next two characteristics are: it is *a self with clear boundaries*, that is, a self that accepts and monitors its own wholeness; and it is *an intimate self*, that is, a self that welcomes the embodied wholeness of the other. Its final and crowning characteristic is: it is *a responsible self*, that is, a self that in its own fullness responds to the other in its fullness.

We consider these six characteristics in order. First, we look at the description each characteristic makes to a being both integral and mutual. With these two descriptions mirroring each other, we affirm again that an adult self *is* a moral self. Then, in order to see each characteristic in perspective, we consider some ways the prevailing culture looks at it. If cultures tend to be "group-differentiating" and rely on "us vs. them" dichotomized thinking, if they are vehicles of tradition, accepted norms and values, and if they often sanction "organized beliefs and convincingly concealed irrationalities," then the characteristics unique to becoming an integral and mutual self offer not only amplify the mosaic of the "whole person" but they can stand as well as a serious countercultural critique.[2]

In speaking of "the culture," we are pointing to some of the dominant features of society that many of us experience, especially if we live in the West or are influenced by globalized thinking. "A culture," suggests Bernard Lonergan, "is simply the set of meanings and values that inform the way of life of a community."[3] Every culture or subculture, every society or community, has "a cultural logic that clusters behaviors, situations, scripts, and values in a coherent, meaningful way."[4] Although taken as normative, these "cultural logics" can be quite contradictory in themselves as well as quite different from each other. We are all *in* cultures, and to a greater or lesser extent cultures are *in* us. Growing up, often we find ourselves critiquing the culture, sorting out the contradictions, comparing one culture to another, and trying to figure out what to accept, to nuance, or to reject in order to relate as ourselves to the other.

A BODY-SELF, A FEELING SELF, A SELF OF INNER DEPTH

These three characteristics—all reflecting developmental fullness—literally reveal the body, feeling or empathy, and depth of the adult-moral self. Without these characteristics, an integral self-in-mutually may be an accurate understanding of the fully human, but it remains too conceptual, too thin or two-dimensional, too skeletal or hollow. Since these three characteristics intimately involve each other, they are best thought of as seamlessly together.

A BODY-SELF

A Body-Self in Adulthood

Although its significance may be somewhat hard to appreciate immediately, the most important characteristic of an integral and mutual self—the foundation on which all of its other characteristics depend—is that it is a body-self. Practically, being a body-self means two things. First, an integral self-in-mutuality is a union of body and mind, a "unit that we can call the body-mind."[5] Second, this self is an organism-environment unity as well.[6] A body-self, quite simply, is a "whole person" within as well as without. As a body-mind unity, "body and selfhood" can be distinguished but they cannot be "disentangled and separated."[7] As an organism-environment unity, the body-self is always in a living relationship with the other.[8] "The living body *is*," as Eugene Gendlin so clearly states, "an ongoing interaction with its environment."[9] Why is being a body-self so important for being an adult self? Being a body-self speaks immediately to the *wholeness* and the *relatedness* of an adult self as the essential cornerstone for understanding it as integral and mutual.[10]

The very idea that we are embodied selves—rather obvious theoretically and practically—is often completely ignored. "We may be *obsessed* with our bodies, but we are often not that accepting of them."[11] Typically, we take our bodies for granted, paying little attention to them unless we are sick, or hurt, or disabled. In some cultures and traditions, there is what Drew Leder calls a "suspicion of embodiment."[12] We think the body should be "feared, mistrusted, despised, punished, discounted, or ignored."[13] Yet, without bodies we would not be alive or have, as Maurice Merleau-Ponty puts it, our own "*point of view on the world*."[14] Our living embodiment makes us unmistakably unique, situated, and relational.[15] Noticed or not, taken into account or not, accepted in empathy or not, our living embodiment—something we all share in com-

this is pivotal to understand—*in being empathic we are negating the two major ways of human disconnection.*[50]

A Feeling Self in Morality

If feeling is the language of an adult self as a body-self and if feeling makes integrity and mutuality possible, it is at the heart of being a fully moral person. In adulthood, the locus of valuing shifts from those who are "outside" of us to a place "inside" the self. In empathy, morality is now intimate to the self-authoring, self-reflective, self-aware self. Most critical to notice in this pivotal shift is that morality is no longer subject-object. Morality is no longer either "subjective," that is, what I believe it is, nor is it "objective," that is, what it is regardless of how I consider it. In its fullness, *morality can no longer be found in the "subject-object dichotomy."* It no longer resides in the "either-or" thinking so presumed as fixed, reasonable, and without exception in the culture.

As the "mind-body" and the "self-other" dichotomies are transformed in adulthood, morality is transformed as well. No longer subjective or objective, it becomes—usually gradually and over time—something that is at once both *inner* and *relational*. The language of the inner and the relational is the language of feeling, the language of empathy.[51] In other words, in adulthood *morality is rooted in empathy, in a felt sensing or a felt knowing of the self and the other.* For example, "As a mature parent, I *feel* the importance of providing proper nutrition for my child." Or, "As a mature teacher, I *feel* the rightness of giving attention to all my students, the bright and the not so bright." Or, "As a mature social worker, I *feel* the need to find a good home for this seriously neglected child." In adult morality, empathy and maturity go together. "With no feeling for what is right or wrong," says Richard Gula, "no one acts in conscience."[52] The morality of an integral self-in-mutuality lives in a connecting empathy that at its essence is inner and relational.

Disconnections and Partial Pictures in the Culture

The influence of the "mind-body dichotomy" is immediately evident in how "reason" and "emotion" are seen in the culture, in academia, in much of philosophy, and in theories of moral development. We have a "reason-emotion dichotomy" so deeply rooted in the culture that it has become a normal way of thinking. Reason is supreme, even though every so often a case is made for the importance of "the emotions."[53] In moral development theory—especially in light of the cognitive theory of Lawrence Kohlberg—a consistent cry has been that "the emotions" have not been taken into account. In most of the critique of reason, however, and in most of the interest in the emotions, *the reason-emotion dichotomy itself is never challenged.*[54] In the culture and in academia, we want a unified understanding of what it means to be a "whole person" or a "living organism," but the only way we have to do that is by relying on the dichotomy that keeps the feeling self split in the first place—split within and split without.[55]

The dictionary defines reason as "the power of comprehending, inferring, or thinking especially in orderly rational ways."[56] The "rational ways," however, are not described. In real life, as Robert Fitterer points out, reason is influenced by "emotions, past experiences, hunches, memories, sudden insights, symbols, imaginary cases, and acquired rules of thumb."[57] Reason is, as Antonio Damasio observes, not "as pure as most of us think it is or wish it were."[58] In fact, on careful reflection it turns out to be, as Hendrik Hart points out, "subjective, historical, limited, and plural."[59] Ultimately, it seems, reason is what we come to believe it is and then, usually, what we think others should come to believe as well.[60] It can be unique and quite different, not only among individuals around the globe who have very different "cultural logics" but also among individuals who have been living together for years under the same roof.[61]

Emotion is "a conscious mental reaction" that is "subjectively experienced as strong feeling" and it is "typically accompanied by physiological and behavioral changes in the body."[62] The different lists of basic emotions often include "happiness, sadness, fear, anger, surprise, or disgust."[63] Emotion is quite different from reason. In fact, as convenient abstractions—and that is all they are—reason and emotion are binary opposites. Reason is of the mind and emotion is of the body; reason is objective and emotion is subjective; reason is control and emotion is the lack thereof; reason is clear and strong whereas emotion is messy and weak. Reason, "the most elevating quality of our species," makes us who we *are* as fully human.[64] Emotion, only a vestige of who we *were*, is "among the most primitive, animal-like, or instinctual of psychological phenomena."[65]

The privileging of reason that is the hallmark of the reason-emotion dichotomy makes paying attention to feeling as the language of the embodied self hard to trust or appreciate. In actuality, we have our experience, and experience is always bodily felt; it is the rationally grasped and the emotionally tinged together as one. However, because of the way "reason" and "emotion" are framed in the culture, not just as abstract, non-developing "things" but as competing parts of ourselves as well, being comfortable as a feeling self can be difficult if not completely countercultural. In adulthood, even though feeling is our inner meaningful aliveness as we relate to the meaningful inner aliveness of the other, it can be hard to value. Why pay attention to what is often characterized in the culture—and especially in academia—as something purely subjective, embarrassingly unscientific, and unworthy of serious consideration.

A SELF OF INNER DEPTH

A Self of Inner Depth in Adulthood

The adult self is a self of inner depth. Depth describes the felt "inner" of the body-self, a reservoir of feeling that is who we are with the other. If feeling is our way of *relating* as a body-self, then inner depth is our way of *being* that self. If empathy is our access to the inner, then depth is that inner. Augusto Blasi's phrase, "deep, preconscious, feelings of rootedness and well-being, self-esteem, and purposefulness" is a good description of depth in adulthood.[66] Depth is the locus of the "spirit," because felt aliveness, concern, and response are celebrated there.[67] Depth is where the "heart" lies, because it is a living center of connection, care, and courage.[68] Depth is the place of "soul," because the "vital animating core of our embodied selves"—and often suffering as well—is there.[69] "We are," says Charles Taylor, "creatures with inner depths; with partly unexplored and dark interiors."[70] Who we are as unique, as inwardly and relationally alive, and sometimes as a mystery to ourselves and to the other, is concealed and revealed in the depth.

Depth is prefigured in our originality. As very young children, at the time of what are called "the terrible twos," we develop a sense of our own autonomy, and to the delight of our parents we become quite proficient in saying "No!" Soon after that, we exhibit a "sense of mineness" that has both emerging agency and a sense of desire.[71] As a complement to this mineness, we begin to take inside the rules and mores of the culture, developing what Sigmund Freud calls the "superego."[72] Later, we have secrets that we decide either "to tell" or "to keep inside."[73] Later still, with the awakening of puberty, we usually experience an array of intense "inner feelings"—enthusiasms, friendships, loves and hates, longings and imaginings—that make us uniquely ourselves and that bring us into a world with others. In time, if all goes well, our inner feelings develop into a "centering whole," a distinctively felt bodily identity out of which we own ourselves and relate to the other.

"As a self," observes Kathleen Fischer, "I am a subject or center of feeling, weaving together many different strands of relatedness into my identity,"[74] In our depth, we have the "place" of our wholeness, of our integrity. A person with integrity, says Gabrielle Taylor, is an "inmost self," a self that is "whole and integrated."[75] In fact, the very definition of integrity offered by Grudin is "an inner psychological harmony, or wholeness."[76] But depth is also the "place" of our mutuality with the other. As Stephanie Dowrick says: "Until you are at home in your inner world, and can accept and trust your own self, it is difficult if not impossible to know, love and trust someone else except in fairly limited and self-seeking ways."[77] Even in solitude, inner depth is a place where genuine intimacy can appear. In solitude, says Donald Evans, "we withdraw from the world in order to be more deeply and widely present in it."[78] With the power of empathy, the *inner* and the *relational* go together. If the self of inner depth is an "innermost," it is also a hospitality that welcomes the depth of the other. Depth is the "place" of integrity and mutuality together.

A Self of Inner Depth in Morality

What is a morality of depth? First and foremost, it is simply a morality of the *inner* and the *relational*. The locus of valuing is no longer found outside with significant others but lies now as a centering whole that is deep within the body-self; I simply cannot find my values outside of myself, even if I should still want to. Second, a morality of depth is self-reflective and self-authoring; my integrity and how I chose to act are now together; in self-empathy, I *go within* to find out what is there. Third, a morality of depth is at the heart of mutuality; the depth in me, through feeling and the power of empathy, finds and welcomes the depth of the other, including the other's "unique character, particular history, and special needs."[79] A living morality of depth—at once deeply inner and deeply relational—is at the heart of integrity and mutuality.

We can present a picture of preadult morality in order to compare it to the adult morality of an integral and mutual self. The former can be called "a superego morality," while the latter can be called "a morality of depth." Superego morality, like the superego itself, comes from significant others outside, while a morality of depth only arises from the inner of the body-self in its relating to the other. Both of these moralities can be spoken of in terms of "voice," simply because—remarkably different as they actually are—they are typically experienced as a kind of bodily resounding voice.[80]

A Superego Morality	**A Morality of Depth**
• a voice that is the internalized values of others	• a voice that is my own way of valuing self and other
• a voice that comes from "the mind" or "the head"	• a voice that comes from feeling, from the body-self
• a voice that is often loud, harsh, critical, and judgmental	• a voice that is often gentle and friendly, with caring and respect
• a voice that is usually a direct command	• a voice of dialogue that is self-reflective
• a voice that is "at me" to make me guilty or to punish me	• a voice that is "from me," from "the inner" to call me forward
• a voice that tends to freeze me in some bad way that I am	• a voice of inner prompting that brings change
• a voice of self-concern, asking "Am I good or bad?"	• a voice of empathy, asking "Are we all OK?"
• a voice that is in the service of control and social conformity	• a voice that is in the service of integrity and mutuality

A morality of depth represents the fullness of our human development. It represents a development from a subject-object grasp of morality to one that is at once inner and relational; a development from conventional morality to a morality that is owned and self-authored; a development from a morality of the culture-living-in-me to a morality forged by me-living-in-the-culture; a development from a morality of external control to a morality constitutive of an adult self as it lives in connection.

Disconnections and Partial Pictures in the Culture

On the one hand, the "hero," the "saint," and the "sage" are beloved archetypal figures that capture the epitome of the human and exist in almost every culture. These figures are greatly admired for their courage, their resoluteness, their compassion, and their vision. They exemplify spirit, or soul, or heart—an inner depth that is culturally acknowledged and often deeply revered. In more recent times, for example, Mahatma Gandhi, Mother Teresa, and Nelson Mandela are figures that might come to mind. On the other hand, however, there is a great deal in the culture that can make the reality of inner depth not only hard to recognize but also hard to appropriate, especially as a developmental reality we all share in our humanness. Three obstacles to the "inner" can be mentioned here: the cultural superego, disembodied rationality, and the external valuing of money, sex, and power.

The Cultural Superego

The superego that we inevitably acquire growing up—it is also archetypal—is not just the internalization of the values of the parents in childhood; it is also the internalization of the values of the culture and society at large. The cultural superego is the culture-living-in-us, in some ways consciously grasped and in some ways not. It is the superego morality we saw above and it has a number of very important characteristics. First, it *is* the morality of all of us, at least for the formative period of life. Second, it is usually very powerful and influential; to think or act in opposition to it can seem as though we are rejecting both ourselves and our culture. And third, it can make trying to honor a sense of inner depth extremely difficult. To realize a morality of our own depth with its openness to the depth of the other, if it is to happen at all, can call for considerable amounts of courage.

Disembodied Rationality

Because it is so thoroughly influenced by the cultural superego and because it is so abstract and non-relational, rationality easily functions in the culture as *the polar opposite of inner depth*. This disembodied rationality—so pervasive in thinking about maturity, so pervasive in theories of moral development, and so linked in the culture with power and sophistication—has little connection with empathy and the felt knowing we have as whole, embodied persons. Disembodied rationality prides itself on having no spirit, no heart, and no soul.[81] As a substitute for the fully embodied reasoning of feeling and inner depth, disembodied rationality is only two-dimensional: it is cold and nearly lifeless. Yet—and this is the great irony—while this detached, relationless rationality is touted as the fullness of the human, our inner depth, where three-dimensional aliveness, relatedness, and profound personal reasoning are actually found, is made to be subjective, irrelevant, or nonexistent.

Money, Sex, and Power

Much like the cultural superego they are part of, money, sex, and power are also archetypal; they are inherently part of being human and part of living in society and culture. Cultures have a lot to say about these three archetypal realities that are so central in our lives. They usually end up being controlled in different ways, so that we can live together in society with some modicum of harmony. Money, sex, and power are celebrated and made to be what life is all about. They are even sacralized, made to be God-like and perhaps even worshipped. In becoming mature, each one of us has the task to find his or her own way with money, with being and acting as a sexual person, and with having the kind of power that is possible and appropriate.

But if money, sex, and power are archetypal, so too is having an inner sense of depth. There are, then, two related questions that we face in becoming adult, moral, and fully human. One question is: "Does the culture define the meaning of money, sex, and power, or do I define their meaning?" The other question is: "How can money, sex, and power—so absolutely necessary to who I am yet so powerfully influenced by the culture—be part of my relational depth, a depth that is essential to being an adult and moral self, an integral and mutual self, a fully human self?"

A SELF WITH CLEAR BOUNDARIES AND AN INTIMATE SELF

These next two characteristics, a self with clear boundaries and an intimate self—both reflecting developmental fullness—deepen the meaning of integrity and mutuality in clarifying ways. If the first three characteristics have more to do with the *being* of an integral self-in-mutuality, these two characteristics—correlatives that are only found together—have more to do with the *relating* of this self.

A SELF WITH CLEAR BOUNDARIES

A Self with Clear Boundaries in Adulthood

An adult self is a self with clear boundaries. Clear boundaries allow for a coherent sense of self and a coherent sense of the other-than-the-self. In adulthood, if I am a body-self, aware enough of my feeling and of my inner depth, then I am going to have boundaries rooted in self-empathy that are definite enough to allow me to be my own wholeness and accept my limits in relating to the other. Clear, consistent, coherent boundaries make for the delineation, constancy, health, and wholeness of the adult self.[82] At the same time, with clear boundaries I am comfortable enough with all my pieces to relate in openness and receptivity to whomever or whatever is other. I can let the other be, in Mario Jacobi's phrase, "a Thou in his or her own right."[83] In other words, as I respect my boundaried wholeness, I can accept and welcome the boundaried wholeness of the other and of reality in general. Clear boundaries are the protection of integrity and mutuality.

Four things about clear boundaries are important to notice. First, the clear boundaries that allow me to be myself go together with my feeling and inner depth. "I set my own boundaries and limits," says Charles Whitfield, "according to and based on my own inner life."[84] As depth forms, clear boundaries form, much like a center allows for a circumference. Second, although clear and consistent boundaries must be held, they must also be *permeable* and *expandable*. In adulthood, clear boundaries are not rigid and they definitely are not meant to exclude the other. They are, in fact, precisely what makes the welcoming of the other in intimacy not only possible but even quite necessary, allowing for an owning of the self and a relating to the other that is growthful for all.

Third, clear boundaries monitor the influence of money, sex, and power in relationships, helping to protect those of us who have few resources and are most vulnerable in our relating.[85] Fourth, clear boundaries allow us to accept what Viktor Frankl calls the "tragic triad" of our humanness: pain, death, and guilt.[86] When we accept all the aspects of our humanness—the loved and the unloved, the comfortable and the uncomfortable, the good and the bad—we find ourselves relating, or at least needing to relate, in ways that are intimate. However, without boundaries that are clear and consistent enough, intimacy is neither possible nor safe enough. Boundaries that are "stable, reliable, and, at the same time flexible" allow us to feel "internally cohesive and interpersonally secure."[87]

A Self with Clear Boundaries in Morality

Clear boundaries and responding as a moral person go together. In fact, respect for the boundaries of the self and of the other is synonymous in the culture with adult morality. This respect is easily seen in professional relationships: with, for example, doctors, or lawyers, or counselors, or religious ministers in their relations with those with whom they are working. "Boundaries—of space, time, financial status, and limits on personal sharing—help to secure the 'safe space' within which mutual respect can take place."[88] Privacy, confidentiality, and professional competence are seen and accepted as boundary issues. But boundary concerns are also alive in our everyday interactions. The moral violations that are experienced all the time—the lying, the stealing, the cheating, the dishonesties, the deceptions, and the taking-of-advantage—are boundary violations.

Only the consistent, coherent, clear boundaries of the self make an integral self-in-mutuality possible. They are "the safe container in which our identity develops."[89] They encircle and protect our bodily inner, giving it the stability and security so crucial for intimate relating. Clear boundaries mean that the "inner"—the feeling and depth of the body-self—is not controlled by someone or something outside, be that another person, an institution, an ideology; be that a substance or an activity; be that a political, a religious, or a social group. Yet, if I am comfortable enough with my own boundaries, I need not be threatened by voices that are different from my own. Clear boundaries allow us to move from a superego morality to a morality of inner depth, from the values others want me to have to the values I find I actually do have.

The clear boundaries holding my integrity make real dialogue possible. At the same time, and quite paradoxically, authentic dialogue—the feeling and inner depth of the self engaging the feeling and inner depth of the other—keeps clear boundaries alive, letting them be held yet flexible, permeable, and expandable. In adulthood and adult morality, dialogue allows us to change inside, not though fear or coercion but by coming to feel differently. In adulthood, dialogue allows us to find something resonating in the feeling and inner depth of the body-self that was not resonating before. Dialogue is the "place" where clear boundaries and intimacy meet.

Disconnections and Partial Pictures in the Culture

If, as Marsha Linehan affirms, "it is the whole that determines the boundaries," the problem many of us suffer from, at least in the West, is *a lack of clear, consistent, coherent boundaries.*[90] For some of us, the problem seems to be one of *getting* enough self-coherence so that we can form clear boundaries and have a sense of integrity in our relating. For others, the problem is one of *losing* clear boundaries that were already well formed—perhaps because of fear, or betrayal, or social pressure, or because of substance abuse, debilitating illness, the experience of trauma, or a devastating loss of some kind. For still others, the problem is one of *avoiding* clear boundaries because of laziness, or a sense of shame or inadequacy, or a fear of having to be responsible, or a sense of privilege and entitlement. Clear boundaries can be a struggle to *have* and to *hold*, and to the extent they are diminished to that extent both our wholeness and our ability to relate to the other are diminished.

The lack of clear, consistent, coherent boundaries are often thought of in the culture in terms of suffering from addiction, of being codependent, and of having a psychological disorder or some other developmental difficulty.

The Addictions

If we have problems in getting, losing, or avoiding clear boundaries, we are prone to suffer from one or more of the addictions. If we are not comfortable enough inside, if we cannot let ourselves be aware enough of our feeling and if we do not have enough inner depth, we can feel empty or dead inside. Alcohol and drugs and activities such as gambling and sexual exploits can fill the void and, at least at first, provide the "intense sense of comfort" we want.[91] As "an abnormal relationship with an object or event," addiction substitutes intensity for intimacy and only leads to isolation and a progressive loss of boundaries.[92] Part of recovery is to learn new ways to relate to ourselves, to our family and friends, to the community, and for some to a "spiritual Higher Power."[93] In the addictions, loss of boundaries, loss of inner depth, and loss of intimacy go together.

Codependency

Our major institutions, says Anne Wilson Schaef, "teach us to think what we are told to think, feel what we are told to feel, see what we are told to see, and know what we are told to know."[94] Codependents have no reliable boundaries; they "take on another's sadness, happiness, fear, or whatever people around them are feeling and/or thinking."[95] I may be dependent on others for my sense of myself. "My good feelings about who I am stem from being liked by you and receiving approval from you."[96] "I am not aware of how I feel. I am aware of how you feel."[97] "I bolster my self-esteem by solving your problems and relieving your pain."[98] "My fear of your anger and rejection determines what I say or do."[99] If I am codependent, it is not safe to be uniquely different from the other. I have no "inner" and so I have no circumference. Recovery begins when I feel safe enough to become aware of my own depth and begin to claim my own boundaries in relationships.

Developmental Difficulties

Clear boundaries give us an excellent way to understand what we variously refer to when we say someone has emotional difficulties, or psychological problems, or a mental disturbance, or a psychiatric disorder. Normally, when we use these phrases to talk about the "vulnerabilities of the self," we have different implicit models of the person at play.[100] Often, these models are elaborated in terms of "the mind," or "behavior," or "disease"—none of which pays much attention to the person in terms of development. Yet, these vulnerabilities of the self—no matter how we choose to label them—involve developmental difficulties of one sort or another that keep us from forming clear boundaries in relating to the other. Along with the addictions and the codependencies, the developmental difficulties—be they somatic, genetic, or psychological—keep us from having and holding the clear boundaries that allow us to function as integral and mutual, as a fully human self.

AN INTIMATE SELF

An Intimate Self in Adulthood

An adult self is an intimate self. "Until we experience intimacy," says Matthew Kelly, "our hearts remain restless, irritable, and discontented."[101] Intimacy is heart-to-heart integrity and mutuality. Often, we do not experience our feeling and inner depth until we come to share them with another. In fact, intimacy is the "whole" of the body-self, in its feeling and its inner depth, loving, accepting, and welcoming the "whole" of the other in its feeling and its inner depth. Intimacy means "being true to yourself in the presence of someone else and accepting the other person being their own self in your presence."[102] Intimacy is "the process of mutual self-revelation that inspires us to give ourselves completely to another person."[103] "We look through each other's eyes, feel through each other's heart, enter each other's mind, and visit one another's soul."[104] If we are integral selves, our clear boundaries allow for the openness, availability, self-forgetfulness, understanding, and love that are intimacy.

In adulthood, inner depth, clear boundaries, and intimacy, along with openness and vulnerability, typically all go together. Brené Brown observes: "sharing appropriately, with boundaries, means sharing with people with whom we've developed relationships that can bear the weight of our story."[105] She goes on to say: "The result of this mutually respectful vulnerability is increased connection, trust, and engagement."[106] When our boundaries are clear enough and when we are at home in our inner depth, we can be intimate with our partner, our children, our close friends, and also with the community, with nature, and with any other that our empathy is able to entertain. In adulthood, being intimate—including, of course, sex that is intimate—nourishes and fosters the wholeness of the self, even as it nourishes and fosters the wholeness of the other.

In adulthood, intimacy is realized in empathy. It is our empathy that welcomes the feeling and the inner depth of the other. "Without empathy," says Judith Jordan, "there is no intimacy, no real attainment of an appreciation of the paradox of separateness within connection."[107] To be myself and to be "in the inner world of the other as if it were your own,"—the classic definition of empathy offered by Carl Rogers—is an exercise of intimacy, even as it is an exercise in our own integrity.[108] Empathy as "the capacity to think and feel oneself into the inner life of another person" is deeply intimate.[109] While intimacy, along with the empathy that makes it real, does not mean that we agree with the other, it does mean that we listen. It means that our "inner" can be challenged in a way that often calls for courage, flexible boundaries, and an ability to respond.

An Intimate Self in Morality

Making the case for intimacy being at the heart of adult morality may seem somewhat strange at first, but it is not a hard case to make, especially if intimacy is "facing who the other person is *in their entirety*."[110] If intimacy, with its attending empathy, is the body-self in its feeling and its inner depth lovingly welcoming the other in its feeling and its inner depth, then intimacy is absolutely essential to morality. How can we be fully moral, if we do not act from our own feeling and inner depth? How can we be fully moral, if we do not know, care about, and respect the feeling and inner depth of the other? As fully embodied, adult morality is necessarily deeply intimate and empathic. Intimacy, with the empathy that attends it, is also no stranger to pain, death, and guilt. Often, in fact, it is the source of strength that allows us to respond appropriately to this "tragic triad" of our humanness.[111]

Interestingly enough, Erikson puts intimacy and morality together in his understanding of adult ethics. Intimacy, he says, is the capacity to commit oneself "to concrete affiliations and partnerships and to develop the ethical strength to abide by such commitments, even though they may call for significant sacrifices and compromises."[112] In this definition, he is saying a number of clarifying things: (1) that adult morality is not only relational but that it is rooted in intimacy; (2) that adult morality calls for a self whole enough to make commitments and to be able to sacrifice and compromise; (3) that adult morality is concerned with caring for others and working justly with them, activities that are at once fully embodied and deeply intimate.

It is important to note that if we describe intimacy as the feeling and inner depth of the self welcoming the feeling and depth of the other, and if we describe empathy as self-empathy and empathy for the other, then we are again describing dialogue. In adult morality, it is essential to dialogue with the self and with the other, with the voice of the self and with the other's "unique character, particular history, and special needs." Self-refection or self-dialogue is the voice of conscience, the voice of inner depth. As we have seen, if we are going to be an adult, this voice is what we listen and respond to. Dialogue with the other is the unique "way of being" of the integral self as it relates to the other in mutuality. *Adult morality always lives in openness to dialogue.* With its subtle way of allowing care and justice to be together, dialogue is the official language of adulthood and adult morality.

Disconnections and Partial Pictures in the Culture

At least in the West, the culture does not easily allow for intimacy as being at the heart of the human and the moral. First, as we have seen, maturity and morality are so often cast in terms of the "rational," the "impersonal," and the "objective"—all reflecting the subject-object or self-other dichotomy—that to see them in terms of mutuality, let alone in terms of intimacy, calls for a near-complete reversal of cultural understanding. In the culture, the one thing to be said definitely about morality is that, of its very nature, it has nothing to do with being intimate. Yet, ironically the word "intimacy" is defined in the dictionary as "belonging to or characterizing one's deepest nature."[113] How strange it is that the sense of the self and of morality in the culture, in philosophy, and in some theories of moral development, has little or nothing to do with our deepest nature.

Second, the notion of "intimacy" is often immediately understood in the culture in terms of having sex. Intimacy is our common code word for sexual relations. As Kelly points out, however, "sex doesn't equal intimacy."[114] "If we are ever to truly experience intimacy," he says, "we must first move beyond the pubescent notion that sex and intimacy are synonymous."[115] Furthermore, we have a worldwide pornographic industry, and we have "adult" films and paraphernalia that have little or nothing to do with the feeling and inner depth of the self and the other. In the culture, sexual encounter and sexual fantasy are made to substitute for genuine adult intimacy. It is not that the culture does not appreciate deep interpersonal sharing or that a loving marriage is not held in high esteem, but the contradictions in how intimacy is characterized makes its central place in being adult and moral hard to grasp. "How can we attempt to think about intimacy," questions Dowrick, "when the very word is mocked by the banal, saccharine or even pornographic imitations of intimacy that permeate every aspect of our public culture?"[116]

A RESPONSIBLE SELF

The culmination and embodied integration of all the other characteristics is the responsible self. Being a responsible self—a notion, as we saw in the introduction, common to being an adult and being moral—is the epitome of being fully human.

A Responsible Self in Adulthood

An adult self is a responsible self. When I am a body-self aware enough of my feeling and of the feeling of the other, when I relate to the other in empathy and intimacy, when I can own my own inner depth and honor the inner depth of the other, when I can respect the boundaries of the other and my own boundaries as well—when all these "whens" are in place—then I am a self defined not only by my ability to respond but also by the wholeness of my actual responding. Being a body-self, a feeling self, a self of inner depth, a self with clear boundaries and an intimate self are all involved in being a responsible self. It is in *actually responding as this inclusive and whole self* that the fullness of human agency lies. Responding in my own integrity—owning "all my pieces" enough—and responding in mutuality to the other—attending to and respecting enough "all the pieces" of the other, including not just other persons, but organizations, nations, nature, the environment, the planet, and the cosmos, is how I act as a fully human self.

This responding as an integral and mutual self has two aspects. It means, of course, "being responsible." It involves "balancing personal concerns and responding to the needs and expectations of others."[117] Howard Gardner captures what we usually mean by being responsible quite well, when he says:

> Productive adults are expected to assume responsibility in a number of realms: for our own health and welfare; for those who depend on us—spouses, offspring, and as they age, grandparents and parents; for those at our workplace; for those in the various communities—such as professional, neighborhood, and regional—in which we live; and to the extent we have the opportunity and the means, for our global society.[118]

Underlying this usual meaning of responsibility, however, there is a second, more comprehensive understanding. In adulthood, responsibility means *actually responding as my own wholeness to the wholeness of the other*. Responsibility means to relate in integrity to myself and to the other as the other is. On one hand, responsibility is necessarily an owning of myself; it is saying: "I am responsible for what I am to be."[119] On the other hand, responsibility is "the activity of receiving and responding to another."[120] It is "the ingrained disposition to answer or respond to others' claims upon us."[121] In adulthood, integrity and responding to the other go together, the one unfolding, enlivening, and deepening the other. Being a fully responding person *is* integrity and mutuality as we actually live them out; it includes much more than the dictionary would suggest. Being an adult, being fully moral, being fully human, and being a person who responds to self and other are one and the same thing.

A Responsible Self in Morality

Being *a responsible self* is the best way we have of naming a fully adult and fully moral person. Whatever we can say about responsibility in adulthood is exactly what we can say about responsibility in morality. If I am a body-self aware enough of my feeling and of the feeling of the other, then I respond in a fully moral way to the other. If I relate to the other in empathy and intimacy, then I respond in a fully moral way to the other. If I can own my own inner depth and honor the inner depth of the other, then I respond in a fully moral way—in a dialogical way—to the other. If I can respect the boundaries of the other and my own boundaries as well, then I am responding in a fully moral way. A responsible self is a moral self as fully alive.

Adult morality means being responsible to and for ourselves. It means that "we are responsible for our own way of being."[122] Being a responsible self also means having loving care and being just in all the relationships that we have, in all of the obligations we have, and in all the different situations in which we find ourselves. Being a responsible self also means nurturing our own wholeness enough to relate to the other in depth, in intimacy, and in dialogue. It means respecting our own boundaries and the boundaries of the other so that the "unique character, particular history, and special needs" of all are attended to. "Mutuality," says Nothwehr, "moves the *starting point for ethical reflection* to a radically inclusive place, where literally everyone and everything is included."[123] Being a responsible self and being a fully moral person is one and the same thing.

Disconnections and Partial Pictures in the Culture

Because being a responsible self incorporates the other five characteristics of being adult and moral, we can see that all the disconnections and distortions of those characteristics are at play when it comes to appreciating what it means. The "mind-body," the "reason-emotion," and the "self-other" dichotomies drive a separating wedge into our ability to take any responsibility at all. The "cultural superego" along with how "money, sex, and power" are seen in the culture are powerfully influential in keeping us from responding as ourselves to the uniqueness of the other. The "addictions," the "dependencies," and the "developmental difficulties" we experience make living as a responsible self difficult if not practically impossible.

The "disembodied rationality" that strikes at the heart of the integral self-in-mutuality, undermines becoming a responsible self in three telling ways. First, disembodied rationality makes for a *disconnection* inside of us even as it makes a *disconnection* in our relating to the other, leaving us to rely on whatever concepts and categories we decide to use to interpret reality.[124] Second, disembodied rationality allows us to use our thinking in ways that are easily influenced by our own rationalizations and by the cultural superego. Third, disembodied rationality, when it holds that "certain doctrines, ideas, or propositions are more important than human beings," is the driving force of the different ideologies we suffer from that easily excuse responsibility.[125]

As it functions in the culture, *disembodied rationality is arguably the major obstacle to becoming a responsible self.* If our reason could be rooted in the body-self, if it could lie in empathy, and if it could come naturally from our inner depth—all of this an adult understanding of reason—then the story would be quite different. A rationality that is empathic and at the heart of the inner—an "embodied rationality"—goes hand-in-hand with being a responsible self, a dialogical self, a self fully adult, fully moral, and fully human.

Finally, one of the things that both disembodied rationality and the cultural superego have in common is their insistence that there is some "external standard" that we need to refer to in order to know that we are being responsible. This external standard must be "objective," that is, "out there" and the same for all of us to see, to accept, and to measure up to. Disembodied rationality holds that this external standard is universal, and the cultural superego holds that it ought to be accepted by all.[126] The problem, however, with this external standard is not just that we can never agree on what it is, on how it is arrived at, or on how it applies in different situations. The real problem with this standard is that it is *external*. It says that adulthood and adult morality is measured by a standard "outside" of us and therefore there is no need to be concerned about our own appropriation of wholeness and relatedness.

The assumption of an objective external standard—so wonderfully comforting in theory, so utterly elusive in reality, and so ultimately frustrating in interpersonal, national, and international dealings—allows us to stay locked up in a subject-object world, a world of disconnection where the inner and the relational do not go together. Without integrity and mutuality implicating each other—and especially without empathy that lets us respond as ourselves to the other as the other is—we can easily conclude: *developing as a human being is of no consequence*. This subject-object thinking is a human tragedy of our own making. No matter how we might struggle to become mature and moral, the source and the measure of being a responsible person always lies in a standard outside of us, a standard that has no connection at all to the "whole person," no connection at all with our becoming fully human.

NOTES

1. *To Kill a Mockingbird*, DVD, directed by Robert Mulligan (1962; Universal City, CA: Universal Pictures Home Entertainment, 2012).
2. Erik H. Erikson, "Autobiographic Notes on the Identity Crisis," *Deadalus* 99, no. 4 (Fall 1970): 757.
3. Bernard Lonergan, *A Second Collection*, ed. William F. Ryan and Bernard J. Terrell (Philadelphia: Westminster, 1974), 232.
4. Dov Cohen and Angela K.-y Leung, "Violence and Character: A CuPS (Culture x Person x Situation Perspective)," in *Human Aggression and Violence: Causes, Manifestations, and Consequences*, ed. Phillip R. Shaver and Mario Mikulincer (Washington, DC: American Psychological Association, 2011), 188.
5. Candace B. Pert, *Molecules of Emotion: Why You Feel the Way You Feel* (New York: Scribner, 1997), 189.
6. Ursula King, *The Search for Spirituality: Our Global Quest for a Spiritual Life* (New York: BlueBridge, 2008), 81.
7. Ibid.

8. For a helpful psychoanalytic understanding of the relational nature of the body, see Lewis Aron and Frances S. Anderson, eds. *Relational Perspectives on the Body* (Hillsdale, NJ: The Analytic Press, 1998).

9. Eugene T. Gendlin, "The Primacy of the Body, Not the Primacy of Perception," *Man and World* 25, no. 3–4 (1992): 349.

10. Judith Butler speaks of "body ontology" as a basic structure of human being "distinct from any and all social and political organization." Judith Butler, *Frames of War: When Is Life Grievable*? (New York: Verso, 2009), 2. Perhaps integrity and mutuality characterized as "a body-self" can be thought of as a basic structure of human being.

11. Susan Bordo, *Unbearable Weight: Feminism, Western Culture, and the Body* (Berkeley: University of California Press, 1993), 15.

12. Drew Leder, *The Absent Body* (Chicago: University of Chicago Press, 1990), 128.

13. Ibid., 153.

14. Maurice Merleau-Ponty, *The Primacy of Perception, and Other Essays on Phenomenological Psychology, the Psychology of Art, History and Politics*, ed. James Edie (Evanston, IL: Northwestern University Press, 1964), 5.

15. Carol Bigwood observes: "we are always already situated in an intersubjective (and thereby already cultural), spatiotemporal, fleshy (and thereby already natural) world before we creatively adopt a personal position in it." Carol Bigwood, "Renaturalizing the Body (With the Help of Merleau-Ponty)," *Hypatia* 6, no. 3 (1991): 66.

16. Juliet M. Corbin, "The Body in Health and Illness," *Qualitative Health Research* 13, no. 2 (February 2003): 258.

17. W. W. Meissner, "The Self and the Body: IV. The Body on the Couch," *Psychoanalysis and Contemporary Thought* 21, no. 2 (Spring 1998): 296.

18. Paul Ricoeur, *Oneself as Another* (Chicago, University of Chicago Press, 1992), 319. The problem with the notion of "embodiment" is pointed out by Thomas Ots, "The Silenced Body—The Expressive *Leib*: On the Dialectic of Mind and Life in Chinese Cathartic Healing," in *Embodiment and Experience: The Existential Ground of Culture and Self*, ed. Thomas J. Csordas (New York: Cambridge University Press, 1994), 117. He says, "The term embodiment may perpetuate the clean subject-object dichotomy of mind and body rather than helping to collapse it."

19. Thomas Csordas observes that it is not true "that the fully developed adult moving about in the world treats his or her body as an object." Thomas J. Csordas, "Embodiment as a Paradigm for Anthropology," *Ethos* 18, no. 1 (March 1990): 36.

20. Gabriel Marcel, *Metaphysical Journal*, trans. Bernard Wall (Chicago: Regnery, 1952), 259.

21. Judith Butler, *Undoing Gender* (New York: Routledge, 2004), 20.

22. J. Kellenberger insists that "fully realized morality is in fact relationship morality." J. Kellenberger, *Relationship Morality* (University Park: The Pennsylvania State University Press, 1995), 5.

23. Parker J. Palmer, *A Hidden Wholeness: The Journey toward an Undivided Life* (San Francisco: Jossey-Bass, 2004), 5.

24. Lewis Aron says: "Mind is inherently dyadic, social, interactional, and interpersonal." See Lewis Aron, *A Meeting of Minds: Mutuality in Psychoanalysis* (Hillsdale, NJ: The Analytic Press, 1996), x.

25. Lawrence J. Walker and Karl H. Hennig, "Differing Conceptions of Moral Exemplarity: Just, Brave, and Caring," *Journal of Personality and Social Psychology* 86, no. 4 (2004): 643.

26. Lorraine Code, *Epistemic Responsibility* (Hanover, NH: University Press of New England, 1987), 101.

27. James Olthuis finds that in addition to rationality we also know "by touch, by feel, by taste, by sight, by sounds, by smell, by symbols, by sex, by trust—by means of every modality of human experience." James H. Olthuis, "Introduction: Love/Knowledge: Sojourning with Others, Meeting with Differences," in *Knowing Other-wise: Philosophy at the Threshold of Spirituality,* ed. James H. Olthuis (New York: Fordham University Press, 1997), 6.

28. Michael J. Mahoney, "Suffering, Philosophy, and Psychotherapy," *Journal of Psychotherapy Integration* 15, no. 3 (2005): 340.

29. *Merriam-Webster's Collegiate Dictionary Online*, 12th ed., https://www.merriam-webster.com/dictionary/mind (accessed November 14, 2015).

30. Ibid.

31. Antonio Damasio notes the "absence of a notion of *organism* in cognitive sciences and neuroscience," and he observes: "The mind remained linked to the brain in a somewhat equivocal relationship, and the brain remained consistently separated from the body rather than being seen as part of a complete living organism." Antonio Damasio, *Descartes' Error: Emotion, Reason, and the Human Brain* (New York: Putnam, 1994), 40.

32. Elizabeth A. Grosz, *Volatile Bodies: Toward a Corporeal Feminism* (Bloomington, IN: Indiana University Press, 1994), 5, argues that "philosophy has established itself on a profound somatophobia."

33. Thandeka, *The Embodied Self: Friedrich Schleiermacher's Solution to Kant's Problem of the Empirical Self* (Albany: State University of New York Press, 1995), 3.

34. For a classical definition of disembodied rationality, see Plato, *Phaedo, The Collected Dialogues of Plato, Including the Letters*, ed. Edith Hamilton and Huntington Cairns (Princeton, NJ: Princeton University Press, 1982), 48. "The mind or psyche," observes Plato, "can best reflect when it is free of all distractions such as hearing or sight or pain or pleasure of any kind—that is, when it ignores the body and becomes as far as possible independent, avoiding all physical contacts and associations as much as it can, in search for reality."

35. Victor Turner, "Dramatic Ritual/Ritual Drama: Performative and Reflexive Anthropology," *The Kenyon Review*, New Series 1, no. 3 (July 1979): 92.

36. For a helpful understanding embodied cognition see Raymond W. Gibbs, Jr., *Embodiment and Cognitive Science* (New York: Cambridge University Press, 2006. For an accessible history of embodied cognition see Lawrence W. Barsa-

lou, "Grounded Cognition: Past, Present, and Future," *Topics in Cognitive Science* 2 (2010): 716–24.

37. Turner, "Dramatic Ritual," 93.

38. Zachary Schaeffer notes: "Modernity itself, with its characteristic mobility and diminished sense of community and connection, is what gives rise both to the atomized conception of the disconnected self and the anxiety and isolation that results from this disconnection." Zachary Schaeffer, "Transference, Countertransference, and Mutuality in Relational Social Work with College Students," *Clinical Social Work Journal* 42 (2014): 13.

39. Matthew Kelly, *The Seven Levels of Intimacy: The Art of Loving and the Joy of Being Loved* (New York: Simon & Schuster, 2005), 19.

40. See Carl Rogers, "A Theory of Therapy, Personality, and Interpersonal Relationships as Developed in the Client-Centered Framework," in *Psychology: A Study of a Science*, vol. 3, ed. Sigmund Koch (New York: McGraw-Hill, 1959), 198, where he calls feeling "an emotionally tinged experience together with its personal meaning."

41. The notions of "felt sensing" and "felt knowing" are used often by Eugene Gendlin. For example, see Eugene T. Gendlin, *Focusing* (New York: Bantam, 1981). See also Eugene T. Gendlin, *Focusing-Oriented Psychotherapy* (New York: Guilford, 1996).

42. Charles Davis, *Body as Spirit: The Nature of Religious Feeling* (New York: Crossroad, 1976), 4.

43. Edward S. Casey, *Spirit and Soul: Essays in Philosophical Psychology* (Dallas, TX: Spring, 1991), xiii.

44. Rogers, "A Theory of Therapy," 210.

45. Robert L. Selman, *The Growth of Interpersonal Understanding: Developmental and Clinical Analyses* (New York: Academic Press, 1980). See also John J. Shea, "The Development of Empathy: Adulthood, Morality and Religion," in *In Search of Healing: Collected Papers from the Annual Conference of the Society for Pastoral Counselling Research*, ed. Augustine Meier (Ottawa, ON: The Society for Pastoral Counselling Research, 2003), 71; Shea shows that Selman's levels of perspective taking throw light on the development of empathy

> As one progresses through the levels there is a move from the person as physical to the person as psychological, from the person as exterior to the person as interior; there is the understanding that the thoughts and feelings of the self and the thoughts and feelings of the other are increasingly important and increasingly differentiated; there is the understanding that mutuality becomes more and more the social reality; there is the understanding that the depth of the self and the depth of the other emerge as the most significant aspects of the self and the most significant aspects of mutual relating; and there is the sense that this personal depth can be felt and communicated, even if not always able to be adequately verbalized.

46. Judith V. Jordan, "Empathy and Self-Boundaries," in *Women's Growth in Connection: Writings From the Stone Center*, ed. Judith V. Jordan, Alexandra G. Kaplan, Jean Baker Miller, Irene P. Stiver, and Janet L. Surrey (New York: Guilford, 1991), 69.

47. Anne J. Vettesen, *Perception, Empathy, and Judgment: An Inquiry into the Preconditions of Moral Performance* (University Park: Pennsylvania State University Press, 1994), 118.

48. See Judith V. Jordan, "Relational Development Through Mutual Empathy," in *Empathy Reconsidered: New Directions in Psychotherapy*, ed. Arthur C. Bohart and Leslie S. Greenberg (Washington, DC: American Psychological Association, 1997), 343–51.

49. For a clear exposition of Roger's understanding of empathy, see Jerold D. Bozarth, "Empathy from the Framework of Client-Centered Theory and the Rogerian Hypothesis," in *Empathy Reconsidered: New Directions in Psychotherapy*, ed. Arthur C. Bohart and Leslie S. Greenberg (Washington, DC: American Psychological Association, 1997), 81–102.

50. Ralph R. Greenson, "Empathy and its Vicissitudes, *International Journal of Psychoanalysis*, 41 (1960): 418.

51. Gisela Labouvie-Vief finds that the language of mature adults tends to be "inner and personal" whereas the language of those younger is more "outer and technical." See Gisela Labouvie-Vief, "Cognitive-Emotional Integration in Adulthood," in *Annual Review of Gerontology and Geriatrics* 17, ed. K. Warner Schaie and M. Powell Lawton (New York: Springer, 1998), 220. See also Paulo Freire, *Pedagogy of the Oppressed*, 30th Anniversary Edition (New York: Continuum, 2009), 35, who talks about a "subjectivity and objectivity in constant dialectical relationship."

52. Richard M. Gula, *Moral Discernment* (New York: Paulist Press, 1997), 35.

53. See, for example, Martha Nussbaum, *Upheavals of Thought: The Intelligence of Emotions* (New York: Cambridge University Press, 2001).

54. For an excellent example of someone who puts reason and emotion together in a unique and helpful way, see Gisela Labouvie-Vief, "Reason and Emotion Across the Life Span: A Personal View," in *A History of Geropsychology in Autobiography*, ed. James E. Birren and Johannes J. F. Schroots (Washington, DC: American Psychological Association, 2000), 173–84. See also Gisela Labouvie-Vief, "Cognitive-Emotional Integration in Adulthood," 206–37.

55. One thinker who offers an expert and Piagetian-inspired understanding of how reason and emotion are integrated is Gisela Labouvie-Vief, *Integrating Emotions and Cognition Throughout the Life Span* (New York: Springer, 2015).

56. *Merriam-Webster's Collegiate Dictionary Online*, 12th ed., https://www.merriam-webster.com/dictionary/reason (accessed November 14, 2015).

57. Robert J. Fitterer, *Love and Objectivity in Virtue Ethics: Aristotle, Lonergan, and Nussbaum on Emotions and Moral Insight* (Toronto: University of Toronto Press, 2008), 6.

58. Damasio, *Descartes' Error*, xxi.

59. Hendrik Hart, "Conceptual Understanding and Knowing *Other*-wise: Reflections on Rationality and Spirituality in Philosophy," in *Knowing Other-Wise: Philosophy at the Threshold of Spirituality,* ed. James H. Olthuis (New York: Fordham University Press, 1997), 37.

60. Alasdair MacIntyre observes that the Enlightenment thinkers and their successors were "unable to agree as to what precisely those principles were which would be found undeniable by all rational persons." Flowing from this, he believes, is "the inability within our culture to unite conviction and rational justification." Alasdair MacIntyre, *Whose Justice? Which Rationality?* (Notre Dame, IN: University of Notre Dame Press, 1988), 6.

61. See MacIntrye, *Whose Justice?*, 8.

62. *Merriam-Webster's Collegiate Dictionary Online*, 12th ed., https://www.merriam-webster.com/dictionary/emotion (accessed November 14, 2015).

63. Antonio Damasio, *The Feeling of What Happens: Body and Emotion in the Making of Consciousness* (New York: Harcourt, Inc., 1999), 50.

64. George E. Marcus, *The Sentimental Citizen: Emotion in Democratic Politics* (University Park: Pennsylvania State University Press, 2002), 134.

65. N. A. Kuiper and M. R. MacDonald, "Reason, Emotion and Cognitive Therapy," *Clinical Psychology Review* 3, no. 3 (1983): 305. Gisela Labouvie-Vief, in talking about reason and emotion, says "the search for integration of these two modes has come to describe many recent theories of development." See Gisela Labouvie-Vief, "Affect Complexity and Views of the Transcendent," in *The Psychology of Mature Spirituality: Integrity, Wisdom, Transcendence*, ed. Polly Young-Eisendrath and Melvin E. Miller (London: Routledge, 2000), 103.

66. Augusto Blasi, "Identity and the Development of the Self," in *Self, Ego, and Identity: Integrative Approaches*, ed. Daniel K. Lapsley and F. Clark Power (New York: Springer-Verlag, 1988), 227.

67. See, for example, Max Scheler, *Man's Place in Nature* (New York: Noonday, 1962). It is interesting to note that, writing on the effects of trauma, Donald Kalsched observes that: "When mind and body split, the animating principle of psychological life, or what we could call spirit leaves." Donald Kalsched, *The Inner World of Trauma: Archetypal Defenses of the Personal Spirit* (London: Routledge, 1996), 67.

68. Parker Palmer calls the heart "that core place in the human self where all our capacities converge: intellect, senses, emotions, imagination, intuition, will, spirit, and soul." Parker J. Palmer, "Toward a Philosophy of Integrative Education," in *The Heart of Higher Education: A Call to Renewal: Transforming the Academy through Collegial Conversations*, ed. Parker J. Palmer and Arthur Zajonc, with Megan Scribner (San Francisco: Jossey-Bass, 2010), 20. See also James Hillman, *The Thought of the Heart* (Dallas, TX: Spring, 1984). See also Christina Becker, *The Heart of the Matter: Individuation as an Ethical Process* (Wilmette, IL: Chiron Publications, 2004).

69. Donald Kalsched, *Trauma and the Soul: A Psycho-Spiritual Approach to Human Development and its Interruption* (New York: Routledge, 2013), 10. See also Farhad Dalal, "Specialists without Spirit: Sensualists without Heart; Psycho-

therapy as a Moral Endeavour," 36th S. H. Foulkes Annual Lecture, *Group Analysis* 45, no. 4 (2012): 419: "At its simplest, soul means the capacity to feel, to feel deeply, and for the feelings to be meaningful." See also Thomas Moore who says that soul "has to do with depth, value, relatedness, heart and personal substance." Thomas Moore, *Care of the Soul: A Guide for Cultivating Depth and Sacredness in Everyday Life* (New York: HarperCollins, 1992), 5.

70. Charles Taylor, *Sources of the Self: The Making of the Modern Identity* (Cambridge, MA: Harvard University Press, 1989), 111.

71. Augusto Blasi, "Neither Personality nor Cognition: An Alternative Approach to the Nature of the Self," in *Changing Conceptions of Psychological Life*, ed. Cynthia Lightfoot, Chris Lalonde, and Michael Chandler (Mahwah, NJ: Lawrence Erlbaum, 2004), 10.

72. See Sigmund Freud, *The Ego and the Id*, trans. Joan Riviere (New York: Norton, 1960).

73. See Max Van Manen and Bas Levering, *Childhood's Secrets: Intimacy, Privacy, and the Self Reconsidered* (New York: Teachers College Press, 1996).

74. Kathleen R. Fischer, *Reclaiming the Connection: A Contemporary Spirituality* (Kansas City, MO: Sheed & Ward, 1990), 31.

75. Gabrielle Taylor, "Integrity," *Proceedings of the Aristotelian Society*, Supplementary Volumes 55 (1981): 143.

76. Robert Grudin, *The Grace of Great Things: Creativity and Innovation* (New York: Ticknor & Fields, 1990), 75.

77. Stephanie Dowrick, *Intimacy and Solitude* (New York: Norton & Company, 1994), 186.

78. Donald Evans, *Spirituality and Human Nature* (Albany: State University of New York Press, 1993), 38. See also Andrew W. Metcalfe, "Solitude as a Community of Difference," *Journal of Spirituality in Mental Health* 15, no. 1 (2013): 3–18.

79. See Arthur P. Ciaramicoli, *The Power of Empathy: A Practical Guide to Creating Intimacy, Self-Understanding, and Lasting Love* (New York: Plume, 2001).

80. One clear source of this contrasting morality is John W. Glaser, "Conscience and Superego: A Key Distinction," in *Conscience: Theological and Psychological Perspectives*, ed. C. Ellis Nelson (New York: Newman, 1973): 167–88.

81. David N. Elkins, "A Humanistic Approach to Spiritually Oriented Psychotherapy," in *Spiritually Oriented Psychotherapy*, ed. Len Sperry and Edward P. Shafranske (Washington, DC: American Psychological Association, 2005), 137, says: "Soul will slip through the bars of every conceptual system and defy all attempts to capture her in abstract terms."

82. William S. Schmidt, *The Development of the Notion of Self: Understanding the Complexity of Human Interiority* (Lewiston, NY: Edwin Mellen Press, 1994), 379, observes: "Boundary intactness becomes a supreme measure for assessing the health or disarray of any self."

83. Mario Jacobi, *The Analytic Encounter: Transference and Human Relationship* (Toronto: Inner City Books, 1984), 64.

84. Charles L. Whitfield, *Boundaries and Relationships: Knowing, Protecting and Enjoying the Self* (Deerfield Beach, FL: Health Communications, 1993), 117.

85. Barbara Glasson, *A Spirituality of Survival* (New York: Continuum, 2009), 71, makes the point that without "real boundaries" one party can become a "victim of either oppression or invisibility."

86. Viktor E. Frankl, *The Will to Meaning: Foundations and Applications of Logotherapy* (New York: New American Library, 1969), ix.

87. Steven Krugman, "Male Development and the Transformation of Shame," in *A New Psychology of Men*, ed. Ronald F. Levant and William S. Pollack (New York: Basic Books, 1995), 114.

88. Karen Labacqz and Ronald G. Barton, "Boundaries, Mutuality, and Professional Ethics," in *Boundary Wars: Intimacy and Distance in Healing Relationships*, ed. Katherine H. Ragsdale (Cleveland, OH: Pilgrim Press, 1996), 103.

89. Rokelle Lerner, *Living in the Comfort Zone: The Gift of Boundaries in Relationships* (Deerfield Beach, FL: Health Communications, Inc., 1995), 14.

90. Marsha Linehan, *Cognitive-Behavioral Treatment of Borderline Personality Disorder* (New York: Guilford, 1993), 31.

91. Craig Nakken, *The Addictive Personality: Understanding the Addictive Process and Compulsive Behavior*, 2nd ed. (Center City, MN: Hazelden, 1996), 8.

92. Nakken, *Addictive Personality*, 15–17.

93. Ibid., 21–23.

94. Anne Wilson Schaef, *Co-Dependence: Misunderstood—Mistreated* (San Francisco: Harper & Row, 1986), 46.

95. Ibid.

96. Whitfield, *Boundaries and Relationships*, 32.

97. Ibid.

98. Ibid.

99. Ibid.

100. The phrase, "vulnerabilities of the self" is from Gil G. Noam, "'Normative Vulnerabilities' of Self and Their Transformations," in *The Moral Self*, ed. Gil G. Noam and Thomas E. Wren (Cambridge, MA: MIT Press, 1993), 222.

101. Kelly, *The Seven Levels*, 8.

102. Dowrick, *Intimacy and Solitude*, 229.

103. Kelly, *The Seven Levels*, 9.

104. Ibid., 218.

105. Brené Brown, *Daring Greatly, How the Courage to Be Vulnerable Transforms the Way We Live, Love, Parent, and Lead* (New York: Gotham Books, 2012), 46.

106. Ibid.

107. Jordan, "Empathy and Self Boundaries," 69.

108. Rogers, "A Theory of Therapy," 210.

109. Heinz Kohut, *How Does Analysis Cure?* (Chicago: University of Chicago Press, 1984), 82.

110. Dowrick, *Intimacy and Solitude*, 196.

111. Frankl, *Will to Meaning*, ix.

112. Erik H. Erikson, "Eight Ages of Man," *Childhood and Society*, 2nd ed. (New York: Norton, 1963), 263.

113. *Merriam-Webster's Collegiate Dictionary Online*, 12th ed., https://www.merriam-webster.com/dictionary/intimate (accessed November 14, 2015).

114. Kelly, *The Seven Levels*, 7.

115. Ibid.

116. Dowrick, *Intimacy and Solitude*, 183.

117. Ann Higgins-D'Alessandro and F. Clark Power, "Character, Responsibility, and the Moral Self," in *Character Psychology and Character Education*, ed. Daniel K. Lapsley and F. Clark Power (Notre Dame, IN: University of Notre Dame Press, 2005), 114.

118. Howard Gardner, "Introduction," *Responsibility at Work: How Leading Professionals Act (or Don't Act) Responsibly* (San Francisco: John Wiley & Sons, 2007), 2.

119. Brian Braman, *Meaning and Authenticity: Bernard Lonergan and Charles Taylor on the Drama of Authentic Human Existence* (Toronto: University of Toronto Press, 2008), 15.

120. Linda Thompson, "Contextual and Relational Morality: Intergenerational Responsibility in Later Life," in *Aging Parents and Adult Children*, ed. Jay A. Mancini (Lexington, MA: Lexington Books, 1989), 259.

121. Kevin Crotty, "Democracy, Tragedy, and Responsibility," in *Taking Responsibility: Comparative Perspectives*, ed. Winston Davis (Charlottesville, VA: University of Virginia Press, 2001). 109.

122. Braman, *Meaning and Authenticity*, 28.

123. Ibid., 262.

124. See Margaret U. Walker, "Moral Understandings: Alternative 'Epistemology' for a Feminist Ethics," *Hypatia* 4, no. 2 (Summer 1989): 15–28.

125. Michael L. Penn and Aditi Malik, "The Protection and Development of the Human Spirit: An Expanded Focus for Human Rights Discourse," *Human Rights Quarterly* 32 (2010): 667–68.

126. For a helpful critique of both objectivity and universality in reason, see Mark Johnson, *Moral Imagination: Implications of Cognitive Science for Ethics* (Chicago: University of Chicago Press, 1993).

Chapter Three

Care and Justice

The Fully Human in Action

In the movie, *A Few Good Men*, Lance Corporal Dawkins and Private Downey are on trial for giving an off-the-books beating—a "code red"—to Private William Santiago, who was later found dead in his barracks. In a dramatic moment near the end of their trial for murder, their lawyer, young Lieutenant Caffey, challenges their crusty commanding officer, Colonel Jessup, about whether he ordered the code red. "I want the truth," insists Caffey. Jessup retorts: "You want the truth? You can't handle the truth." Caffey demands again: "Did you order the code red?" Jessup finally explodes: "You're damn right I did." The courtroom gasps. Dawkins and Downey were following orders when they gave Private Santiago the fatal beating. Although not guilty of the major charges against them, they are convicted of conduct unbecoming a marine and are ordered to be dishonorably discharged. A disbelieving Private Downey says: "What did we do wrong? We did nothing wrong." Then, in perhaps the most telling moment of the film, Lance Corporal Dawkins responds: "Yeah, we did. We were supposed to fight for people who can't fight for themselves. We were supposed to fight for Willy."[1]

In this chapter, we describe care and justice in light of an integral self-in-mutuality and its defining characteristics. We move from describing what an adult-moral self "is" to describing how this self "acts." Being caring and just—together as one—is the best description we have of an integral and mutual self in action. Likewise, it is the best description we have of how we act as a responsible self. This move from "is" to "acts" could not be more important for understanding the fully human. More than two virtues among many, care and justice are, in their developmental fullness, a foundational core of adult-moral activity. Together as one, being caring and acting justly is how we relate when we are fully human.

An explanation of why this move from "is" to "acts" is so important may be as surprising as it is critical. Two things can be said. The first is that understanding care and justice from an adult-moral perspective radically transforms the meaning these two notions usually have in the culture and in academia. The second is that as the notions of care and justice are transformed, it becomes clear how impoverished and dysfunctional their typical understandings are. In fact, if we cannot entertain a serious critique of care and justice in the culture and academia, if we allow them to remain in developmental atrophy and disconnection, we are left not only with no adequate understanding of either notion but also with no actionable blueprint of how to act as a responsible human being.[2]

WHAT DO CARE AND JUSTICE MEAN?

While being caring and acting justly are somehow at the core of our humanity, the meaning of these notions can be hard to grasp. Does care have its primary importance in family relationships? Is it more natural to women than it is to men? Is it something essentially connected to mothering? As it is so often characterized in the literature, is care subjective, emotional, concrete, and personal? What is justice about? Does justice have to do primarily with our broader societal relationships? Is justice more natural for men than it is for women? Is justice meant to be an application of universal principles? As it is so often characterized in the literature, is justice objective, rational, abstract, and impersonal?[3]

Because care and justice are often paired, we cannot help wondering about their connection. Are these two notions in opposition to each other, describing ways of responding that are essentially separate or disconnected? Or are these two notions self-contained silos that should stand next to each other? Or are these two notions meant to be complementary, so that the picture we have of maturity and morality is incomplete if both are not included in some way? Or are these two notions mutually involving, so that in actual practice we cannot be just if we are not caring or caring if we are not just? Lastly, we can ask the kind of question we have been asking all along: "Do care and justice have to be understood as *disconnected*, or is there a way to see them together as one?"

The dictionary tells us that care means "painstaking and watchful attention."[4] To care for means "to do the necessary things for someone who needs help or protection."[5] The dictionary defines a carer as a person "who is responsible for attending to the needs of a child or dependent adult."[6] A caregiver is "a person who provides direct care (as for children, elderly people, or the chronically ill)."[7] Although these dictionary definitions of care do mention needs that certain others have, they are incredibly limited and narrow.

In the dictionary, care is framed primarily in terms of the physical needs of those who are not able to help themselves. The importance of loving and competent caring, especially in the early years, is not mentioned. The idea that all of us need to care and to be cared for from cradle to grave is given no attention at all. The dictionary suggests that care is something we may need when we are not whole; it fails to see that care is actually how we respond to the self and to the other when we are whole. Unfortunately, there is nothing at all in the dictionary definitions of care to suggest that it is an indispensable quality, a quality so essential, in fact, that without it we would not be human.

The dictionary tells us that justice is "the quality of being just, impartial or fair." It is also "the maintenance or administration of what is just," and "the determination of rights according to the rules of law or equity,"[8] Although these definitions are concise and clarifying, the different ways that justice is actually considered in the culture could hardly be more disparate. Down through the centuries—and still very much today—justice has come to mean: the law; crime and punishment; revenge and retribution; contracts, obligations and what is owed to the other; personal rights and duties; what a person has earned or is entitled to; vindication; virtue; what is useful for society; a social contract; restitution; the restoration of wholeness; the happiness of a good life; human flourishing; and the common good.

If all of this were not enough for justice to include, since the time of the Enlightenment it has also been paired—especially in academia—with a disembodied rationality that honors the subject-object dichotomy and tends to privilege facts over values in the human. Justice lies in "abstract principles" or "rules of reason" that are not only objective but universal as well. With all of this, we can rightfully ask, as Robert Solomon and Mark Murphy do, "given the enormous amount of disagreement among us concerning the right conception of justice, can we suppose with any confidence that there is, ultimately, some single standard or 'definition' to be found?"[9]

Critical questions need to be asked about the meaning of care and justice. Is there a fullness to care that is missing? Could care be much more than an action so often completely discounted, so often dismissed as insignificant in human affairs? Is there a fullness of justice that is missing? Could justice be much more than abstractions that must be formulated objectively as universal principles? Thankfully, the answer to these questions is in the affirmative. As care and justice mature, they become much easier to recognize. Coming into their own wholeness, they relate to each other in mutuality. Coming into their own wholeness, they describe quite well how we act when we are fully human. In maturity, care and justice are not disconnected at all. In fact, as Susan Hekman puts it, they "inhabit" each other.[10]

WHAT IS MATURE CARE?

In its fullness, *care is attending to the needs, rights, and freedoms of the self and the other for wholeness*. In relating as an adult-moral person, caring means to look after the needs for wholeness of the self and the other and it means to be concerned about the rights and freedoms that safeguard these needs.[11] Interpersonally, caring is "the ability to perceive other people in their own terms and to respond to their needs."[12] On a broader scale, caring is about responding in empathy to the need for wholeness of whatever is other, be that animals, natural resources, the environment, or the planet. In order to care, "I must understand the other's needs and I must be able to respond properly to them."[13]

Needs, says Selma Sevenhuijsen, are the "quintessential object" of care, and the care they call for runs the gamut from micro to macro, "from child-rearing practices and intimate relationships, to social services and education and political deliberations."[14] Yet, care is also about responding in empathy to the needs of the self. Care for the self and care for the other work well when they work together. If love is defined as an active concern for the growth and wholeness of the self and the other, then loving and caring go together in an adult-moral self. A mature care is a loving care. "To be moral and to be loving imply one another."[15]

WHAT IS MATURE JUSTICE?

In its fullness, *justice is respect, fairness, and equity in caring for the needs, rights, and freedoms of the self and the other for wholeness.* In relating as an adult and a moral person, to be just means to be accurate and evenhanded in attending to these needs, rights, and freedoms of self and other and it means that we are all equal when it comes to the consideration our needs, rights, and freedoms deserve.[16] Equity only nuances equality. It recognizes that the actual needs for wholeness that each of us has may be different and that, as Jean Piaget observes, the "real situation" of the self and of the other has to be taken into account.[17] Justice is about treating the self and the other appropriately in a context of mutuality.[18] Furthermore, if justice is rooted in caring, then mature love is as much a part of justice as it is a part of caring.[19] It is fair to say: "To love is to seek justice, to seek justice is to care."[20]

CARE AND JUSTICE: INTEGRITY AND MUTUALITY

As we reflect on care and justice as being the power of our integrity and the practice of our mutuality, what do we find? We find that our caring, our *attending* to the needs, rights, and freedoms of the self and the other, comes directly from our integrity and mutuality. If we are whole selves, if we can own all of our own "pieces," and if we are mutual selves, if we take the other's individuality, differences, and circumstances into account, not only are we are able to care for ourselves and for the other, but we need to do that. Likewise, we find that our justice, our *respecting*, our ability to be fair and equitable as we relate to self and other, also comes directly from our integrity and mutuality. We realize that being caring and just are imperatives. We see that *being caring and acting justly is how we acknowledge, confirm, and further wholeness and mutuality.*

Can care and justice exist in disconnection? While care and justice are so often split in the culture as well as in higher education, they are not split in an adult and moral self. In an integral self-in-mutuality, there is no "ethic of care" that is not intimately connected to an "ethic of justice." To be caring is to attend to the needs, rights, and freedoms of the self and the other for wholeness; to be just is to be respectful, fair, and equitable as we do that. Caring is not fully human if it is not framed by respect for the self and the other. Justice is abstract, arbitrary, and elusive—often a perversion and even a sign of contradiction—if it is not connected to the need for wholeness of self and other. Our relating in integrity and mutuality is always a "just caring" or a "caring justice."

How do we know that integrity and mutuality always involve a just caring or a caring justice? In reality, it is not at all difficult to tell. In family life and in all our wider relating, the more whole we become the more we experience caring separated from justice stretching along a continuum that has imposition at one end and serious exploitation at the other. Likewise, the more whole we become the more we experience justice separated from caring stretching along a continuum with disrespect at one end and serious dehumanization at the other.

In the culture, however, and especially in academia—where fact is often privileged over value and analysis often privileged over synthesis—care and justice are often seen to be in disconnection. As their cultural understandings suggest, they are made out to be two quite different "things"—things that turn out to be neither whole nor connected to each other. Not only does this lack of wholeness and connection seriously distort the meaning of both notions but it also seriously distorts our understanding of human development, including what it means to be a woman or a man.

In the culture, at least stereotypically, women are expected to be naturally caring but not especially skilled or interested in justice; men are expected to be naturally just but not especially skilled or interested in caring. It is if these two foundational human ways of acting, along with the genders thought to embody them, were stand-alone entities in some kind of competition. Regardless of our gender, the clarifying questions for us have to be: "Is it possible to integral and mutual and not be caring? Is it possible to be integral and mutual and not be just?" Is George Vaillant not right when he says that true wisdom is "a fusion of caring and justice"?[21]

CARE AND JUSTICE IN LIGHT OF THE SIX CHARACTERISTICS

The meaning of care and justice and how they are intimately connected is seen most clearly, perhaps, in light of the six characteristics of an integral and mutual self. If we are interested in understanding the fully human in action, if we are looking for a living mosaic of what it means to act as an adult and moral self—a mosaic not seriously disfigured by disconnection—these six characteristics provide the kind of descriptive detail that both amplifies and confirms the meaning of care and justice in the fully human.

If we consider care and justice in relation to being a body-self, what do we find? As Erik Erikson's thinking helps us see, we begin to embody care and justice from birth.[22] We take in care and respect from our being fed and held, from all the administrations of our mother or those who are caring for our needs. As we become aware of ourselves in relation to the other, Jean Piaget's work helps us see that care and justice naturally go together, that fairness is a kind of calculus for care.[23] We know this because if we had siblings we probably said quite often in early indignation: "He got a bigger piece than I did!" The care and justice we begin to embody as very young children becomes the foundation of our human growth and becoming. Later, if all goes well enough, the interplay between care and justice continues to develop throughout childhood and adolescence. In time, if we are fortunate and courageous enough, we find that care and justice emerge as an essential core of our embodied relationality.

Do care and justice have to be embodied? It is easy, perhaps, to see that there is no such thing as disembodied care. Images of mothers feeding infants and physical therapists helping those who have been injured readily come to mind.[24] It is not hard to see that "care cannot be fully understood without attending to its embodied dimension."[25] It may be harder, however, to see that there is no such thing as disembodied justice. Yet, as Diemut Bubeck reminds us, justice is never done to "abstractions" but to "concrete, real people."[26] The fairness and equity of justice are merely idealized concepts unless they are rooted in respect for an actual self or an actual other—*this* person, *this* institution, *this* animal, *this* aspect of the ecology. "Justice," John Caputo points out, "is there, on the spot, in the individual situation."[27] As a body-self, we know what care and justice are because in life we find ourselves consistently needing to experience them.

From the perspective of being a feeling self, we naturally, if not automatically, experience care and justice together. In the last chapter, we saw that feeling is the emotionally tinged and the rationally grasped as they exist together in our experience. The examples were: "As a mature parent, I *feel* the importance of providing proper nutrition for my child." Or, "As a mature teacher, I *feel* the rightness of giving attention to all my students, the bright and the not so bright." Or, "As a mature social worker, I *feel* the need to find a good home for this seriously neglected child." Caring and justice are not separate "things" but are felt together, often seamlessly in the moment. The dichotomized thinking that categorizes justice as the "reasonable" and care as the "emotional" is an analytic maneuver that is not primarily operative in a feeling self. We can say: "When empathy is born, care is born, and with it morality."[28]

If we look at care and justice in light of being a self of inner depth, how does that impact our understanding of these two notions? The hero, or the saint, or the sage—figures of inner depth known for their greatness of spirit, or soul, or heart—are also known for their exceptional caring and their concern for justice. In addition to these wonderful exemplars, we also have powerful examples of caring and justice in our own families, friends, and communities. Most of us know, either personally or by reputation, people whose very identity lies in being caring and just. We say of these people that they are *deeply caring*; that they are *just to the core*; that they are the *soul of compassion*; that they have *exceptional courage*; that they relate to the other with a *profound generosity of spirit*. We understand that for these people—adult and moral as they are—caring and justice are a practiced part of their embodied *innermost*.

Care and justice can be seen as one in a self with clear boundaries. If we are suffering, for example, from one of the addictions, or from codependency, or from some other developmental difficulty, we may not be enough of a "reasonably coherent whole" to relate in mutuality to the other. Without clear boundaries, the self is not aware enough either of its own needs, rights, and freedoms or of the needs, rights, and freedoms of the other. Unfortunately, caring for the self and for the other is often hard to sustain in any serious way, and the meaning of care is itself easily distorted. Likewise, without clear boundaries our diminished respect for self and other is going to make relating in fairness and equity diminished as well. As this happens, acting justly is inevitably compromised.

It is important to note that Gil Noam's "vulnerabilities of the self" described in chapter 1 are also vulnerabilities in our ability to care and to be just. As described, the "vacillating self" that is "so preoccupied with its own survival and cohesion"[29] and the "alienated self" that has "little empathy either for itself or for others"[30] are going to find a mature practice of care and justice beyond the pale of their concern. Yet, a self with clear boundaries finds care and justice in their innermost, each having appropriate boundaries yet relating as one.

It is in terms of an intimate self that the true nature of care and justice can, perhaps, be seen most clearly. If empathy—self-empathy and empathy for the other—is at the heart of intimacy, it is also at the heart of caring. Caring—attending to the needs, rights, and freedoms of the self and the other—requires that I be in touch enough with my own feeling and depth and that I welcome the feeling and depth of the other. Justice—being fair and equitable in respecting the needs, rights, and freedoms of the self and the other—also requires that I be in touch enough with my own feeling and depth and have enough understanding of the feeling and depth of the other. Although in conventional thinking justice is often thought of as cold and impersonal, in an adult-moral self it cannot avoid being deeply intimate.[31] In the empathy that accompanies intimacy and genuine friendship, a mature caring and a mature justice are realized as one.[32]

Finally, being caring and acting justly—these adult ways of being that function together—is a perfect definition of what it means to act as a responsible self. Quite simply, anyone who attends to the needs, rights, and freedoms of the self and the other for wholeness and who does so with respect, fairness, and equity *defines* what it means to act responsibly. Responsibility *is* to be just and caring to myself and to attend to the unique character, particular history, and special needs of the other. A morality of inner depth with its voice of concern for self and other *is* responsible, caring, and just at the same time.

In *A Few Good Men*, the film that introduces this chapter, Private Downey protests: "What did we do wrong? We did nothing wrong?" When Lance Corporal Dawkins responds: "Yeah, we did. We were supposed to fight for people who can't fight for themselves. We were supposed to fight for Willy," in his own martial way he is describing care, justice, and responsibility together. An integral and mutual self, a responsible self, a fully human self is a self that is caring and just.

CAN WE MAKE ROOM FOR CARE IN THE CULTURE?

At this point, the important question to ask is: What needs to change in cultural thinking for care to be seen in its wholeness, to be seen at the core of an adult-moral self, a fully human self? In answering this question, it is helpful to keep in mind the way care is so often taken for granted in the culture, the way it is equated with the familial and the private, the way it often figures so little in the economies of the world, and the way it is so often described in complete disconnection from justice. In fact, a good place to begin making room for care in the culture is to critique the idea that care is the opposite of justice: if justice must be objective, rational, abstract, and impersonal, then care must be subjective, emotional, concrete, and personal. As we critique this fourfold belief about the nature of care, we necessarily critique the dichotomized thinking that so powerfully and so effectively keeps the notions of care and justice so anemic and so disconnected from each other.

"Care must be subjective, emotional, concrete, and personal."

Care Is Subjective

Although seeming to be the definitive put down of the importance of care, it is not at all clear what this belief actually means. Does it mean that caring has more to do with the one who cares than who or what is cared for? Does it mean that the object of our care is not taken seriously into account? Does it mean that a caring person cannot perceive the needs, rights, and freedoms of the self and the other very accurately? Is this belief a direct consequence of the subject-object dichotomy in our thinking? If justice must be objective, then does care have to be subjective? Could this belief that care is subjective also be quite sexist? Is caring something that women do, women who cannot be very objective?

Care Is Emotional

Again, it is not at all clear what this belief means. If everything we do is bodily felt, if feeling is the emotionally tinged and the rationally grasped together, why do we not include the emotional and the rational together in our understanding of care?[33] Is the reason-emotion dichotomy at play? If justice must be rational, does caring have to be emotional? Is this belief also quite sexist? Is caring something that women do, women who are not very rational? If men are caring, are they also emotional? Do real men not care? When we separate emotion from reason, what does that do to the place of care in a culture that worships justice as disembodied rationality?

Care Is Concrete

If being concrete means that care *actually attends to the needs of the self and the other*, then caring is very concrete. It is *this* caring person attending to *this* other. A mother taking care of her child is doing something very concrete. A corporation negotiating benefits with its employees is engaged in something very concrete. A country providing for refugees from a neighboring country is engaged in something very concrete. If, however, "being concrete" is meant to be pejorative, if it means that care is not abstract and universal the way that justice is thought to be, then care is seen in disconnection from justice and as having little or no importance for being either adult or moral.

Care Is Personal

It could not be otherwise. Care is personal, interpersonal, and relational all at the same time. Care is attending to the needs, rights, and freedoms of the self and the other, and as we know from experience it is often deeply felt and deeply intimate. If, however, "being personal" means not being impersonal or not having the kind of universal application that principles of justice are thought to have, then thinking of care as "being personal" is a way of disparaging this inherently human way of being. Seen as necessarily in disconnection from standards of impersonal justice, care as personal has little or no connection with the understanding in the culture of what it means to be a fully moral person, a fully human person.

LIBERATING CARE IN THE CULTURE

Fortunately, a number of thinkers see care at the heart of what it means to be a human being, and they are interested in liberating it from the confines of subject-object thinking. In the last century, the continental philosopher, Martin Heidegger, saw care as the essential "source" of our humanness as embodied beings.[34] "For Heidegger care is inevitable; all aware human beings care. It is the mark of being human."[35] More recently, Carol Gilligan—opening up a new era in moral thinking—proposed a developmental "ethics of care" as a complement to the "ethics of justice" proposed by Lawrence Kohlberg.[36] Nel Noddings is a powerful proponent of an "ethic of caring" over an "ethic of principle" focused on moral reasoning and moral judgment.[37] For Annette Baier, Joan Tronto, Selma Sevenhuijsen, Leonardo Boff, and any number of others, it is care that allows for "the flourishing of that which is truly humanizing: deep feeling, willingness to share, and the requirements of love."[38]

Three thinkers in particular are helpful in making room for care in the meaning of being an adult and a fully moral person.

WENDY HOLLWAY

Wendy Hollway, a social scientist and psychoanalytic thinker, believes that "care is the psychological equivalent to our need to breathe unpolluted air."[39] As she explains, "good-enough care, like good-enough air, is inside and outside us—inevitably—all the time, whether in its presence or lack."[40] For her, the essence of care lies in "meeting needs," both physical and relational, and this requires "attentiveness and compassion" on the part of the carer.[41] Compassionate caring depends on "adequate recognition" of the other.[42] The "absence of attentiveness" is not just a problem; it is "a moral failing."[43] "We can only know what another person is experiencing through empathy or 'fellow feeling'; that is, through using ourselves as an instrument of understanding."[44]

For Hollway, the capacity to care is developmental, and "the early primary relationship between mother and infant" is crucial for this development.[45] As she says, it is through "the mother's sensitive response to the baby's experiences" that the baby "first experiences the integrity of its own body."[46] Families are "the crucible of subsequent caring relationships."[47] Then, Hollway says, in perhaps the most critical point of her book, *The Capacity to Care*: "The experience of being cared for is essential in developing the capacity to care."[48]

The capacity to care is actually "a model for all adult development."[49] Hollway holds that a differentiated self, a self able to "recognize the other as a subject in her own right," is "an essential precondition for the capacity to care."[50] As a model of development, care has four distinguishing abilities: (1) adults are "capable of reciprocal, interdependent care receiving and care giving; (2) adults are capable of providing the "the non-negotiable, asymmetrical" care that is required of mothers, fathers, and others; (3) adults are "capable of self care"; and (4) adults can extend their care "to both human and non-human objects."[51]

Not only does Hollway see caring as a profoundly human adult ability, but also *she clearly equates this adult ability with being a moral person.* As she puts it: "to care for others and the environment that sustains them is to live an ethical life."[52] "Ethics" she says, "is another way of talking about the capacity to care; one that belongs more to the public than the private sphere, more to the care for strangers than for intimates, more to citizenship than mothering."[53]

VIRGINIA HELD

Virginia Held, a feminist and a philosopher, states: "I find care the most basic moral value. Without the actual practice of care, there cannot be human life at all."[54] Held contrasts an "ethics of care" with an "ethics of justice." Care for her is about "attentiveness, sensitivity, and responding to needs," needs that can be basic and simple as well as psychological and cultural.[55] In an ethics of care, "trust, solidarity, mutual concern, and empathic responsiveness have priority."[56] She finds that justice "in all its forms requires impartiality, treating persons as equals, and recognizing their rights." In an ethics of justice, "equality, impartiality, fair distribution, and noninterference have priority."[57] For Held, *care has primacy over justice*. She points out: "unless we have strong motives to care about our fellow human beings and unless we value this caring, we will not care whether their rights are respected or not, especially in the case of people who are too weak to make serious trouble for us."[58]

Care for Held is about "actual relationships" and it is based on what she calls "mutual autonomy." Whereas individual autonomy is thought of in terms of "self-sufficiency, noninterference, self-direction, rational control, and the like," mutual autonomy involves "mutual understandings and acceptances of how much sharing of time, space, daily decisions, and so on" will characterize the relationship.[59] A "liberal individualism" fosters "a false picture of society and the persons in it."[60]

> Instead of seeing the corporate sector, and military strength, and government and law as the most important segments of society

> deserving the highest levels of wealth and power, a caring society might see the tasks of bringing up children, educating its members, meeting the needs of all, achieving peace and treasuring the environment, and doing these things in the best way possible to be that to which the greatest social efforts of all should be devoted.[61]

ERIK ERIKSON

Erik Erikson describes mature adulthood in terms of generativity versus stagnation. Adult fullness lies in being generative, in "establishing and guiding the next generation." The virtue or strength of this adult stage, a stage that is so pivotal in human evolution, is care. His definition of this care is all-inclusive: "*Care is the widening concern for what has been generated by love, necessity, or accident; it overcomes the ambivalence adhering to irreversible obligation.*"[62] Not only is Erikson saying that care is the quintessential strength of mature adulthood, but also he is saying that there is really no reason for an adult not to be caring. He is saying that *the need for care is the only calculus for care*. For Erikson, the intimacy and love of young adulthood naturally lead us into the generativity and care of mature adulthood.

Loving care *is* mutuality: it forms "a relationship in which partners depend on each other for the development of their respective strengths."[63] Caring "*strengthens the doer even as it strengthens the other*."[64] In caring, both the self and the other are engaged in a lifelong process of growth that furthers the wholeness of all who are involved. The care of the mother begets trust and hope in the child. In this mutuality, the child actually incorporates the care of the mother; outer good becomes "inner certainty."[65] Care is the engine of generativity, carrying the human forward from one generation to the next. It is "a quality essential for psychosocial evolution."[66] Care renewing itself in each generation makes the human possible. In other words, the fullness of human life revolves around the loving care that the adult self provides.

If we are interested in hearing from the "better angels" of our human nature, doing whatever we can to make room for care in the culture, in academia, and in social policies is a good place to start.

CAN WE REDEFINE JUSTICE IN THE CULTURE?

It is equally important to ask: What is it about justice in the culture that makes it so hard to see in its human wholeness? Interestingly enough, the answer to this question—the most telling answer—is that justice is so often presented as completely separate from caring. The disastrous effects of this *disconnection* can be found in three beliefs so many people throughout the world seem to share. The first belief is that: "Justice must be objective, rational, abstract, and impersonal." The second belief, a belief that appears to be more common with the breakdown of cultural constraints, is: "To be just is to follow the law." The third belief, a belief thoroughly entrenched in a great many cultures, is: "Justice is punishment."

"Justice Must Be Objective, Rational, Abstract, and Impersonal"

The first belief—a belief that so many philosophers, moral theorists, and others in academia hold with exceptional tenacity—is the requirement that justice be objective, rational, abstract, and impersonal. In critiquing this fourfold belief about the nature of justice, three questions can be kept in mind. First, why are so many thinkers and academicians so certain of this belief? Second, what does this fourfold belief do to the marginalization of care in the culture? Third, what does this fourfold belief mean if we understand justice in adulthood as respect, fairness, and equity in caring for the needs and rights of the self and the other for wholeness?

Justice Must Be Objective

For something to be objective, we usually mean that it is "out there in the real world," separate from the knower (this is implicit in "the subject-object dichotomy"), and the same for all to observe. What this means for acting justly is, however, hard to comprehend. I am the person who needs to be just, yet who I am and how I see the other is not to be taken into account because the locus of morality is "out there in the real world." No doubt the reason that so many ethicists insist that morality be "objective" is that they are trying to protect justice from our propensities for distortion, emotional bias, wishful thinking, and superstition. The irony is, however, that for justice to be objectively known by a perceiving subject, the perceiving subject is made to disappear.[67] For justice to be objective, the person needing to be just—let alone any actual qualities this person might have developed—is not even part of the equation.

Justice Must Be Rational

If "being rational" means that I must be respectful, fair, and equitable as I relate to whomever or whatever is other, then reasoning is, of course, an inherent part of being a just person. If, however, "being rational" is taken to mean that nothing "emotional," nothing of the situated embodied self, can be taken into account, then "being rational" is not an adequate understanding of justice at all. As we have seen, a disembodied rationality reflecting the "mind-body dichotomy" negates who we are as embodied selves and negates the feeling and inner depth that make us human and able to respond to the other. Justice as a function of mind-body dualism is not relational at all, let alone caring. In fact, an approach to justice through disembodied rationality is often very dehumanizing, paying no attention to the respect, fairness, and equity for the self and the other that we embody as adults.

Justice Must Be Abstract

If "being abstract" means stepping back from the actual situation and *reflecting on* it from a number of different perspectives before we act, then this kind of abstraction can be very helpful in acting justly. If, however, "being abstract" means *prescinding from* the concrete situation in order to decide fairness and equity by appealing to selected concepts or general principles—concepts or principles that may be neither relevant nor adequate to the actual situation—then it is simply another way of honoring the "mind-body" and the "self-other" dichotomies so present in the culture. As it actually flows from integrity and mutuality, justice is inherently relational and developmental. In actual practice, justice as respect, fairness, and equity in caring for the needs, rights, and freedoms of the self and the other for wholeness is something very concrete. It may often call for very serious reflection on our part, but its practice neither begins nor ends in abstract principles.

Justice Must Be Impersonal

Like being objective, rational, and abstract, "being impersonal" may be another way of saying that justice must always be fair and equitable and that it should never be tainted by prejudice, favoritism, or personal preference. If, however, "being impersonal" is taken as a disembodied mind making adult-moral decisions by paying no attention to self-empathy and empathy for the other, then it is another synonym for being objective, rational, or abstract. Again, the mind-body dichotomy has us thinking that acting justly can only be achieved by pretending that who we actually are and who or what the other actually is must not be taken into account. How is this even possible? How can something as deeply challenging and often gut-wrenchingly personal as acting justly be said to be not personal at all? If justice is impersonal, how could care for either the self or the other even be considered?

An understanding of justice as objective, rational, abstract, and impersonal is so disembodied, so ambiguous, so laced with contradictions, and so steeped in "either-or" thinking that it fosters confusion and obfuscation rather than the clarity it claims to serve. To the extent we are guided by these beliefs, to that extent an adult understanding of justice is impossible. If justice is necessarily framed by the subject-object dichotomy—as each of these four beliefs support—then it is not about the wholeness of the self as it relates to the wholeness of the other. If the practice of justice is to be free of bias, prejudice, favoritism, and whatever else harms its fairness and equity, the way to achieve this is not by turning justice into some less-than-human, disembodied, unfeeling, non-relational, idealized, and universalized "object" or "principle." On the contrary, the way to practice justice can only be to own our humanness completely, to see the inner and the relational together, to honor our embodied wholeness as we relate in mutuality to the other. For "a proper concept of justice we need caring empathy as well as a firm sense of the equality of all persons."[68]

"To Be Just Is to Follow the Law"

A second belief that so many of us as individuals or as members of a profession, an institution, a government, or a corporation seem to subscribe to is: "To be just is to follow the law." In a culture of disembodied rationality, the law easily becomes a necessary, if not privileged, external standard of justice. The question we ask is: "Is it legal?" Our thinking is: "If it isn't against the law, then I can do it." In fact, for many people the law *is* morality, a seemingly "objective" morality to be sure and one that is ready-made in the culture. The law says what we have to do and what we cannot do. In fact, obeying the law is often equated with being a responsible person. The phrase we hear is: "You are responsible in the eyes of the law."

Unfortunately, however, the law is often little more than the least common denominator among us. Often the law only reflects the values of the cultural superego, and often the law only protects the interests and prejudices of those who have the most political, religious, and economic power in the society. Although the law can be very helpful at times in safeguarding care and justice, it can also do just the opposite. Even when it is helpful, however, *the law is never a substitute for personal responsibility*. "Laws are always oversized or undersized, too sweeping or too narrow, more or less bad fits."[69] Following the law may have little or nothing to do with my integrity as I respond in mutuality to the other. Following the law may have little or nothing to do with being an adult and moral person. Even when it is the best it can possibly be: "The law is a schema that tries to cover as many areas as it can, as fairly, equitably, and evenhandedly as it can. But it never quite can."[70]

"Justice Is Punishment"

A third belief, a belief that seems to be deeply engrained in so many of us and in so many cultures, is: "Justice is punishment." This belief—the defining aspect of retributive justice—operates in most systems of criminal justice. Its dictum is: If you break the law you will be punished. In the popular mind, there seem to be two aspects to this belief. First, we seem to believe: "If you break the law, you owe a debt to society, a debt you are obliged to pay in full." Second, we seem to believe: "If you cause serious harm to some person or property, you are liable to serious harm in retribution." If harm has caused the other some deprivation, then, as Lucius Garvin says: "What is more natural than the demand that the evildoer shall suffer a similar deprivation?"[71] In this "just desserts mentality," the measure of the pain and damage we cause to the other is the measure of the pain and damage we must expect to suffer ourselves.

The thinking in support of the practice of justice as punishment is: first, that somehow it *repays a debt* to society; second, that it *deters* crime because of the negative consequences the offender suffers and because, if only for a time, it takes the offender out of a broader circulation; third, it may *reform* the offender, although often few resources are allocated for this specific purpose; and fourth, it provides for the *law and order* that allows the rest of us in society to be safe, to feel a sense of security and perhaps even a sense of righteousness. Whether, or to what extent, justice as punishment actually accomplishes these four things is often seriously questioned. Prisons often turn out to be schools for criminals. Putting criminals in prison to remove them from society seems to be more geographical than actual. And ironically, the societies that seem to be the most violent are the societies that have a larger percentage of their population in prison.

The critique of this practice of justice is: first, its fairness is often very *uneven and unpredictable* because there are so many variables in society and in the justice system; second, the *actual needs* of the victim, the offender, and the community are often not taken into account by this rather impersonal way of practicing justice; third, this way of punitive justice allows us to consider it, and perhaps even to welcome it, as a form of *sanctioned vengeance*; and fourth, what actually transpires in prison is often in the service of *violence* and *dehumanization*. In the culture, in fact, it is easy to conclude that justice, violence, and dehumanization are all meant to go together.

Were we to ask: "What it is about justice in the culture that makes it so hard to see it in its wholeness?" then "justice is punishment" would undoubtedly have the place of primacy. If in its wholeness, justice is understood as respect, fairness, and equity in caring for the needs, rights, and freedoms of the self and the other for wholeness, then "justice is punishment"—the practical justice of so many of us in so many societies—has little if anything to do with justice at all. In the culture and in the law, justice is intimately tied to punishment. Yet—and this is an amazing irony—in adulthood and adult morality justice is intimately tied to care.

If we are interested in hearing from the "better angels" of our human nature, doing whatever we can to redefine justice in the culture, in academia, and in social policies is a good place to start.

JUSTICE: THREE TRADITIONAL STRANDS

Although we consider care and justice together as the fullness of human action in terms of peace in the next chapter, it is helpful to consider their connection in light of how *justice alone* has been traditionally described. Down through the centuries, justice has been understood in three strands that intersect with each other in various ways. First and foremost, there is distributive justice (and more recently social justice) which relies on some notion of the equality of all parties involved.[72] Then, there is rectificatory justice (and more recently restorative justice) which can come into play when distributive justice is violated.[73] Finally, there is retributive justice which, as we have seen, is directly related to punishing those who commit crimes.

(1) In *distributive justice*, there is the understanding that assets, or benefits, or rights—the "goods of the earth," the "goods of society"—need to be shared on the basis of some notion of equality. Often with this thinking, there is also the understanding that "responsibilities" need to be shared equally as well. Not surprisingly, perhaps, there are a lot of distinctions made by different thinkers about what might or might not be included in the goods to be shared, how these goods are to be shared, the role of government in the sharing, whether some individuals or groups are more equal than others, and what the responsibilities of the individuals in the society are. Still, fairness, and especially the notion that "equals are to be treated equally," is the foundation of this notion of justice.

Distributive justice is in harmony with an adult notion of justice as respect, fairness, and equity in caring for the needs and rights of the self and the other. The "respect, fairness, and equity" of the later definition is really a nuancing of the "equality" of the former. What may be somewhat different in the two understandings is the "caring for the needs and rights of the self and the other" that specifies justice in adulthood. It may well be, however, that a mention of "caring" makes explicit something that is already implicit in at least some understandings of distributive justice, especially in that needs, rights, and freedoms are to be considered. The notion of social justice—attending to the needs of those most disadvantaged—is considered an inherent part of distributive justice. In other words, if "care" can be included in the notion of distributive justice, then it is quite similar to the care and justice of an adult and moral self. As we will see in the next chapter, an amplified notion of distributive justice is foundational to an understanding of peace.

(2) In *rectificatory justice* there is the understanding that one person has done harm to or wronged the rights or the property of another and that the wrong needs to be "set right" or rectified. Typically, in this strand of justice there is restoration of what has been taken or there is fitting compensation for the harm that has been done. This is a "corrective," or "commutative," or "remedial" form of justice. The wrongdoing—addressed as crime in the legal system—has created an imbalance or inequality and its rectification is a return to the equality that was present before the wrong occurred. Different thinkers disagree on how directly rectificatory justice is related to distributive justice, but the notion of equality seems to be common ground for both.[74]

Rectificatory justice is also in harmony with an adult notion of justice as respect, fairness, and equity in caring for the needs, rights, and freedoms of the self and the other. In rectificatory justice, the needs, rights, and freedoms of the other have been violated in some way and this form of justice sets the injustice right and restores the equality or the *status quo ante* that previously existed between the two parties. This strand of justice applies, of course, to current transactions that are unjust, but it also applies to the descendants of people who have been wronged historically, for example, the Australian Aborigines, or the First Nation of Canada, or the Native Americans of the United States. Although at times an apology may be offered and forgiveness may be expressed, the importance of "caring" is not necessarily a major focus in this strand of justice.[75] As we will see in the next chapter, *restorative justice*, an amplification of rectificatory justice, is quite explicitly relational and it is a notion that takes caring directly into account.

(3) In *retributive justice*, there is, as we have seen, a direct connection between justice and punishment. In this strand of justice, retribution, the need for an offender "to pay back" is paramount. If the offender gains an unfair advantage over another, he or she deserves to be punished. Punishment removes the unfair advantage "by imposing a penalty that in some sense balances the harm inflicted by the offense."[76] Although the notions of fairness, equality, and even equity can be important in this strand of justice, the focus is on the offender, on the offense, and on the punishment to be exacted rather than on the impact of the offense on the victim. As we have seen, the way punishment is carried out in this strand of justice often allows for violence and dehumanization. This strand of justice has the least "caring" in it and is the least relational of the three.

From this brief consideration of these traditional strands of justice, four points can be taken. First, it is very clear that "equality," if not "equity," is seen in the culture to be foundational to the understanding of justice. Second, it is very clear that the notion of caring is not very prominent in the traditional cultural understandings of justice, and to the extent that it is present in these understandings it is often there only in an implicit and quite unthematic way. Third, in the more recent notions of social justice and restorative justice, there is some evidence that justice is beginning to be redefined and that caring is beginning to find room in the culture. Fourth, each of these three traditional strands of justice—especially in the notion of equality—is foundational for an understanding not just of how the self is meant to relate to the other but also for how societies are meant to function.

CARE AND JUSTICE IN SOCIETY AND CULTURE

Finally, it is important to note that in the notions of care and justice as found together in adulthood and adult morality there is no *disconnection* between self and society. There is no "self-other dichotomy." An integral self-in-mutuality is at once personal and social. The characteristics that amplify this self—a body-self, a feeling self, a self of inner depth, a self with clear boundaries, an intimate self, and a responsible self—describe what it means to be a mature and moral self in society. Care is attending to the needs, rights, and freedoms of the self and the other. Justice is respect, fairness, and equity in caring for the needs, rights, and freedoms of the self and the other. Both are about something that is always *inner* and *relational* at the same time. To talk about being caring and acting justly is to talk about what it means to be an adult-moral self in relation to whomever or whatever is other, whether that other be, as we have seen, "family member, spouse, friend, events, groups, communities, institutions, animals, or the environment."

NOTES

1. *A Few Good Men*, DVD, directed by Rob Reiner (1992; Culver City, CA: Columbia Tri-Star Home Video, 2001).

2. Robin West says: "Our ideals as well as our practices, of justice have been uncaring, and our ideals as well as our practices, of care have been unjust, and the consequence has been the deflation of *both* virtues. Our justice is not just when it is not caring, care is not caring when it is not just." Robin West, *Caring for Justice* (New York: New York University Press, 1997), 9.

3. For a thorough discussion of these positions, see Virginia Held, ed., *Justice and Care: Essential Readings in Feminist Ethics* (Boulder, CO: Westview Press, 1995).

4. *Merriam-Webster's Collegiate Dictionary Online*, 12th ed., https://www.merriam-webster.com/dictionary/care (accessed November 14, 2015).

5. *Macmillan Dictionary*, http://www.macmillandictionary.com/us/dictionary/american/care-for (accessed November 14, 2015).

6. WordWeb Online, https://www.wordwebonline.com/en/CARER (accessed November 14, 2015).

7. *Merriam Webster*, 11th ed. s.v. "Caregiver."

8. *Merriam Webster*, 11th ed. s.v. "Justice."

9. Robert C. Solomon and Mark C. Murphy, *What Is Justice? Classic and Contemporary Reading*, ed. Robert C. Solomon and Mark C. Murphy (New York: Oxford University Press, 1990), 5.

10. Susan J. Hekman, *Moral Voices, Moral Selves: Carol Gilligan and Feminist Moral Theory* (University Park: Pennsylvania State University Press, 1995), 32.

11. H. Hart says "the core notion of rights is neither individual choice nor individual benefit but basic or fundamental needs." See H. L. A. Hart, *Essays of Bentham: Studies in Jurisprudence and Political Theory* (New York: Oxford University Press, 1982), 293.

12. Carol Gilligan, "The Conquistador and the Dark Continent: Reflections of the Psychology of Love," *Deadalus* 113, no. 3 (Summer 1984): 77.

13. Milton Mayeroff, *On Caring* (New York: HarperPerennial, 1972), 19.

14. Ibid., 22. See also Rianne Mahon and Fiona Robinson, eds., *Feminist Ethics and Social Policy: Towards a New Global Political Economy of Care* (Vancouver: University of British Columbia Press, 2011). See also Virginia Held, *The Ethics of Care: Personal, Political, and Global* (Oxford: Oxford University Press, 2006).

15. Richard M. Gula, *Moral Discernment* (New York: Paulist Press, 1997), 37.

16. See W. G. Maclagan, "Respect for Persons as a Moral Principle—I," *Philosophy: The Journal of the Royal Institute of Philosophy* 35, no. 134 (July 1960): 193–217. See also his "Respect for Persons as a Moral Principle—II," *Philosophy: The Journal of the Royal Institute of Philosophy* 35, no. 135 (October 1960): 289–305.

17. Jean Piaget, *The Moral Judgment of the Child*, trans. Marjorie Gabain (New York: Free Press, 1965), 383.

18. John Rawls, "The Sense of Justice," *Philosophical Review* 72 (1963): 281, observes that "if men did not do what justice requires, not only would they not regard themselves as bound by the principles of justice, but they would be incapable of feeling resentment and indignation, and they would be without ties of friendship and mutual trust. They would lack certain essential elements of humanity."

19. Paul J. Wadell, "The Family as a Crucible of Grace: Finding God in the Mutuality of Love," in *Mutuality Matters: Family, Faith, and Just Love*, ed. Herbert Anderson et al. (Lanham, MD: Rowman & Littlefield, 2004), 14.

20. Darlene Ehinger, "Toward an Ethic of Mutuality: An Integrated Concept of Justice," *Sewanee Theological Review*, 36, no. 3 (1993): 413.

21. George E. Vaillant, *Triumphs of Experience: The Men of the Harvard Grant Study* (Cambridge, MA: Harvard University Press, 2012), 156.

22. See Erik H. Erikson, "Eight Ages of Man," *Childhood and Society*, 2nd ed. (New York: Norton, 1963), 247–74.

23. See Piaget, *The Moral Judgment of the Child.*

24. Maurice Hamington defines care as: "an approach to individual and social morality that shifts ethical emphasis and consideration to context, relationships, and affective knowledge in a manner that can be fully understood only if its embodied dimension is recognized." Maurice Hamington, *Embodied Care: Jane Addams, Maurice Merleau-Ponty, and Feminist Ethics* (Chicago: University of Illinois Press, 2004), 12.

25. Ibid., 4.

26. Diemut E. Bubeck, *Care, Gender, and Justice* (Oxford: Clarendon, 1995), 215.

27. John D. Caputo, *Against Ethics: Contributions to a Poetics of Obligation with Constant Reference to Deconstruction* (Bloomington: Indiana University Press, 1993), 98.

28. Gula, *Moral Discernment*, 37.

29. Gil G. Noam, "'Normative Vulnerabilities' of Self and Their Transformations in Moral Action," in *The Moral Self*, ed. Gil G. Noam and Thomas E. Wren (Cambridge, MA: MIT Press, 1993), 228.

30. Ibid., 232.

31. Wadell, "The Family as a Crucible," 14.

32. Ibid.

33. Lawrence Blum says: "Knowing what to do involves knowing others and being connected in ways involving both emotion and cognition. Caring action expresses emotion and understanding." Lawrence A. Blum, "Gilligan and Kohlberg: Implications for Moral Theory," *Ethics* 98, no. 3 (1988): 476. Ruthellen Josselson finds that "emotion and thought are integrated in care, experienced as deriving from the heart as well as the mind." Ruthellen Josselson, "Relationship as a Path to Integrity, Wisdom, and Meaning," in *The Psychology of Mature Spirituality: Integrity, Wisdom, Transcendence*, ed. Polly Young-Eisendrath and Melvin E. Miller (London: Routledge, 2000), 98.

34. Martin Heidegger, *Being and Time*, trans. John Macquarrie and Edward Robinson (New York: Harper & Row, 1962), 243.

35. Nel Noddings, *The Challenge to Care in Schools: An Alternative Approach to Education*, 2nd ed. (New York: Teachers College Press), 18.

36. For the foundation of her groundbreaking work see Carol Gilligan, *In a Different Voice: Psychological Theory and Women's Development* (Cambridge, MA: Harvard University Press, 1982).

37. Nel Noddings, *Caring: A Feminine Approach to Ethics and Moral Education*, 2nd ed. (Berkeley: University of California Press, 2003), 5.

38. Leonardo Boff, *Essential Care: An Ethics of Human Nature* (Waco, TX: Baylor University Press, 2007), 75.

39. Wendy Hollway, *The Capacity to Care: Gender and Ethical Subjectivity* (London: Routledge, 2006), 11.

40. Ibid.

41. Ibid.

42. Ibid., 14.

43. Ibid., 13.

44. Ibid., 14.

45. Ibid.

46. Ibid., 57.

47. Ibid., 6.

48. Ibid.

49. Ibid., 80.

50. Ibid., 85.

51. Ibid., 18.

52. Ibid., 101.

53. Ibid.

54. Virginia Held, "Liberalism and the Ethics of Care," in *On Feminist Ethics and Politics*, ed. Claudia Card (Lawrence: University Press of Kansas, 1999), 202.

55. Held, *The Ethics of Care*, 39.

56. Ibid., 15.

57. Ibid.

58. Ibid., 89.

59. Ibid., 55.

60. Ibid., 14.

61. Ibid., 19.

62. Erik Erikson, *Insight and Responsibility: Lectures on the Ethical Implications of Psychoanalytic Insight* (New York: Norton, 1964), 131.

63. Ibid., 231.

64. Ibid., 233.

65. Erikson, "Eight Ages of Man," 249.

66. Erik H. Erikson, "The Roots of Virtue," in *The Humanist Frame*, ed. Julian Huxley (New York: Harper & Brothers, 1962), 159.

67. As William Desmond, *Perplexity and Ultimacy: Metaphysical Thoughts from the Middle* (Albany: State University of New York Press, 1995), 67, says: "There is an oblivion of the self in the very success of self as objective mind." From another perspective, Augusto Blasi comments on Piaget: "He seemed to believe that objectivity, the goal of knowledge, can only be arrived at by progressively controlling and eliminating the intervention of the subject in the cognitive process." Augusto Blasi, "Neither Personality nor Cognition: An Alternative Approach to the Nature of the Self," in *Changing Conceptions of Psychological*

Life, ed. Cynthia Lightfoot, Chris Lalonde, and Michael Chandler (Mahwah, NJ: Lawrence Erlbaum Associates, 2004), 23.

68. Ville Päiväsalo, "Taking Viewpoints of Fairness and Care," *Studia Theologica* 58 (2004): 129.

69. Caputo, *Against Ethics*, 88.

70. Ibid., 87.

71. Lucius Garvin, "Retributive and Distributive Justice, *Journal of Philosophy* 42, no. 10 (1945): 274.

72. As David Miller, *Principles of Social Justice* (Cambridge, MA: Harvard University Press, 1999), 4, observes: "Social justice requires the notion of a society made up of interdependent parts, with an intuitional structure that affects the prospects of each individual member, and that is capable of deliberate reform by an agency such as the state in the name of fairness."

73. See the next chapter for a consideration of restorative justice.

74. See, for example, Wojciech Sadurski, "Social Justice and Legal Justice," *Law and Philosophy* 3 (1984): 239–354.

75. See Rodney C. Roberts, "Justice and Rectification: A Taxonomy of Justice," in *Injustice and Rectification*, ed. Rodney C. Roberts (New York: Peter Lang, 2005), 24.

76. Wesley Cragg, *The Practice of Punishment: Towards a Theory of Restorative Justice* (New York: Routledge, 1992), 15.

Chapter Four

Violence and Peace

Dialectic of the Fully Human

In the movie, *Dead Man Walking*, Matthew Poncelet is convicted of raping and stabbing Hope, a teenage girl, and shooting her and her boyfriend, Walter, in the back of the head. On death row and believing his time is at hand, Matthew asks Sister Helen to visit him. Nervous, but caring and wanting to respect him, she agrees. Insisting: "I didn't kill nobody," he asks her to help him with his appeal. Sister Helen does all she can, finding a good lawyer and getting Matthew's mother involved, but the appeal is denied. The day is set for the execution. Matthew asks Sister Helen to be his spiritual advisor. At first, when she asks him to "talk about what happened," he says: "I won't talk about that." Later, during the intimacy of his last meal, she asks "What about Matthew Poncelet, where is he in the story?" He admits: "Walter, the boy, I killed him." "And Hope, did you rape her?" "Yes, ma'am," he responds. "Do you take responsibility for both of their deaths?" "Yes, ma'am," he responds. Then, turning to her, he says: "Thank you for loving me." In his last words a few minutes later, Matthew apologizes to Walter's father. And to Hope's parents he says: "I hope my death gives you some relief."[1]

In this chapter, violence and peace define each other as opposites in a context of the fully human in action. With all of the concerns we face in ourselves, in our communities, in the society, and in the culture, nothing is more important or more urgent for us to consider than violence and peace, especially as they measure who we are. Crucial for us to understand as we look without, they are also crucial for us to understand as we look within. From the perspective of an integral self-in-mutuality and its characteristics, the mature definitions we have of care and of justice are pivotal. They offer us an understanding of violence and peace, revealing them as ultimately at stake in the development of integrity and mutuality.

Violence is a phenomenon all too frequent in our world. It is there in individual lives, in troubled families, in the life of our schools, in the problems and tensions of the neighborhood, the countryside, and the city. It is there—both abhorred and celebrated—in our different games and media. It is there in and between ethnic groups, political groups, economic groups, and religious groups; it is there in the wars that are waged in and between nations; and, of course, it is there in the terrorism that knows no boundaries at all. Violence is a cavernous black hole at the heart of the human. It is often devastating when it occurs yet it occurs quite frequently.[2] It is often a momentary act yet its consequences can last forever. It is often quite senseless yet it can completely destroy the deeper meanings that nourish the human spirit and give purpose to our lives. The violence that lives in us is our humanness in contradiction.

Peace is often thought of as the longed-for time that, when it comes, marks an end to war and conflict, to hatred and recrimination, to feuds and reprisals, to quarrels and hostilities. For so many people in so many places, peace is an imagined state of rest and restoration that would soothe the beleaguered soul, if only it could be found. Yet, although often spoken of first as a respite from outer violence, peace is an inner quest as well. In fact, although we rarely speak of peace in developmental terms, from the perspective of an adult and moral self peace is not only profoundly wished for but—and this is rarely acknowledged either in the culture or in academia—it is actually the goal and the pinnacle of human development. Amazingly powerful and vitally dynamic, peace is ultimately what being human is about. Peace is the fullness of the human in action.

How can we go about understanding violence? How can we go about understanding peace? Although simple enough at first glance, these questions are not only critical but they are the very questions that have to be carefully pursued if we are concerned about the future of humanity. The best answer—the most human, the most relational, and the most developmentally formed answer—we have is: *to understand violence and peace is to understand care and justice*. The seeds of violence lie in the denial of care and justice for the wholeness of the self and the other; the promise of peace lies in embracing care and justice for the self and the other as the only hope for human survival and flourishing. The adult-moral actions that make care and justice a reality are precisely what deter violence and allow peace to thrive. Being adult, being moral, being fully human, and being a peaceful person go together as one. All four are violated and made to count as nothing when they are at the mercy of disconnection and human violence.[3]

To idealize or mystify the reality of either violence or peace is neither clarifying nor helpful. Opposite as they are in so many ways, neither is an external beyond-the-human force. Thinking of violence as some strange and horrible occurrence, as some terrible virus that takes us by surprise whenever it "breaks out," is not helpful. Even when it is brutally dehumanizing, violence must be understood as an intimate part of the human. Likewise, thinking of peace as a utopian dream or as an incredible blessing that may suddenly appear bringing harmony, compassion, and wonderful accord, is not helpful either. Peace is only as real as it is a part of the human. The first and most important thing to be said, therefore, about violence and peace is that they are not alien to who we are. In fact, violence and peace are the two main paths—paths in contradiction—that human development can take.

Violence—in abuse, robbery, bribery, or corruption; in discrimination, shaming, defaming, or terrorizing; in rape, murder, torture, or genocide—is our humanity in its developmental failure. Peace—made real by all the myriad ways we engage in taking care and being just—is our humanity at its developmental best. It is important to realize that, wherever else they may be, one or the other can be found embodied in each of us as we relate to self and other. Although they draw us in opposite ways, one or the other characterizes our feeling and inner depth.

Human violence is always in our rejection of care and justice. Peace—peace that does not "paper over" violence, peace that is authentic and can be trusted—always lies in the care and justice we are able to receive and give. As we pursue our quest for wholeness and strive to relate to the other in mutuality, each of us necessarily ends up negotiating a path that leads either toward violence or toward peace. Over time—perhaps more than anything else—one or the other is the contemporary test of our humanness. Each of us is called to take responsibility for the reality of one or the other in the self's being and relating.

VIOLENCE AND THE HUMAN

As we look more closely at human violence, three questions are especially relevant. The way we answer these questions determines not only how we understand the violence we find in ourselves and in the world but also how we can effectively respond to this devastating aspect of our humanity. The first and most crucial question is: What is the nature of violence in the context of the human? The second question is: How is violence, along with peace, part of human development? The third question is: Why is violence so powerful and so pervasive in so many of us and in so many cultures? Interestingly enough, as we address these three questions, it becomes quite clear that we can neither understand violence without understanding peace nor can we understand peace without understanding violence. They are actually their own kind of dialectic. Each is a key that unlocks the meaning of the other.

What Is the Nature of Violence in the Context of the Human?

What is violence? Typically, violence is defined as an action, for example, as "exertion of physical force so as to injure or abuse."[4] Although we know that violence is part of our humanness, we tend to objectify it, to turn it into an "event" or a "thing." But if violence is part of our humanness, the full magnitude of violence is understood best in light of the full magnitude of the human. If we ask, therefore: "What does violence do to our quest for integrity?" we find that it attacks it directly—physically, psychologically, and morally—doing whatever it can either to break the "pieces" of our integrity apart or to keep them from coming together in the first place. If we ask: "What does violence do to our mutuality?" we find that it destroys relating—at best treating the other with indifference or disdain and at worst obliterating the other in wanton and total destruction. As human action, therefore, violence is best understood as *annihilating integrity and mutuality*, literally making our wholeness and relatedness to be as nothing.

In annihilating integrity and mutuality, violence annihilates loving care and justice. Care is attending to the needs, rights, and freedoms of the self and the other for wholeness, but violence considers these needs, rights, and freedoms to be of no account. Justice is respect, fairness, and equity in caring for the needs, rights, and freedoms of the self and the other for wholeness, but violence considers these needs, rights, and freedoms as unworthy of respect, or fairness, or any kind of consideration at all. In annihilating care and justice, violence is human action that only dehumanizes. If loving care and justice is the blueprint for human action in its fullness, then violence stomps all over this blueprint, destroying it in any way it can. Annihilating care and justice not only is violence but unfortunately it also invites violence, begets violence, and escalates violence. As a contradiction of care and justice, violence is only able to perpetuate itself.

Violence often comes in three interwoven strands. First, there is *personal* or direct violence, the violence we do as individuals that violates the basic needs, rights, and freedoms of self or other.[5] Then, there is *structural* violence, that is, the violence in our social institutions—often hidden and harder to notice—that makes for inequality through exploitation or repression.[6] Overarching these two, there is *cultural* violence that serves "to justify and legitimize personal and structural violence."[7] An example of all three of these strands can be seen, for example, in the man who is physically beating his wife. The laws or community resources to protect her from this violence may be weak or lacking, and the culture may convey—perhaps in the way it names violence and responds to it—that "boys will be boys" and that women are not as important as men. Structural and cultural violence often compound personal violence. Johan Galtung observes: "With the violent structure institutionalized and the violent culture internalized, direct violence also tends to become institutionalized, repetitive, ritualistic, and like a vendetta."[8]

As we are describing violence, it is important to notice that *disconnection* is usually in the room. Violence divides, splits apart, tears down, cuts off, severs, and dismembers. It "does not know," says Jean-Paul Sartre, "how to put things together."[9] Its roots are in whatever separates us within and without. Domestic violence of women, for example, often comes from a disconnection between the status of women and men as human beings. For a broader example, many individuals, many institutions, and many cultures, disconnect care from justice, and the consequences are played out in different forms of violence—neglect, disrespect, unjust decisions, denial of rights, impoverishment, and death. Not surprisingly, disconnection is "a kind of reverse intimacy."[10] It is a calculus for violence that sabotages empathy, care and justice, and our best efforts at being peace.

In the culture, the language of *disconnection* is often confused with a language of *difference*. A language of difference is a language of differentiation, of uniqueness, of disagreement, and of perceived conflict. It is an adult language, a careful and respectful language, a language that lets us name the presence or the absence of wholeness and mutuality, fairness and equity, and of course, care and justice. A language of disconnection, however, is an "over against" language, a dichotomizing language, a language of mind-*versus*-body, of self-*versus*-other. In the eventuation of the Rwandan genocide of 1994, for example, the Tutsi, ostensibly separate from the Hutu, were said to be "cockroaches" and then were systematically exterminated. "Living tissue of connection and difference must be cauterized," says Michael Ignatieff, "before a neighbor is reinvented as an enemy."[11]

The definition of violence is also a definition of evil. Evil, as John Kekes sees it, is "an attack on the fundamental conditions of human well-being."[12] It "involves depraved, malignant, monstrous actions that violate universal human values and required conventions in a way that breaches the bulwark between civilized life and barbarism."[13] "Any act," says Ronald Miller, "that destroys our trust in the reciprocity of human relationships and creates the belief that individuals need only look out for themselves and not one another is human evil."[14] "Evil creates and builds upon brokenness in the world by threatening, attacking, destroying and desecrating the integrity of the relational nature of life."[15] Claudia Card makes the case that terrorism, torture, and genocide are today's paradigms of evil.[16] Without question, violence and evil define each other.

How Is Violence, along with Peace, Part of Human Development?

If violence and peace are inherently human and relational—the case we have been making—can we also see that they are inherently developmental? One thinker, who shows in some detail how this is so, is Erik Erikson. Erikson's thinking lets us see that human development is toward peace when it is growthful and toward violence when it is not. If we are able to take in the care and the justice provided by the love of those who raise us, then eventually we may become adults who embody these essential human qualities. If, however, we are not able to embody care and justice as we grow up, then we may find ourselves on a path that leads to violence instead of peace. There is, of course, any number of influences—biological as well as societal and cultural—contributing to becoming a violent person. As Johan Galtung puts it, "human beings are easily overshadowed by structure, culture, and institutions."[17] Still, Erikson's thinking lets us see clearly that violence is always one possibility in the development of each one of us.

THE FIRST FIVE STAGES OF DEVELOPMENT OF ERIK ERIKSON

Although Erik Erikson does not focus directly on peace and violence in his understanding of the stages of life, his seminal thinking shows that care is the quintessential strength of mature adulthood, and if care and justice go together in his thinking—and they do—a case can be made that becoming a peaceful person is a definite goal of adult development.[18] Violence, although a negation of that development, is not just something "unenlightened and uncivilized" for Erikson; he sees it as a "vital aspect of life."[19] In a dialogue with Richard Evans, he points to violence developmentally by stating: "when future growth becomes unfulfillable, a deep rage is aroused in man comparable to that of an animal driven into a corner."[20] For Erikson, violence is explained by human development, not by human evolution. As we walk briefly through his first five stages of life, the stages that bring us to adulthood, the genesis of our development toward either peace or violence can be seen.[21]

Stage 1: Trust vs. Mistrust

This is a time of *taking in*. The infant in the first year of life develops a sense of trust by taking into the body all that the mother and others provide through care. In this incorporative stage, if it is satisfying enough, the infant finds two things that bode well for the future. First, the infant senses that being a needy body is safe enough, because basic human needs can be met in the world. Second, the infant senses that being with others is safe, secure, and at times quite delightful. If this incorporative stage is not satisfying enough, however, a sense of mistrust develops. This mistrust, if not addressed, may become a way of relating. If our significant others are not attentive and respectful, if the world is a threatening place, if my own basic needs cannot be satisfied, then apathy, emptiness, rage, and disconnection can be expected. Trust in the world and trust in the self—the very foundation of relationship both inner and outer—is at stake.[22]

If the beginnings of the care and justice that lead to peace lie in an initial sense of trust, the beginnings of violence lie in an initial sense of mistrust. Violence lives in a sense of betrayal by the other and also by the self. Later, if trust is shattered by violence, by loss, or by some other traumatic occurrence, it is easy for us to be so disconnected to self and other that violence can get a foothold. In mistrust, the beginning of *disconnection* in the self and from the other is a segue for violence.

Stage 2: Autonomy vs. Shame and Doubt

This is a time of *holding on* and *letting go*. The toddler in the second and third years of life needs to develop a sense of autonomy, a sense that "I am a self." This autonomy is realized through will-power and the ability to be in control of the body in its dependent dealings with others and the world. Others are now experienced as separate from the self. In fact, autonomy sets the initial boundaries of what is self and what is other, and it prefigures the mature sense of boundaries that are realized in an adult-moral self. If, however, there is too much self doubt and humiliation, and especially if there is too much shame, then this fledgling self may develop the sense: "I cannot be me; there is something wrong in the very makeup of who I am." Shame and rage—captured in the notion of "the terrible twos"—typically feed each other at this stage.

The beginnings of violence are often in the experience of unbearable shame. Later, if the child continues to be ashamed, whether at home, or in school, or in the community, or later still in marriage, at work, or in the society, some kind of violent behavior, either against the self or against the other, can be expected. Shame, as any number of writers attest, is one of the best schools we have for psychopathology and violence.[23] Fed by ridicule, belittlement, derision, and humiliation, shame can become utterly destructive, blotting out empathy and creating a disconnection within the self so powerful that it defies healing and creating a disconnection from the other so powerful that it cannot be overcome. At its worst, shame comes to mean: "No matter what, I am never OK; no matter what I do, I will never receive the care and respect that I so desperately need to be a self."

Stage 3: Initiative vs. Guilt

This is a time *to make like*, *to play* in a purposeful way. The young child in the third, fourth, and fifth years of life needs to develop a sense of initiative, a sense of what he or she can actually do in the world as an autonomous self. At this stage, both imagination and sexual desire come alive, and the child plays at being an adult. As a way of controlling imagination and sexual desire, the superego, an inner agency of dependence and control, makes its appearance. Initiative, for Erikson, is the beginning of an imagined adulthood and the superego is the precursor of adult morality.

If the child experiences too much guilt, however, if too much of what he or she does is labeled as bad or wrong, then anger, frustration, resentment, and shame easily surface.[24] If little care or justice is experienced, the child may give up trying to do what is seen as right and "act out," either to get attention or to get care and respect. If guilt is going to be inevitable, if care and justice cannot be had, and if forgiveness is not offered, then violence can become inevitable as a way of being in the world.

Stage 4: Industry vs. Inferiority

This is a time to *make things*, to go to school and learn the skills needed for living in society and culture. The child, in dependent relating with competent adults, must acquire the kinds of knowledge that will be useful in being a self in the society, and the child also must develop the skills of relating to others that will pave the way for being an adult. Industry, which is the ability to work in a purposeful and collaborative way, is the immediate precursor of adult identity and mutuality.

If, however, inferiority sets in too strongly, the skills necessary for making a living and finding a satisfying place in the world, the skills that allow for self-esteem and esteem from others, cannot develop. It should be no surprise that a sense of inferiority is a natural breeding ground for nonacceptance, illegal activity, and violence. Inferiority, and the shame and humiliation that so often bind with it, is a basic ingredient in most of the recipes we have for genocide. Violence is often a natural response to an unremitting sense of inferiority.[25]

Stage 5: Identity vs. Identity Diffusion

This is a time to *be oneself.* As the self approaches adulthood, it needs to bring all of its "pieces" together into what Erikson calls a "reasonably coherent whole," that is, a self whole enough to be able, in Freud's famous phrase, "to love and work." This "reasonably coherent whole," which includes personal, sexual, and social identity, allows for fully mutual relating, relating which respects the integrity of the other even as it respects the integrity of the self. For Erikson, it is in the advent of identity-in-mutuality that the adult-moral self, the self that begins to own being caring and acting justly, is born.[26] It is in the advent of identity-in-mutuality with the other that peace can be recognized as a personal project.

At this stage, however, Erikson describes the possibility of developing an identify diffusion that manifests as an inability to find enough wholeness and sense of mutuality. In a worst-case scenario, he also mentions the possibility of developing a *negative identity*, an identity that is the *opposite* of wholeness and respect for the other. This negative identity is a breeding ground for antisocial behavior and violence.[27] "A specific rage can be aroused wherever identity development loses the promise of a traditionally assured wholeness."[28] In fact, this negative identity may become so pronounced—given personal, social, and historical circumstances—that it brings about what he calls a "crisis of wholeness."[29] Instead of the wholeness and mutuality that lead to loving and caring relationships, the self may find itself engaging in "organized terror" and even "major industries of extermination."[30]

What can we draw from this brief tour of Erikson's first five stages, especially in terms of understanding violence? In addition to showing how violence is a "failure of the normal developmental process," the developmental thinking of Erikson is insightful for three reasons.[31]

First, it allows us to see how a person's violent development might have been in the direction of peace if the quality of care and justice had been different. Second, it allows us to see how a person's violent development—precisely because it is a process of development—might be addressed and perhaps rectified. And third, it allows us to conclude that if there is any variable able to rectify violence, that variable is care and justice woven together.

In the case of a violent offender, for example, what caring and justice might turn out to be would have to be uniquely tailored. To think, however, that anyone is going to change in the absence of care and justice, or to think that a superego morality, let alone a morality of inner depth, is going to develop in the absence of care and justice, or to think that *there is something humanly more powerful than care and justice* is simply not realistic. In the last analysis, is not the question we have to ask: "At what point do we decide to consider those who are violent in a context of human development?" Does not our question have to be: "Can anything take the place of care and justice in human development?" Is not our question: "What realistic alternative to peace do we have in our attempt to understand human development?"[32] The movie, *Dead Man Walking*, is helpful in letting us consider these three questions.

SHAME AND VIOLENCE IN MEN

James Gilligan, a forensic psychiatrist and the former director of mental health for the prison system of Massachusetts in the United States, discusses a young inmate who murdered a woman his own age and then cut out her eyes and her tongue.[33] Gilligan finds the roots of this atrocity in "shame, humiliation, weakness, inferiority, incompetence," and in "sexual and financial inadequacy."[34] This man, he believed, suffered from "a collapse of self-esteem" resulting in the death of his sense of self. After killing his victim, he had a complete absence of remorse or guilt, saying "I didn't like the way she was looking at me" and "I didn't want her talking about me."[35] He was not the problem; the woman he murdered and mutilated was the problem. He could not take responsibility for his actions; he could not look bad; he could not allow himself to be "overwhelmed by shame and ridicule." Ironically, the binary "logic of shame"—so central in prison life—was such that the violence he could not be responsible for was the very thing that bolstered his self respect as a man.[36]

"I have yet to see," says Gilligan, "a serious act of violence that was not provoked by the experience of feeling shamed and humiliated, disrespected and ridiculed."[37] Perpetrators ward off the effects of shame, humiliation, inferiority, and impotence by replacing them with actions that give a sense of pride, honor, superiority, and power. Yet, says Gilligan, shame by itself is not a sufficient cause of violence. There are three preconditions. First, the perpetrator's shame is so overwhelming that it brings about a state of "numbness and death more tormenting than any pain could be."[38] Second, the perpetrator cannot experience the emotions that inhibit or neutralize violence, emotions such as guilt and remorse, or love and empathy, or the normal fear of the consequences of one's actions. Third, the perpetrator does not see himself as "having sufficient *non*violent means available with which to maintain or restore his self-esteem, such as education, social status, wealth, or socially honoured achievements."[39]

SHAME AND VIOLENCE IN WOMEN

Judith Jordan offers a clear understanding of shame, especially as it tends to be experienced by victims of violence:

> Shame seeks isolation and dwells in silence. It interferes with movement back into relationship. Our shamed parts are the last

ing others, if not from our own self-reflection, there is often an enormous investment of energy involved in trying to find the attending-that-provides-care and the respect-that-provides-justice that validates us as human beings. If there is nothing more powerful in the human than the care and justice that is peace, then, in a kind of deficit reckoning, violence is the testament to that power.

Violence makes little sense except as the absence of peace. Understood developmentally, it is the futile fulfillment of the unmet need for wholeness and relatedness. Violence is care for the self in the absence of loving care; it is the respect or justice for the self when respect and justice cannot be had. Untutored by care and justice, the power of violence is a primal protest against mistrust, shame, guilt, inferiority, and the inability to find identity, or self-esteem, or wholeness. It is a rage born of *disconnection*, a rage proclaiming that integrity and mutuality along with care and justice are nothing but a lie, or an absence, or a devastating contradiction. Violence is an impassioned and entitled lashing out against the self and the other for an attending-to-need and a respect-for-fairness that cannot be had.

PEACE AND THE HUMAN

As we look more closely at peace, what do we find? So far, with the help of Erikson, we have seen that peace is one of two primary paths of human development; it is the path of growth, the path of health, the path of human fullness. We have said that peace is not just the absence of violence, that it is not simply a time of blessed calm or welcomed rest. We have claimed that peace is a reality that is vitally alive and dynamic in its own right. We have said several other things as well: that peace cannot be had in the absence of care and justice; that the strength of peace can only come from care and justice; that there is nothing more humanly powerful than the care and justice that are the substance of peace. Finally, we have proposed that peace is the fullness of the human in action. Peace is ultimately what being human and relating in the fullness of that humanness are all about.

Simply said, a self that is integral and mutual is a peaceful self. From the perspective of being adult and moral, peace is always *inner* and *relational*. There is a unity, a wholeness, an "at-oneness" that this self *is* in itself because all the "pieces" of this self, "the loved and the unloved, the comfortable and the uncomfortable, the good and the bad," live together as one. There is also a unity, a wholeness, an "at-oneness" that this self *is* with the other because in an adult-moral self a unity of integrity and mutuality defines this self. If we ask then: "Is there a concise definition of peace in its full humanness?" the answer is: *peace is the "at-oneness" of an integral self-in-mutuality*. The peace of an adult-moral self—a self that is inner and relational, a self acting in care and justice—is a *unity in action*. It is an amazingly powerful "at-oneness" of the self's relating within and without that makes it fully human.

PEACE AS THE EPITOME OF HUMAN DEVELOPMENT

There are three prominent ways of describing peace as the epitome of human development. First, peace can be seen in its relational fullness if we amplify and nuance the notion of distributive justice that has been handed down to us. Second, the "wholing" and "mutualizing" nature of peace can be understood in describing the process of restorative care and justice that has become prominent in the last few decades. Third, peace in all of its dimensions can be seen in a careful description of nonviolence as it has come to be known and practiced.

Peace as Distributive Care and Justice

If peace flows directly from our actions of caring and being just and if in itself it is an "at-oneness" as it relates within and without, then "distributive care and justice" is a basic and practical description we can take from the culture to name the fullness of peace. To see care and justice together as being distributive picks up the intuition about equality and the concern for human rights that lie in the traditional notion of distributive justice. When it comes to care—attending to the needs, rights, and freedoms of the self and the other—we are all equal. When it comes to justice—to respect, fairness, and equity in caring for the needs, rights, and freedoms of the self and the other—again we are all equal. None of us has needs, rights, and freedoms that are more important than anyone else.

The fragile and putative sense of justice that has been present down through the centuries is that there is a basic equality common to the needs and rights of all. In an adult-moral self, therefore, care and justice in tandem are—and are meant to be—distributive. Human resources and responsibilities are meant to be shared equally by all in service of the wholeness that all are meant to realize. The primary way, therefore, that peace is alive in an adult-moral self is seen in actions that are distributive. *Peace as an at-oneness within and without is inherent in the notion of distributive care and justice.*

In describing the fullness of peace as distributive care and justice, four points need to be mentioned. First, it is always an ongoing process of attending to and respecting the needs, rights, and freedoms of the self and the other. Second, while every person is included in this mutual process of attending and respecting, the unique circumstances of individuals, societies, and cultures need to be taken into account. Third, to the degree that distributive care and justice are not accepted either by individuals or within countries and cultures, to that degree peace is not able to be realized. Attending to and respecting the needs, rights, and freedoms of all—equality tutored by equity—is the *sine qua non* of any real and stable peace. Fourth, in the ongoing process of attending to the needs, rights, and freedoms of all, it can be expected that our understanding of what these are may develop and become increasingly clearer. In other words, the actual practice of care and justice is the actual practice of peace.

Making, building, and safeguarding peace—articulated in the notion of peace as distributive care and justice—is meant to be the ongoing struggle of human development in each one of us. Peace as distributive care and justice is the first, the natural, and the ongoing way of peace of an adult and moral self. Peace as distributive care and justice is the way of peace that promotes wholeness and forestalls violence in both the self and the other. This is the kind of peace that underlies notions of the just society and the common good. This is the kind of peace that Johan Galtung seems to be speaking of when he says: "the basic measure of peace is what happens to human beings, the extent to which their basic needs and basic rights are met."[45]

Peace as Restorative Care and Justice

A second way of peace that is naturally present in an adult-moral self is in restorative care and justice. The notion of restorative justice, a nuancing of the rectificatory justice of the tradition, has become prominent across the globe in the last few decades. With its roots in the notion of *ubuntu* in some African Nations and in the practices of the Māori people of New Zealand, the First Nations of Canada, and the Native Peoples of the United States among others, it has come to be a notion that is increasingly significant in how public justice is understood and pursued.[46] What is unique about this notion of restorative justice, however—and what makes it so fully human—is that *it is a notion of rectifying justice firmly rooted in a notion of caring*. In other words, restorative justice is more accurately described as restorative care and justice.[47]

In the practice of restorative care and justice—called for when distributive care and justice has been violated—the central question is not: How should we punish the offender? The central question is: What can be done to make things right?[48] In answering this question—a question of care and justice together—Howard Zehr, raises five more questions:

1. Who has been hurt?
2. What are their needs?
3. Whose obligations are these?
4. Who has a stake in this situation?
5. What is the appropriate process to involve stakeholders in an effort to put things right?[49]

In restorative care and justice, the crime—the uncaring and injustice—is understood as personal and relational, as possibly involving a number of different relationships that may require healing, reconciliation, and a return to whatever wholeness and mutuality can be realized for all the parties going forward.

The *victim* or *survivor* is the primary focus of restorative care and justice. Since the victim is the one whose right to equal care and justice has been violated, the needs of the victim are paramount in any process of restorative care and justice. The victim may need to tell the story of what happened, or to explain the impact of the offense on self, family, and friends, or to tell of re-victimization that occurred in the justice system, or to hear an apology from the offender, or to ask for some other response: "Why did this happen?" "Why did you do this to me?" "How could you do this?" "Do you have any understanding of what you have done to my life?" "Can you be responsible for what you have done?" The actual needs of the victim for care and respect, for healing and wholeness, are the focus of restorative care and justice.[50]

The *offender* or *perpetrator* needs to be held directly accountable to the victim for his or her actions. The offender needs to understand the consequences of his or her actions and take responsibility for those consequences. The offender may need to explain why he or she harmed the victim or the community. The offender may need to apologize to the victim and to others who were harmed. The offender may need to make some kind of restitution and to ask for forgiveness. In responding to how the victim has been violated as an integral-self-in-mutuality, the offender is called to address the harm to his or her own integrity and mutuality: "I'm sorry for what I did." "What can I do to make amends?" "I am taking responsibility." "I am taking these steps to change." Along with some empathy for the victim, the offender is challenged to move from shame to responsibility. If the offender needs to show some care and respect for the victim, the offender also needs to find some care and respect for himself or herself as well.[51]

The *community* of those most directly affected by the harm is very important, at times as victim, at times as context, at times as witness, at times as source of support. Those in the community are often stakeholders in the harm or crime as well as in its restoration. One of the little-focused-on facts about incidents of violence is the "ripple effects" visited on who or what is other in addition to the victim—on spouses, children, parents, grandparents, the unborn, friends, identified groups, neighborhoods, regions, cities, and budgets. The community almost always feels the negative impact of crime in a number of disintegrating ways. At the same time, the community can serve as a holding environment and a container without which restorative care and justice would not be possible. If crime is relational, restorative care and justice is relational as well. The role of the community, when patiently, carefully, and skillfully organized, is critical in restorative care and justice.

The *appropriate process* that can put things right is the crucial component of restorative care and justice. Taking a number of forms, it may unfold through a *victim-offender dialogue* willingly entered into. It may unfold through *community conferencing* of some kind. It may unfold in *peacemaking circles* that are periodically held. In a safe space with respect for all, the harm can be honestly faced and acknowledged; pain and shame can surface from the inner depth; the heart, or the soul, or the spirit can be touched; and all can find themselves involved in a dialogue that is often poignantly intimate and transformative. With an appropriate process carefully crafted, restorative care and justice can bring healing, wholeness, reconciliation, and peace for all involved in a way that nothing else may be able to do.[52]

Peace as Nonviolence

Is there any way to pursue peace that involves the use of violence? Is there any way to respond to violence that does not involve an exercise of the care and justice that are the actions of peace? Nonviolence is a third way of peace, a way of being and relating to self and other that is rooted in a number of religious traditions down through the centuries, a way of peace that is completely in harmony with being an adult and moral self, an integral and mutual self, and a caring and just self. Three recent versions of this way of peace are briefly presented here: one in Mahatma Gandhi (1869–1948), whose understanding of nonviolence is clearly rooted in the Hindu religious tradition; one in Martin Luther King, Jr. (1929–1968), who is influenced by Gandhi yet has a notion of nonviolence firmly rooted in the Christian religious tradition; and one in Barbara Deming (1917–1984), who is influenced by Gandhi, King, and a number of others yet is rooted in no religious tradition at all.

MOHANDAS KARAMCHAND GANDHI

Mahatma ("the great soul") Gandhi, a spiritual leader and activist, has a commitment to nonviolence that is steeped in a search for truth which for him is also a search for God. Truth, *satya*, is "the substance of all morality," but it is only found in a sustained and selfless inward quest characterized by honesty and purity of intention.[53] If we are not "relatively free from anger, selfishness and hatred," we "will never find the truth."[54] Even external authority, "if it is in conflict with sober reason or the dictates of the heart," must be rejected.[55] "There is," says Gandhi, "an inmost centre of us all, where Truth abides in fullness."[56] Our fears and our desires that keep us from finding the truth are only conquered by selfless love. "In order to be fearless we should love all and adhere to the path of truth."[57]

For Gandhi, truth and nonviolence, *ahiṃsā*, go together. As "the deliberate abstention from harm and from ill will," nonviolence is "the supreme moral principle."[58] This principle—found only in the heart—includes not just killing or the physical harm of another but also "hurt by every evil thought, by undue haste, by lying, by hatred, by wishing ill to anybody, and by our holding onto what the world needs."[59] *Ahiṃsā* means "no coercion." "Those who coerce others in order to gain advantage are acting untruthfully."[60] Nonviolence "does not mean meek submission to the will of the evil-doer, but it means pitting one's whole soul against the will of the tyrant."[61] Nonviolence is *satyagraha* or "truth force," an active resistance to oppression in the service of truth that honors—as it did with the British colonizers in India—the need to love and respect the unjust other in peace, and yet it has the power to "melt the stoniest heart."[62]

MARTIN LUTHER KING, JR.

Martin Luther King, Jr., a spiritual leader and activist who greatly admired Gandhi, is deeply rooted in the Christian tradition, especially in terms of a God of universal love and liberation. "The innate worth referred to in the phrase the image of God," says King, "is universally shared in equal portions by all men."[63] King speaks of love as *agape*, "an overflowing love which seeks nothing in return." He goes on to say: "When you love this way, you begin to love men not because they are likable, not because they do things that attract us, but because God loves them and here we love the person who does the evil deed while hating the deed that the person does."[64] For King, the Christian tradition calls us to confront evil with "nonviolence and love rather than violence and hate." Nonviolence "is not passive nonresistance to evil," but rather "active nonviolent resistance to evil."[65]

King, a man who finds himself "obliged by conscience," makes five points about nonviolence. First, it is "not a method for cowards; it *does* resist."[66] Second, "it does not seek to defeat or humiliate the opponent, but to win his friendship and understanding."[67] Third, "the attack is directed against forces of evil rather than against persons who are caught in those forces."[68] Fourth, it avoids not only external physical violence but also internal violence of spirit." And fifth, it is "based on the conviction that the universe is on the side of justice."[69] For King: "Power at its best is love implementing the demands of justice."[70] In one sermon, he says: "As you press on for justice, be sure to move with dignity and discipline, using only the weapon of love."[71] "If you succumb to the temptation of using violence in your struggle, unborn generations will be the recipients of a long and desolate night of bitterness, and your chief legacy to the future will be an endless reign of meaningless chaos."[72]

BARBARA DEMING

A theorist of nonviolence and a civil rights marcher in the United States during the 1960s, Barbara Deming is a powerful advocate of nonviolence. She argues clearly that "nonviolence does not need a religious basis."[73] She does not believe that "the universe is on the side of justice" nor does she rely on the presence of a "higher power." Religious people "expect too much from their oppressors" and "use petition and prayer rather than force to achieve their goals."[74] She believes: "to resort to power one need not be violent, and to speak to conscience one need not be meek. Sometimes our most effective action *both* resorts to power *and* engages conscience."[75] Nonviolence calls for "self-assertion," for aggressively acting out the truth, as we see it, as well as for restraint toward others, for "acting out of love for them" with "respect for their human rights."[76] In nonviolence, we lay two hands on the oppressor, "the one calming him, making him ask questions, as the other makes him move."[77]

Like King, Deming is looking toward the future when we "will act out a basic respect, for each and all others" and nonviolence is the way to achieve this. [78] To those who say nonviolence has been tried and does not work, she says: "It has *not* been tried. We have barely begun to try it. The people who dismiss it now as irrelevant do not understand what it could be."[79] If we use violence, violence escalates; if we are nonviolent, "one can count on reaching a point where de-escalation begins."[80] If we "wage battle without violence, we can remain much more in control—of our own selves, of the responses to us which our adversaries make, of the battle as it proceeds and for the future we hope will issue from it."[81] The person "who acts violently forces another to do *his* will" but the person "who acts nonviolently insists upon acting out his *own* will."[82] Honoring integrity, mutuality, and connection means that we do not confuse the "offerings of radical change" with the "resort to violence."[83]

Nonviolence not only defines peace with exceptional clarity, but as it does so it also brings a similar clarity to an integral and mutual self, to the person who actually is that peace. In fact, nonviolence defines the peace of an integral and mutual self in a way that nothing else can.

- Nonviolence is a peaceful response to violence, a response that rejects violence completely.

- Nonviolence, put positively, is a way of relating to the violent other in love, care, and justice, even as it informs the actual meaning of love, care, and justice.
- Nonviolence is a direct response to human evil, a response that may entail considerable danger and personal suffering; nonviolence holds evil in clear relief, not through a logical binary lens of "good vs. evil" but simply by not participating in evil no matter the cost.
- Nonviolence calls for an integrity that is strong and for a mutuality that is unwavering. Responding to violence with nonviolence not only *demands* integrity and mutuality but it *safeguards* integrity and mutuality even as it *validates* integrity and mutuality for all concerned.
- Nonviolence not only takes into account the needs, rights, and freedoms of the self and the other for wholeness, but it also is a practical way of sorting out for all involved what those needs, rights, and freedoms actually are. Yet seemingly exceptional, nonviolence is the normal response of an adult-moral self. Nonviolence is fully human conscience.
- Nonviolence as peace in action is anything but passive or disengaged. As the opposite of disembodied rationality, it often calls for fistfuls of courage and an undaunted sense of self-control; it is a profoundly embodied way of being, not just a tactic or a strategy.
- Nonviolence is a morality of inner depth; it comes from the depth and it helps to define that depth; it brings the heart, or the soul, or the spirit to life, even as it shapes the meaning of these three dimensions that distinguish our innermost.
- Nonviolence is a direct challenge to the inner depth of the other as well as to the inner depth of the self; it appeals directly to the conscience of all involved; it is an implicit invitation to dialogue on the basis of integrity and mutuality.

- Nonviolence engages all the other characteristics of an integral and mutual self: it is a stance of the whole self, with mind and body as one; it is deeply felt, with reason and emotion as one; it immediately sets and tests clear boundaries for the self and the other; it is inescapably and vulnerably intimate; and it epitomizes the responsible self, the self that responds to the other as its own uniqueness in the uniqueness of the situation.

PEACE AND EMPATHY: THE POWER OF TRANSFORMATION

From the way that peace functions in distributive care and justice, in restorative care and justice, and in the nonviolent response to violence, it is clearly an amazingly transformative power. Where does this power lie? It lies in the power of being caring and just and it lies in the conversation, the exchange, the encounter, the dialogue. The power of peace is ultimately interpersonal. It is the power of one embodied self, in feeling and depth, engaging the other, in feeling and depth, in ways that all are touched and able to move toward wholeness. In distributive care and justice this encounter is the very basis of our relating to each other. In restorative care and justice, this encounter takes place as the parties are willing and able. In nonviolence, this encounter or dialogue may be implicit in the unfolding situation. If we ask: "What makes this kind of exchange between the feeling and depth of one person with that of the other possible?" the answer is: *it is the power of empathy that makes this exchange possible.*[84]

Peace and empathy are intimately connected. Peace is an integral and mutual self in action. Empathy—self empathy and empathy for the other—is at the heart the *feeling self*, the *self of inner depth*, the *intimate self*, and of all the other characteristics of an integral self-in-mutuality. Peace is not possible except in the presence of care and justice, and care and justice are only possible with empathy for both the self and the other. What peace and empathy have in common—both so often misunderstood and underappreciated in the culture—is that *they involve attending to and respecting the self and the other*. Paying attention to and having respect for the self and for the other are liberative, transformative, and integrative. In the fullness of the human, peace and empathy necessarily go together. Empathy is a *sine qua non* for peace. Without empathy there is no peace. In *Dead Man Walking*, Matthew Poncelet's transformation shows this.

VIOLENCE VERSUS PEACE

If violence is understood as *the annihilating of the integral and mutual self*, and if peace is understood as *the fullness of this self*, then these two human powers are the opposite of each other. Violence, as we noted, is always found in *disconnection*. Peace is always in the service of overcoming disconnection. The very nature of peace is that it is an "at-oneness" of an integral self-in-mutuality, an amazingly powerful "at-oneness" in attending and respecting, in relating within and without. Empathy—self-empathy and empathy for the other—is also an "at-oneness" in its attending and respecting within and without. As we have seen, empathy makes an integral self-in-mutuality possible. If *disconnection* is the right hand of violence, if disconnection is always in the room when violence is present, then the "at-oneness" that is peace and the "at-oneness" that is empathy are together the power we are and have that corrects violence. As practiced, it is the nature of neither peace nor empathy to give an opening to *disconnection*.

At this point, we can contrast violence and peace in light of the fully human.

This contrast speaks directly to the fully human: (1) as a way of showing these two opposing paths of human development with as much clarity as possible; (2) as a framing of the ultimate human struggle between good and evil in a way that everyone is at stake; and (3) as a way to help the first part of this book about the fullness of the human to come to its rightful conclusion.

Violence as Human Action	**Peace as Human Action**
• dehumanizes and is the failure of human development	• humanizes and is the fullness of human development
• directly attacks integrity, keeping the "pieces" of the self from coming together	• is the "at-oneness" of integrity, harmonizing all the "pieces" of the self
• completely violates mutuality for the other	• lives in mutuality and is impossible without it
• is the active annihilation of care and justice	• is the active result of care and justice working together
• attacks the body-self, bringing trauma that would separate mind from body in horrible and fearful ways	• respects the body-self, bringing healing and wholeness and fostering connection
• deadens the feeling self, blocking empathy	• enlivens the feeling self and only lives in empathy
• seizes the inner depth, filling it with rage	• becomes the inner depth as a core of caring and justice
• rides roughshod over boundaries of self or other	• honors the clear boundaries of both the self and the other
• mocks the intimate self in an invading closeness of disregard or contempt	• is an openness to, a welcoming of, and an honoring of the intimate self
• destroys the responsible self	• is the responsible self
• is "evil," developmentally understood	• is "good," developmentally understood

• is always in the service of disconnection	• is always in the service of connection

NOTES

1. *Dead Man Walking*, DVD, directed by Tim Robbins (1995; Santa Monica, CA: MGM Home Entertainment, 2005).

2. Judith L. Herman, *Trauma and Recovery* (New York: Basic Books, 1992), 33, observes: "Traumatic events are extraordinary, not because they occur rarely, but rather because they overwhelm the ordinary adaptation to life."

3. For a broadly conceived article on violence, peace, and basic needs, see Ervin Staub, "Notes on Cultures of Violence, Cultures of Caring and Peace, and the Fulfillment of Basic Human Needs," *Political Psychology* 24, no. 1 (2003): 1–21.

4. *Merriam Webster*, 11th ed. s.v. "Violence."

5. Johan Galtung, "Violence, Peace, and Peace Research," *Journal of Peace Research*, 6, no. 3 (1969): 170.

6. Johan Galtung, *Peace by Peaceful Means: Peace and Conflict, Development and Civilization* (London: Sage, 1996), 40.

7. Johan Galtung, "Cultural Violence," *Journal of Peace Research*, 27, no. 3 (1990): 291.

8. Ibid., 302.

9. Jean-Paul Sartre and David Pellauer, *Notebooks for an Ethics* (Chicago: University of Chicago Press, 1992), 173.

10. Edward Tick, *War and the Soul: Healing Our Nation's Veterans from Post-traumatic Stress Disorder* (Wheaton, IL: Quest Books, 2005), 20.

11. Michael Ignatieff, *The Warrior's Honour: Ethnic War and the Modern Conscience* (New York: Henry Holt, 1997), 53–54.

12. John Kekes, *The Roots of Evil* (Ithaca, NY: Cornell University Press, 2005), xi.

13. John Kekes, *The Human Condition* (Oxford: Clarendon Press, 2010), 114–15.

14. Ronald B. Miller, "Deny No Evil, Ignore No Evil, Reframe No Evil: Psychology's Moral Dilemma," in *Humanity's Dark Side: Evil, Destructive Experience, and Psychotherapy*, ed. Arthur C. Bohart, Barbara S. Held, Edward Schneider, and J. Kirk (Washington, DC: American Psychological Association, 2013): 232.

15. J. Jeffrey Means, *Trauma and Evil: Healing the Wounded Soul* (Minneapolis, MN: Fortress, 2000), 98.

16. Claudia Card, *Confronting Evils: Terrorism, Torture, and Genocide* (New York: Cambridge University Press, 2010).

17. Johan Galtung, "Peace Studies and Conflict Resolution: The Need for Transdisciplinarity," *Transcultural Psychiatry* 47, no. 1 (February 2010): 22.

18. Erik H. Erikson, "Reflections on the Dissent of Contemporary Youth," *Daedalus* 99, no. 1 (Winter 1970): 164, talks about care in connection with values consciously chosen "with insight and foresight," making it clear that justice with its respect, fairness and equity is an intimate part of care. While insight and foresight can easily be seen as cognitive qualities they can also easily be seen as qualities of empathy.

19. Erik H. Erikson, "Autobiographic Notes on the Identity Crisis," *Daedalus*, 99, no. 4 (Fall 1970): 756.

20. Richard I. Evans, *Dialogue with Erik Erikson* (New York: Praeger, 1981), 68. It is interesting to note that Erikson is not making the case that we are animals in an evolutionary way, as so many thinkers tend to assume; he is saying that when we cannot be human we may act in a way that some animals act.

21. It is important to note that Herman, *Trauma and Recovery*, relies on Erikson's first five stages to understand both the traumatic effects of violence and to understand the relational process of recovery.

22. Erik H. Erikson, "The Roots of Virtue," Julian Huxley, ed., *The Humanist Frame* (New York: Harper & Brothers, 1962), 151.

23. See Helen Block Lewis, "Introduction: Shame—the 'Sleeper' in Psychopathology," in *The Role of Shame in Symptom Formation*, ed. Helen Block Lewis (Hillsdale, NJ: Lawrence Erlbaum Associates, 1987), 1–28; see Thomas J. Scheff, "The Shame-Rage Spiral: A Case Study of an Interminable Quarrel," in Lewis, *The Role of Shame in Symptom Formation*, 109–49; see Thomas J. Scheff, *Emotions and Violence: Shame and Rage in Destructive Conflicts* (Lexington, MA: Lexington Books, 1991); see J. Brooks Bouson, *Embodied Shame: Uncovering Female Shame in Contemporary Women's Writings* (Albany: State University of New York Press, 2009); see James Gilligan, *Violence: Reflections on a National Epidemic* (New York: Putnam, 1996); see James Gilligan, *Preventing Violence* (New York: Thames & Hudson, 2001).

24. For a helpful discussion of the relationship between shame and guilt, see Helen B. Lewis, *Shame and Guilt in Neurosis* (New York: International Universities Press, 1971); see also James Gilligan, "Shame, Guilt, and Violence," *Social Research: An International Quarterly*, 70, no. 4 (2003): 1149–80.

25. See William I. Miller, *Humiliation: And Other Essays on Honor, Social Discomfort, and Violence* (Ithaca, NY: Cornell University Press, 1993); see Julian Walker and Victoria Knauer, "Humiliation, Self-esteem and Violence," *Journal of Forensic Psychiatry and Psychology*, 22, no. 5 (2011): 724–41.

26. See Erik H. Erikson, "Eight Ages of Man," *Childhood and Society*, 2nd ed. (New York: Norton, 1963), 247–74.

27. Erik H. Erikson, *Identity: Youth and Crisis* (New York: Norton, 1968), 25.

28. Erikson, "Autobiographic Notes on the Identity Crisis," 733.

29. Erikson, *Identity: Youth and Crisis*, 89.

30. Ibid.

31. Peter Fonagy, "Toward a Developmental Understanding of Violence," *British Journal of Psychiatry* 183, no. 3 (August 2003): 190.

32. See Liz Elliott, "Security, Without Care: Challenges for Restorative Values in Prison," *Contemporary Justice Review*, 10, no.2 (June 2007): 193–208.

33. James Gilligan, "Exploring Shame in Special Settings: A Psychotherapeutic Study," in *Forensic Psychotherapy: Crime, Psychodynamics and the Offender Patient*, Vol. 2: Mainly Practice, ed. Christopher Cordess and Murray Cox (London: Jessica Kingsley, 1996), 475–89, 477.

34. Ibid., 481.

35. Ibid., 478.

36. Ibid., 480.

37. James Gilligan, "Sex, Gender and Violence: Estela Welldon's Contribution to Our Understanding of the Psychopathology of Violence," *British Journal of Psychotherapy* 25, no. 2 (May 2009): 244.

38. Ibid., 245

39. Ibid., 247.

40. Judith V. Jordan, "Personality Disorder or Relational Disconnection? In *Handbook of Personality Disorders: Theory and Practice*, ed. Jeffrey J. Magnavita (Hoboken, NJ: John Wiley, 2004), 129.

41. Eli Buchbinder and Zvi Eisikovits, "Battered Women's Entrapment in Shame: A Phenomenological Study," *American Journal of Orthopsychiatry* 73, no. 4 (2003): 355–66.

42. Ibid., 360.

43. Ibid., 361.

44. Farhad Dalal, "Specialists without Spirit: Sensualists without Heart: Psychotherapy as a Moral Endeavour," 36th S. H. Foulkes Annual Lecture, *Group Analysis* 45, no. 4 (2012): 423.

45. Galtung, "Peace Studies and Conflict Resolution," 20.

46. For an understanding of *ubuntu*, see Susan C. Marks, chapter 8: "Ubuntu, the Spirit of Africa: Example for the World," in *Watching the Wind: Conflict Resolution during South Africa's Transition to Democracy* (Washington, DC: United States Institute for Peace, 2000), 181–90. Desmond Tutu says: "A person with *ubuntu* is open and available to others, affirming of others, does not feel threatened when others are able and good, for he or she has a proper self-assurance that comes from knowing that he or she belongs in a grater whole and is diminished when others are humiliated or oppressed, or tortured as if they were less than who they are." Desmond M. Tutu, *No Future without Forgiveness* (New York: Doubleday, 1999), 31.

47. For a very accessible introduction to restorative justice see Howard Zehr, *The Little Book of Restorative Justice* (Intercourse, PA: Good Books, 2002). See also Dennis Sullivan and Larry Tifft, eds., *Handbook of Restorative Justice: A Global Perspective*. London: Routledge, 2008.

48. See Howard Zehr, "A Restorative Lens," *Changing Lenses: A New Focus for Crime and Justice*, 3rd ed. (Scottsdale, PA: Herald Press, 2005), 186.

49. Zehr, *Little Book*, 38.

50. See Howard Zehr, "The Victim," *Changing Lenses: A New Focus for Crime and Justice*, 3rd ed. (Scottsdale, PA: Herald Press, 2005): 19–32.

51. See Howard Zehr, "The Offender," *Changing Lenses: A New Focus for Crime and Justice*, 3rd ed. (Scottsdale, PA: Herald Press, 2005): 33–44.

52. For an understanding of how restorative care and justice might apply in a much larger context see Ivo Aertsen, Jana Arsovska, Holger-C. Rohne, Marta Valiñas, Kris Vanspauwen, eds., *Restoring Justice after Large-scale Violent Conflicts: Kosovo, DR Congo and the Israeli-Palestinian Case* (Devon, UK: Routledge, 2008).

53. Raghavan N. Iyer, *The Moral and Political Thought of Mahatma Gandhi* (Oxford: Oxford University Press, 2000), 150.

54. Ibid., 172.

55. Ibid., 173.

56. Ibid., 176.

57. Ira Chernus, *American Nonviolence: The History of an Idea* (New York: Orbis, 2004), 99.

58. Iyer, *The Moral and Political Thought*, 184.

59. Ibid., 180.

60. Chernus, *American Nonviolence*, 100, says this about Gandhi's political thought.

61. Mahatma Gandhi, *Non-Violent Resistance (Satyagraha)* (New York: Schocken Books, 1961), 134.

62. Chernus, *American Nonviolence*, 107.

63. Martin Luther King, Jr., "The Ethical Demands for Integration," in *A Testament of Hope: The Essential Writings of Martin Luther King, Jr.*, ed. James Melvin Washington (Washington, DC: Harper & Row, 1986), 119.

64. Martin Luther King, Jr., "The Power of Nonviolence," in *A Testament of Hope: The Esse ntial Writings of Martin Luther King, Jr.*, ed. James Melvin Washington (Washington, DC: Harper & Row, 1986), 14.

65. Martin Luther King, Jr., "An Experiment in Love," in *A Testament of Hope: The Essential Writings of Martin Luther King, Jr.*, ed. James Melvin Washington (Washington, DC: Harper & Row, 1986), 18.

66. Martin Luther King, Jr., "Nonviolence and Radical Justice," in *A Testament of Hope: The Essential Writings of Martin Luther King, Jr.*, ed. James Melvin Washington (Washington, DC: Harper & Row, 1986), 7.

67. Ibid.

68. Ibid., 8.

69. Ibid.

70. Martin Luther King, Jr., *Where Do We Go from Here: Chaos or Community?* (New York: Harper & Row, 1967), 37.

71. Martin Luther King, Jr., "The Most Durable Power," in *A Testament of Hope: The Essential Writings of Martin Luther King, Jr.*, ed. James Melvin Washington (Washington, DC: Harper & Row, 1986), 10.

72. Ibid.

73. Ira Chernus, *American Nonviolence*, 183.

74. Ibid.

75. Barbara Deming, "On Revolution and Equilibrium," in *Nonviolence in America: A Documentary History*, ed. Staughton Lynd and Alice Lynd (Maryknoll, NY: Orbis Books, 1995): 413.

76. Ibid., 427.

77. Ibid., 416.

78. Barbara Deming, "New Men, New Women: Some Notes on Nonviolence" in *We Cannot Live without Our Lives* (New York: Grossman, 1974), 4.

79. Deming, "On Revolution and Equilibrium," 409.

80. Ibid., 416.

81. Ibid., 406.

82. Ibid., 414.

83. Ibid., 411.

84. See Arthur P. Ciaramicoli, *The Power of Empathy* (New York: Dutton, 2000).

Part II

Chapter Five

Education and the Fully Human

In the movie, *To Sir, with Love*, Mark Thackeray, a kind and gentle person, is hired at the working-class North Quay Secondary School in London's East End in the middle of the term. He replaces Mr. Hackman, who was so abused and defeated by his students in their final term that he resigned. These students do everything possible to torment their new teacher, disrespecting him at every turn, cutting off a leg of his desk, dropping a bag of water on him, and finally setting an unmentionable object on fire in the classroom stove. In disgust, he storms into the staff room. "Those kids are the devil incarnate," he screams. Then he catches himself and says in a eureka moment: "Kids, kids, that's it." Returning to the class, he dumps the text books into the basket, and he tells his students that they are becoming adults and that they need to learn what that involves before they leave. Things turn around dramatically. The students are intrigued by him and attracted by his integrity and his genuine respect and care. By term's end—in the simple words of the movie's title song—"Sir," as he is called, is loved and revered—"a friend who taught us right from wrong and weak from strong."[1]

In this chapter, we consider education in light of the fully human. First, we articulate a foundational and ultimate goal of education. Second, we consider six practical questions that help to focus on this goal. Third, we elaborate a pedagogy of connection, a pedagogy that takes into account not only the development of a peaceful self but also the failure of development that may result in a self that is violent. In this pedagogy, we look at the central role of empathy in education and we observe examples of teaching empathy, teaching care and justice, and teaching peace. The chapter ends by looking at four exemplary educators, each of whom makes her or his own unique contribution to the practice of education as well as to a pedagogy of connection.

THE GOALS OF EDUCATION

Education has any number of explicitly articulated goals: acquiring literacy; learning how to think; learning the culture and the wonders of the world we live in; gaining knowledge in important subject areas; stimulating intellectual curiosity; developing particular skills; learning to cooperate; preparing for appropriate work; getting a job; lifting us out of poverty; becoming a productive member of society; achieving proficiency; success in life; and competing in a global world. These goals, along with others that could be mentioned, are worthy, desirable, and necessary. They are complemented by other goals: for example, concern for "whole child" education that has personal growth as a major focus; and fostering discipline and maturity, especially as these concerns are thematic in understandings of moral development, character development, and citizen development.

Along with all these goals, a basic, pervasive, and holistic goal of education is for each student to develop into a whole person, an integral and mutual self. The goal is for each student to become a felt-from-within, self-authoring whole who relates in mutuality to whomever or whatever is other. Since being caring and just is how an integral and mutual self acts, these two ways of acting need to be the *sine qua non* of educational policy and practice. If education is for full livingness, could there be anything more important than learning care and justice? Education has to be about genuine caring, about learning to respond in empathy to the needs and rights and freedoms of the self and the other. It has to be about human justice, about learning to respect, to be fair, and to be equitable in caring for the needs not only of the self but also for all of our "others"—including the needs of other human beings, our human institutions, cultural attainments, the expansion of knowledge, the living environment, and the planet.

Ultimately, the goal of education is, therefore, about becoming a peaceful self—a self that is in, of, and for peace. With its integrity and mutuality and with its care and justice, the peaceful self—the pinnacle of the human—is a unity in action, an "at-oneness" in its relating within and without. Nurturing the peaceful self is not only a foundational and ultimate goal of education but it is one that could not be more consequential—individually, socially, multiculturally, nationally, internationally, and globally. If the future of our shared humanity is to be respected and furthered, nurturing the peaceful self needs to be bedrock in family life as well as in formal education.

A FEW PRACTICAL FOCUS QUESTIONS

As a way to focus on education in service of the fully human and as prologue to a pedagogy of connection, six practical questions may be helpful.

Is education for violence or is it for peace?

If we hope to move together with confidence through the twenty-first century, this is the first question we ought to be asking. The immediate answer we would probably want to give is: "Of course, education must be for peace." But if education is for peace and if peace is the fullness of human development, then the way to realize the peaceful self through education must be to approach the whole educational endeavor by fostering integrity and mutuality. If we believe that education must be for peace, there is a clear and definite way to implement this understanding. In other words, when we ask: "Is education for violence or is it for peace?" this question is anything but idealistic, or naïve, or vague, or peripheral. It is essentially a question—one that is crucial to our human survival and flourishing—about whether or not to seriously foster care and justice as the best way to counteract violence and celebrate peace.

Is seeing care and justice at the heart of education primarily a sectarian idea?

Akin to our understanding of care, justice, and empathy seamlessly working together is the notion of compassion. As we will see in chapter 7, all the world religions talk about showing compassion for the suffering of the other. But if care and justice are serious sectarian values that reflect some of the most cherished spiritual aspirations found in the culture, it is because first they are values that flow from and directly further integrity and mutuality. Whether we think of ourselves as spiritual or not—even if we find that the notion of spirituality has no useful purpose at all—as individuals and as members of the community we ought to be able to say with conviction: "Education is for care and justice as they complement and support each other." We can say this because of our shared humanity, because being caring and just with ourselves and the other is how we act when we are fully human.

Is it important in education to see human development and moral development as one?

Once we see that an adult self is a moral self, we realize that separating human and moral development is impossible. In educating for integrity and mutuality, in educating for care and justice, and in educating for peace we have a mosaic of the "whole person" in mind. We can understand what human development is—and we can come to take it seriously—if we realize that morality is inherent in it. We can understand what moral development is—and we can come to take it seriously—if we realize that it is not a stand-alone enterprise. Moral development, like human development, is learning to embody care and justice. The fully human is not a special concern of a few of us. It is the concern of all of us.

Is education meant to be for the-culture-in-us or for us-in-the-culture?

Seeing an integral and mutual self, along with the care and justice it embodies, as an ultimate goal of education, lets us say: "Education must be for the-culture-in-us and it must also be for us-in-the-culture." On the one hand, it is imperative that we learn and respect the different cultures we are in, that we learn to appreciate "the cultural superego" in all its different facets. On the other hand, it is imperative that we learn how to be caring and just. By embodying care and justice not only do we become fully ourselves but we are also able to challenge and transform the culture in ways that foster the full humanness that is peace.[2] In other words, the essence of education is to be formative and transformative, to embrace a paradox of cultural continuity and cultural change. Care and justice working as one supports this paradox.

Do we need to distinguish between moralism and morality in education?

Moralism is usually understood as "a conventional moral attitude."[3] It is usually the accepted rules and norms for action in the culture and it goes hand-in-hand with the "superego morality" that we saw in chapter 2. Moralism, as "the socially acceptable way to be," has a sense of conforming to cultural values, and its dynamic is the outside-influencing-the-inside. A teacher relying on moralism might say, for example: "If I catch anyone making fun of the new girl because she does not speak English, that person is going to be in trouble." While moralism can help with control and compliance, it tends to have a short shelf life; its sense of conformity and coercion can leave it alien and unowned, inviting us to challenge it if we can. In education, moralism may put us on an acceptable path, but without a focus on feeling and inner depth often it does not take us very far in a direction that is either appropriate or growthful.

Although easily confused with moralism, morality is best thought of as an animal of an entirely different species. If moralism is about "the-culture-in-me," morality is about "me-in-the-culture." Morality directly involves the empathy of the feeling self; it directly addresses our inner depth; and it directly challenges our need to be caring and just. Morality is "how I need to act." Its dynamic is the inside-influencing-the-outside. For example, a teacher trying to foster maturity and morality together might say: "Our newest member of the class grew up speaking no English at all; I am asking all of you to help her in any way that you can." If education needs occasional doses of moralism to avoid confusion, chaos, and immediate inequalities, that moralism is only a "surface exhibition" and must give way to empathy and a morality of depth. Unfortunately, nothing confounds genuine morality in us and in society more surely than the conformity that outlasts whatever usefulness it may once have had.

Is education for realizing the just society and the common good?

Educating for care and justice is directly in the service of realizing integrity and mutuality. The more each one of us is able to become an integral and mutual self, the more the just society and the common good are enhanced. The more we become fully human, the more we become caring and just, the more we contribute to and live in a world that is peaceful. There is no reason to separate what is personal from what is social and global. Becoming an integral and mutual self, a caring and just self, and a peaceful self is inherently something that at once is personal, social, and global. Yet, the wonderful paradox of this self is that, although it is a call to connection and peace that each one of us has, it stubbornly remains a unique individual quest until the day we die.

A PEDAGOGY OF CONNECTION

In light of these questions that help us focus on the overarching goal of education, the question arises: Is there a specific approach to education we can consciously pursue? There is such an approach, and it can be described at least in outline. In education, if we want to take human development seriously, to take violence and peace seriously, and to take our world seriously, the best way to proceed is to subscribe to a pedagogy of connection. This pedagogy of connection is the place from which to start if we want our students to understand who they are in their world.[4] It has three essential components.

- A pedagogy of connection sees education in the service of becoming integral and mutual, caring and just, and at peace within and without. This pedagogy makes a point of honoring the connections between integrity and mutuality and between care and justice. Since peace is at the heart of both of these connections, in actual practice this pedagogy is a pedagogy of peace.
- A pedagogy of connection recognizes, pays attention to, and creatively challenges the disconnections and the violence that we find in the culture as well as in ourselves. It is necessarily a critical pedagogy that takes the dialectic between violence and peace seriously. It makes a point of being a pedagogy of connection, of healing, and of nonviolence. In actual practice, this pedagogy is a pedagogy of peace.

- A pedagogy of connection never sees the student as a disconnected self living in disconnection from whatever is other to it—other people, the community, the environment, the country, the world, nature, history, the hard sciences, the social sciences, the arts, sports, citizenship, etc. It is a pedagogy of self and other together, a pedagogy of the "within" and the "without" *understood as inseparable*. In actual practice, this pedagogy is a pedagogy of peace.

In education, if we do not get the notion across—in terms clear, unmistakable, and often countercultural—that the self and the other, the *inner* and the *relational*, are connected from the beginning, then the whole enterprise is subverted from the start. Education loses its heart, its soul, its spirit. Thinking that is dualistic, either-or, and subject-object rules the day. Learning becomes objectified and disconnected, even as the learning self becomes objectified and disconnected. "The opposite of objectification," says Tobin Hart, "implies connection, even oneness, but this has not been what education has allowed."[5] *If the self and the other, the inner and the relational, are not together in education, then the concern for our development as persons is sidetracked from the beginning*. The entire project ends up doing little more than proposing secondary gains for the particle self, gains that may have little if anything to do with how we become fully human.

The very definition of an adult-moral self, a self that is integral and mutual as well as caring and just, is the definition of a self that is only alive in connection. The atom-like, self-sufficient, nondeveloping self that is so celebrated in the culture is not just a tolerated conceit born of Enlightenment philosophy. It is a self predicated in *disconnection*. It is a nonfeeling, nonrelational self that is normalized not just in the philosophical world but also in economics, in ethics, in politics, and in so many of our other academic and social pursuits.[6] To counteract this disconnection, educators, including those involved in higher education, must insist that being whole and being relational go together. As educators—and many of us are educators in different ways—one thing is crystal clear: if we want to avoid violence and assure peace, we can neither model nor teach disconnection.

NURTURING THE INTEGRAL AND MUTUAL SELF IN EDUCATION

In a seminal article, "Identity Education: A Conceptual Framework for Educational Researchers and Practitioners," Elli Schachter and Yisrael Rich understand identity as the aim of education in a way quite similar to how becoming an integral and mutual self is its aim.[7] Schachter and Rich define "identity education" as "the deliberate active involvement of educators with the psychosocial processes and practices that are involved in students' identity development."[8] They understand coming to identity not as an area of focus in addition to "academic, social-emotional, and moral education," but as what education essentially is all about.[9] This, of course, is what coming to integrity and mutuality is all about.

In their article, the authors talk about three over-all goals of identity education. Borrowing the terminology of Zvi Lamm, who sees these goals in conflict, they are: socialization, enculturation, and individuation.[10] *Socialization* is learning "the skills, norms, or attitudes required to participate constructively in social life or to assume significant adult roles."[11] *Enculturation* is learning the "values, dispositions, and bodies of knowledge that are deemed by educators to be true, moral, holy, or beautiful *regardless* of their functional value."[12] *Individuation* is learning to develop "a critical stance toward hegemonic social structures that cause social inequities" and learning "the skills and resilience to uphold their own desired identities rather than accept society's attempt to enforce debilitating ones."[13] Whether or not these goals are "compatible, complementary, or mutually exclusive" can be debated, say

Schachter and Rich, but clearly these primary goals of identity education are not elaborated in disconnection.[14]

Seeing an integral and mutual self as the overarching aim of education allows us to affirm individuation, socialization, and enculturation as not only clear goals in education, but it also allows us to realize that, even if these goals seem to be in some tension, they cannot be realized if they are mutually exclusive. Ultimately, each one of these goals is in the service of the other two, and when all three tutor each other and work together, then education is seen as a process of integral and mutual development that is inclusive and does *not separate the self and the other*.

At the end of their article on identity education, Schachter and Rich raise a few appropriate questions. Likewise, we can ask some appropriate questions of our own. “What are my educational goals and how are they informed by integrity and mutuality?” “How do I see care and justice as important to me personally, and does my personal understanding of these embodied ways of being influence the way that I administrate or teach?” “In what ways do care and justice influence the ethos of the school, and in what ways could they be part of the school’s mission statement?” “Given the nature of the student body of the school and given the different backgrounds students have, are there times when individuation, or socialization, or enculturation need special attention?” “If violence is a problem hampering individuation, socialization, or enculturation, can all who are impacted either in the school or in the surrounding community have a voice in naming the violence and finding practical solutions?” “Does not education inherently have to be a pedagogy of peace?”

FOSTERING THE SIX CHARACTERISTICS IN EDUCATION

If we consider each student we teach as an integral and mutual self in the making, then becoming a body-self, a whole person, is foundational in education. Education has to take embodiment seriously. "Our children," says Nel Noddings, "are physical entities enlivened with spirit and reason."[15] Engaging nature, engaging the world with all of our senses is clearly a full-bodied, organism-environment learning that nothing else can replicate. Learning patience, learning endurance, learning discipline, testing the other in fairness, selecting goals that have a sense of achievement—all these can be very helpful for connection. Learning about the body is all important. Sex education and nutrition education provide vital knowledge. Laughing and having a good time are indispensable for connection. Three good questions: Do I see my students in terms of a mind-body dichotomy? Do I see the essential humanness of my students in terms of care and justice or in terms of rationality? Do I want to educate minds or do I want to educate whole embodied persons?[16]

Taking the feeling self as who the student is meant to become, even as it is who I am meant to be as a teacher, is immensely freeing. Honoring reason apart from emotion or emotion apart from reason directly honors disconnection. Keeping the emotionally tinged and the rationally grasped together makes connection possible. Showing empathy, practicing empathy, and allowing students to be empathic with themselves and each other are essential for connection. Avoiding embarrassing, scapegoating, and labeling is imperative. Three good questions: Do I ask my students how they feel about important things considered in class? If I am not consistently empathic with my students, then how do I relate to them? As appropriate, can I share my own feelings as a teacher or an administrator?

Seeing that each of my students is meant to become a self of inner depth is invaluable. In fact, it is helpful to think of each student as an *inner* to be concerned about, to be addressed, to be fostered, to be protected. Honoring the uniqueness of each student is important, especially in the hopes and dreams and talents that each student has. Honoring achievements of different kinds—artistic, athletic, relational, and academic—makes an inner connection. Honoring courage and spirit acknowledges inner depth. Honoring acts of caring and justice touches the soul even as it lets everyone know that trust and community can be counted on. Three good questions: Do I honor the unique inner of each of my students? As appropriate, can I ask my students about their dreams for the future? Do I honor the times when a question, or an issue, or an action touches inner depth?

Honoring clear boundaries and the intimate self—and especially honoring them as connected—is extremely helpful in education because it lets our students know that their feeling and inner depth are connected with the feeling and the inner depth of the other. As appropriate, sharing is an exercise in intimacy that can be very helpful. Boundaries have to be respected—personal boundaries, physical boundaries, family boundaries, ethnic and racial boundaries, cultural boundaries—because these boundaries protect the student's emerging wholeness and relating to the other. When boundaries are crossed and the inner depth is encroached upon, these violations must be dealt with, but always with care and respect. Three good questions: How well do I respect boundaries while encouraging the developing inner depth of my students? Do I speak to the importance of boundaries, especially at appropriate times? Can I see my students both as unique persons and as a community?

Finally, it is imperative to honor the responsible self, not in demanding or fear-evoking ways, but as an expectation, that each student knows he or she is becoming a responsible person. Paying attention to acts and failures of responsibility is vitally important because this is exactly what nourishes the responsible self. Talking about responsibility as an opportunity rather than a burden is helpful. Seeing responsibility as care and justice enhancing the wholeness of self and other is incisive. Three good questions: Do I find myself relying on shaming or blaming in order to have control? Am I aware enough of how my students can be responsible and do I encourage that? Am I enough of a responsible self with and for my students that they can see that becoming such a self is an attainable and worthwhile goal?

THE CENTRALITY OF EMPATHY IN EDUCATION

Empathy is the foundation of a pedagogy of connection, of a pedagogy of integrity and mutuality, of a pedagogy of care and justice, and of a pedagogy of peace. Ironically, however, although empathy is foundational in education—and, in fact, foundational for all aspects of our humanness—it is a notion that is often completely misunderstood. Often, it is mystified or it is dismissed as "fraught with ambiguity."[17] Three major difficulties in particular help to make the role empathy plays in a pedagogy of connection hard to appropriate: first, empathy as a notion was born in disconnection; second, empathy is easily conflated with sympathy; third, empathy is the antithesis of the disembodied rationality so valued in the culture and in academia. If we do not have a clear-enough picture of what empathy is and if we do not describe it in some practical detail, then empathy can be—as so many seem to consider it—a somewhat idealized notion that is hard to define and that does not come with a user's manual.

A Very Brief History of Empathy

The first major difficulty in appreciating empathy lies in the history of the notion itself. Early in the last century, this notion evolved in two distinct and very separate traditions, traditions that had two distinct and very separate literatures. Briefly put, there was *cognitive empathy*, often called "perspective taking," which was concerned with understanding the other's mind or reasoning, and there was *affective empathy*, often characterized as "subjective feeling," which was basically an emotional resonance with the feeling of the other. The notion of empathy—exquisitely split by the "mind-body" and "reason-emotion" dichotomies—was conceived and born in separation. Because of this history, empathy was a confusing and contentious notion that spoke, ironically, to disconnection much more than connection.

Fortunately, in the last few decades, this split in empathy has been substantially healed in academia, allowing the cognitive and the affective, or reason and emotion, to be taken together and allowing empathy to become about inner and outer as felt together. The healing of the split can be seen in the recent work in multicultural education, as for example, in *Rethinking Multicultural Education for the Next Generation: The New Empathy and Social Justice.*[18] Bringing empathy into focus as a bodily felt phenomenon in education is made possible by the dramatic discovery in brain science of "mirror neurons." Mirror neurons are cells in the brain that respond not only when we perform a particular action but also when we perceive someone else performing the same action. In other words, these neurons let us *feel* the actions of the other much as if these actions are our own.[19] If the notion of empathy needed rehabilitation in order to have its rightful place in the human, neuroscience supports that rehabilitation exceptionally well.

The Conflation of Empathy and Sympathy

The second major difficulty in appreciating empathy is that it is so easily conflated with sympathy. Both notions are concerned with feeling; both have been used interchangeably; and both have been defined in ways that overlap each other.[20]

The dictionary describes empathy as: "the action of understanding, being aware of, being sensitive to, and *vicariously experiencing the feelings, thoughts, and experience of another*" [italics mine].[21] It is also: "the ability to share someone else's feelings."[22] The dictionary describes sympathy as: "an affinity, association, or relationship between persons or things wherein *whatever affects one similarly affects the other*" [italics mine].[23] It is also: "the act or capacity of entering into or sharing the feelings or interests of another."[24]

Three ways that empathy and sympathy can be further distinguished may be helpful:

(1) *Empathy "feels into" the self or the other*. Empathy wants to "go into" and "go deeper."[25] Its goal is to understand the self or the other; it is active and initiating; it is a practice and a skill that is intimate yet not judgmental; it is a practice and a skill that *wants to be with feeling and inner depth* just as it is; and it is always in the present. For example, in empathy I may ask myself: "Can you take a minute and become aware of just how you are feeling right now?" Or I may say to another: "You are still feeling hurt and misunderstood by what the other students said yesterday about your project?" In being with feeling and depth and in being intimate, empathy is in the service of becoming adult and moral.

Sympathy "shares in" the feeling of the self or the other; it aligns with or merges with the other's feeling, often as a spontaneous response of "condolence, agreement, or pity." Although this *shared feeling* can be deeply felt, I may hold it privately and not respond to the other at all.[26] For example, in sympathy I may say to myself: "Poor me; it's terrible; he didn't even need the scholarship; things never work out for me." Or in sympathy I may say about another: "That brave person in the Ebola outbreak; how can anyone possibly handle that kind of incredible suffering so publicly and with such dignity?" Sympathy is a "being with" that typically does not "go into" or "go deeper."

(2) *Empathy is clear about the boundaries of self and other*; I feel my present feeling, and I know that it is my feeling; I feel the feeling of the other, and I know that it is the other's feeling. For

example, in self-empathy I might say: "I am surprised how deeply I feel the breakup of this relationship; it's like a huge part of me is just gouged out." Or in empathy for another, I may say: "I get the sense that what is happening right now is extremely painful for you." Then I may wait for a response because I want to know what is inner for the other. In *distinguishing clear boundaries*, empathy is in the service of becoming adult and moral.

Sympathy shares boundaries; self and other are in it together, often in a general way. For example, in sympathy I may observe: "It was such a bad day for me that I found myself pretty much wallowing in misery; I had a real pity party just for myself." Or I may say what all of us seem to feel: "I cannot believe how pleased we all were when Mrs. Benjamin walked with such pride across the stage to accept the award for being the best teacher in the district." Sympathy—even when very authentic and deeply felt—is not necessarily connected with being adult and moral.

(3) *Empathy discriminates, and we may not even agree with the feeling*, but it feels the feeling no matter what it is. Again, it is nonjudgmental. For example, in self-empathy I might say: "What was said to me at dinner last night really upset me; I thought I was beyond getting bothered by things like that." Or on an international level, in empathy I may say: "You feel that torturing and murdering these citizens is an acceptable response to all the injustice that has been done to your own country." In *feeling the feeling no matter what it is*, empathy is often personally or interpersonally challenging in an adult-moral way.

Sympathy comforts and affirms the feeling of self or other. For example, in sympathy I may say to myself: "I am feeling rather proud of myself in all of this." Or it may say to the other: "I really want to support you in what you are going through; I am touched by your patience and by the humility you have shown these last few days." Sympathy need not be personally or interpersonally challenging at all.

In summary, if we contrast empathy and sympathy, empathy is *inherently relational*; it has clear boundaries, is intimate, and welcomes depth; it welcomes dialogue and has a definite focus on the self and the other; it wants the self or the other to feel what is being felt; it wants to respond to this feeling just as it is; it is disciplined and often waits patiently for the feeling—the emotionally tinged and the rationally grasped—to surface; empathy knows that meaning is in the feeling. As relational and *nonjudgmental*, empathy is at the heart of a pedagogy of connection.

Compared to empathy, sympathy need not be very relational or very intimate at all; it is occasioned by the feeling of the self or the other but it usually does not explore that feeling. It is, for example, how we feel about "the serious accident several students were in," or about "the loss of the championship game," or "adding on more school days at the end of the year." Sympathy is *a felt sharing* of experience that—helpful or supportive as it often is—may or may not be nonjudgmental or an aspect of a pedagogy of connection.

Empathy vs. Disembodied Rationality

The third major difficulty in appreciating empathy is that it is the antithesis of the disembodied rationality so dominant in the culture. If disembodied rationality is abstract and non-relational, empathy is concrete and inherently relational. If disembodied rationality is cold and nearly lifeless, empathy is warm-hearted and alive. If disembodied rationality makes for disconnection within and without, empathy makes for connection within and without. If disembodied rationality is often truncated, selective, self-serving, and easily manipulated, empathy can be understood as an embodied reasoning that seriously attempts to take the self-as-a-whole and the other-as-a-whole into account. Yet, because they are at opposite ends of the knowing seesaw, the more disembodied rationality is valued in a given culture, the more empathy—precisely *because it is embodied reasoning* and *because it may be personally and inter-*

personally challenging—can be dismissed as trivial, lowly, and of little or no value.

A FULLER PICTURE OF EMPATHY

In order to get a practical picture of the role that empathy plays in a pedagogy of connection, we look briefly at a number of thinkers whose common understanding of empathy as the *emotionally tinged* and the *rationally grasped* reinforces the notion of empathy even as it amplifies it. This fuller picture not only lets us see what empathy is in education but also it helps us understand why empathy is so central in all of our human relating. We look briefly at the thinking of Carl Rogers, Judith Jordan, Beverly Musgrave, Cornel West, Arthur Ciaramicoli, and George Lakoff.[27]

CARL ROGERS

Carl Rogers, as we have seen, has a classical definition of empathy: "to perceive the internal frame of reference of another with accuracy and with the emotional components and meanings which pertain thereto, as if one were the other person, but without ever losing the 'as if' condition."[28] Rogers is concerned for the practice of empathy in education as well as in psychotherapy.

- Empathy means "entering the private perceptual world of the other and becoming thoroughly at home in it" so that you are "a confident companion to the person."[29]
- Empathy "involves being sensitive, moment by moment, to the changing felt meanings which flow in this other person."[30]
- Empathy means "temporarily living in the other's life, moving about in it delicately without making judgments."[31]
- Empathy "means frequently checking with the person as to the accuracy of your sensings, and being guided by the responses you receive."[32]

For the educator, Rogers's thinking suggests that empathy is, if we want it to be, a way of being for us; it reminds us that empathy calls for *bracketing our judgments* while we listen to the feeling of the other and our own feeling together; it reminds us that empathy calls for honesty, self-possession, and courage; and it reminds us that empathy needs to be communicated lest it remain a priceless gift that is never actually given. Empathy—especially empathy for the other—is an expressive skill that is "complex, demanding, and strong yet also a subtle and gentle way of being."[33]

JUDITH JORDAN

Judith Jordan, a feminist psychotherapist and developmental thinker, defines empathy as being at the heart of human development and the development of mutuality: "Empathy is a complex cognitive-affective experience of joining in understanding, a feeling-resonance that leads to a more differentiated understanding of self, other, and the relationship."[34]

- "Empathy is central to an understanding of that aspect of the self which involves we-ness, transcendence of the separate, disconnected self."
- "Often, self-empathy develops along with a general increase in empathic attunement to others."[35]
- Empathy, when it is mutual, is at the heart of human development.[36]

For the educator, Jordan is saying that when there is mutual empathy—an educator with the faculty, an educator with the students, students with each other, students with those who educate them—all are learning and growing. Education is meant to be an inherently mutual and empathic relationship.

BEVERLY MUSGRAVE

Beverly Musgrave, a professor and psychotherapist, defines empathy "as the ability to tolerate the tension of being truly open to the experience of another person, while simultaneously attempting both to understand the subjective world of the other and to remain a differentiated self."[37] Reflecting on a saying of photographer Freeman Patterson: "the camera looks both ways," she holds that "we cannot see anything until we are ready to see it" just as "we cannot engage in empathic listening and genuine encounter until we are ready for it."[38] For Musgrave:

- Empathy is possible for a differentiated self.
- "Empathy is at the heart of intimacy."[39]

For the educator, Musgrave's thinking suggests that our own integrity, our own "differentiation," is all-important and that it is this, along with our ability to respect boundaries, which makes education the appropriately intimate activity it is meant to be.

CORNEL WEST

A professor, a philosopher of religion, and an activist, West sees empathy at the heart of being a responsible self.

- "Empathy is not simply a matter of trying to imagine what others are going through, but having the will to muster enough courage to do something about it."[40]
- "In a way, empathy is predicated upon hope."[41]

For the educator and for all of us, empathy is not passive but active; it is responsible; it responds as it can to the needs of self and other; it draws us forward.

ARTHUR CIARAMICOLI

Arthur Ciaramicoli, a clinical psychologist, defines empathy as "the capacity to understand and respond to the unique experiences of another."[42]

- Empathy "seeks to go deeper, to listen with rapt attention, to understand, to mix in, and, even if it is just for brief moment, share another person's heart and soul."[43]
- "Empathy is the force that completes the soul's craving for connection, giving us the courage and the energy to reach out to others."[44]

Ciaramicoli describes empathy at the heart of values that are often classified as "moral or spiritual."[45] He considers empathy's role in "honesty, humility, acceptance, tolerance, gratitude, faith, hope, and forgiveness."[46] Whether or not we are educators and whether or not we think of ourselves as spiritual, these are the empathy-based values that go to describe the depth of humanness of our daily lives that education is able to touch.

GEORGE LAKOFF

George Lakoff, a professor of language, metaphor, and cognition, sees empathy as "the capacity to put oneself in the shoes of others—not just individuals, but whole categories of people; one's countrymen, those in other countries, other living beings, especially those who are in some way oppressed, threatened, or harmed."[47]

- "Empathy is the capacity to care, to feel what others feel, to understand what others are facing and what their lives are like."[48]
- "Empathy is at the heart of real rationality, because it goes to the heart of our values, which are the basis of our sense of justice."[49]

For the educator, Lakoff is allowing the reach of empathy to be as far and as deep as it can be—other cultures, those most in need, the living environment. He makes the case that empathy's rationality underlies care and justice.

TEACHING EMPATHY

There is any number of creative age-appropriate ways to teach empathy. Although it is inherently natural and human, as it turns out it is also a skill that can be modeled, learned, and practiced. Two approaches to teaching empathy developed by seasoned educators are mentioned here as examples of a pedagogy of connection.

(1) In a seminal article entitled, "Supposing That . . . ," Deborah Meier recalls that she had several goals when she started out as a kindergarten teacher: "I wanted to prepare students to be comfortable in the 'big conversations' that grown-ups engage in. I wanted them to feel confident that nothing, or very little anyway, was beyond their capacities. I wanted them to have a reasonable shot at being able to do anything that seemed important or worthwhile to them."[50] Early on, she discovered two things. The first was that *informed skepticism* is natural to "the human species," especially in childhood.[51]

The second thing Meier found was that *informed empathy*, "developing the habit of stepping into the shoes of others—both intellectually and emotionally," is central to a society that asks us "to suspend belief long enough to entertain ideas contrary to our own," and to realize that "our ideas are forever 'in progress,' unfinished and incomplete."[52] She points out: "Imagining ourselves as other people and even other species is part of all good story telling." She also points out: "When a child is injured, we can model empathy by our quick response to the wounded one, rather than by our immediate search to determine who is at fault. What we praise, what we attend to, and what we announce as valuable all help to predispose children one way or another."[53]

Later in her article, Meier says: "The kindergarten comes closest to encouraging openness and empathy, but each year thereafter schools strip away, one by one, all the kindergarten-like features that help sustain such qualities."[54] "We increasingly glorify 'objectivity' over subjectivity, the impersonal over the personal, external standardization over the development of internal standards, certainties over ambiguities, and the one right answer over possible alternative paths."[55] In a summary reflection, she remarks pointedly about higher education: "Oddly enough we felt that our approach prepared young people better for the world of hard knocks than for the insular world of academe. In fact, the intellectual habits and dispositions we tried to foster—focused as they were on the development of informed skepticism and empathy—would have their roughest and toughest survival test on the college campus, not in life itself."[56]

(2) In *Roots of Empathy: Changing the World Child by Child*, Mary Gordon, also a seasoned educator, describes training in empathy that is centered on classroom visits of a mother with her infant child.[57] These visits are every several months; they begin when the infant is two to four months old, and they go on for the year. A green blanket is put on the floor, and the students in the class—in kindergarten or the primary grades—sit around the blanket and observe the activity of the child with his or her mother. They watch the infant grow, see how the mother cares for it, and observe its milestones like being able to turn over or sit up. With the teacher's tutoring before, during, and after the session, the students understand together what the infant is feeling and they are invited to say what they are feeling. By the end of the year, the quality of empathy in the classroom is wonderfully enhanced. Interestingly enough, students who may have experienced quite poor parenting can be profoundly changed.[58]

"Empathy is frequently defined," says Gordon, as the ability to identify with the feelings and perspectives of others." She continues: "I would add *and to respond appropriately* to the feelings and perspectives of others."[59] Gordon is convinced that empathy is "our deepest connection with one another."[60] It is only when it is absent that "we begin to grasp the profound, complex and fundamental role it plays in the healthy function of human relations." We see this clearly, she says, when we "think of the Holocaust or South Africa under apartheid."[61] "Were the people who participated in these affronts to human rights, or stood by and watched them happen, fundamentally different from us?"[62] The failure of empathy in our development "leads to complicity and apathy" at best and to "cruelty and violence" at worst.[63]

TEACHING CARE AND JUSTICE

In a pedagogy of connection, being empathic as an educator—embodying empathy, modeling empathy, teaching empathy, encouraging empathy—naturally flows into teaching care and justice together. There is, of course, any number of creative ways care and justice can be taught.[64] Two examples are mentioned here: one is illustrative of the restorative care and justice focus that has been so influential, especially in juvenile justice; the other is from the Kohlberg tradition of moral development on the forming of a caring and just community.

(1) In their article, "Restorative Justice: Pedagogy, Praxis, and Discipline," Brenda Morrison and Dorothy Vaandering make the case for restorative justice as a pedagogy of engagement as opposed to a more traditional pedagogy of control. They begin by saying: "Violence is most often framed and regulated in moral and legal terms, asking: How evil is this action and how much punishment does it deserve"?[65] As an alternative to a "zero tolerance" approach to school discipline and the exclusionary practices of "of-

fice referral, suspensions, and expulsions," they make the case for a pedagogy of restorative justice as "a promising praxis for safe and caring schools."[66] Violence, they say, needs to be "considered in the context of understanding what happened, listening to the needs of those who have been most affected, and responding to the harm done."[67]

In the move from a pedagogy of control to a pedagogy of connection, the authors comment on process and research. In terms of process: (1) students have a "rich opportunity for collective problem solving, learning, and growth"; (2) students "build positive affect (empathy, interest, and excitement) and discharge negative affect (anger, humiliation, fear, and disgust)"; and (3) the community nurtures the "human capacity for *restitution*, *resolution*, and *reconciliation*."[68] In terms of research: (1) "whole-school" programs of restorative justice seem to be most effective;[69] (2) in one school district "referrals for physical aggression in an elementary school were reduced from 773 to 153"; "suspensions in a junior high school were reduced from 110 to 55"; and "in a senior high school suspensions dropped from 132 to 95."[70]

(2) The "just community," an approach to education of Lawrence Kohlberg first introduced in the 1970s, is also a move from a pedagogy of control to a pedagogy of connection. Organized as a program within the larger school, it is limited in size "to allow face to face discussion and continuous interaction."[71] Typically, between twenty-five to ninety students and three to eight faculty are involved.[72] The members have: (1) a *democratic meeting* of the whole on a regular basis for developing the rules and policies of the community; (2) smaller *advisory "family" groups*, with perhaps ten students and one faculty member, for more intimate relating and for planning the meetings of the whole;[73] and (3) a *fairness committee* with several students and one or two faculty; this committee—rotating on a regular basis—handles disciplinary issues to show

"violators that what they did has an effect of the whole group" and to elicit from them an intent to change.[74]

The just community approach to education ensures that the students involved "have regular legislative experience and frequent opportunities for democratic leadership."[75] "In this approach, students share responsibility for forming community, and community seems to mean "a valuing of the ideal of group solidarity and a commitment to norms of care and responsibility."[76] "Just communities have," says Clark Power, "a concern for the common good." "While most schools are not communities in the strict sense of the term, a case can be made that in the interest of moral education they ought to be."[77] Power believes that "the just community approach should be measured not in terms of how many schools adopt it, but in terms of how it stimulates practitioners and researchers to raise fundamental questions about the nature of moral education."[78]

TEACHING PEACE

In a pedagogy of connection, if we are teaching care and justice we are also teaching peace; the empathy that underlies care and justice is an active element in peace education. Defined by UNICEF, peace education is: the "promotion of the knowledge, skills, attitudes and values" needed by "children, youths and adults to prevent conflict and violence, both overt and structural; to resolve conflict peacefully; and to create the conditions conducive to peace, whether at an intra-personal, interpersonal, inter-group, national or international level."[79] Two examples of peace education—both elaborated in the starkness of conflict-ridden societies—are considered here. One example is from the work of Michalinos Zembylas, a peace educator who has written extensively about national conflict, especially in his native Cyprus.[80] The other example is from the work of H. B. Danesh, a Canadian psychiatrist and educator who is the creator of Education for Peace in Bosnia and Herzegovina.

(1) As a peace educator, Michalinos Zembylas is concerned about the perpetuation of narratives of trauma in societies such as Cyprus that are divided by ethnic conflict. How is it possible to address the destructive "ethos of conflict" in these societies, to address the "dehumanization of the opponent," to address "the systematic cultivation of hatred for *the enemy*."[81] These conflicted societies beget a "politics of trauma"—both personal and societal—a politics that memorializes fear, hatred, and victimization, that becomes hegemonic, and that rests clearly on "*us-and-them* dichotomies."[82] In light of this politics, Zembylas is asking if younger students can be relieved of "the burden of 'remembering' unlived memories."[83] Is it possible for students and teachers "to create a new psychic and socio-political order where they do not simply remain traumatized 'objects' of history?"[84] In other words, is it possible to devise "pedagogies that do not get stuck in trauma?"[85]

To overcome the intensive negative feelings of trauma narratives, "the door of empathy has to open," says Zembylas."[86] As he sees it, "empathy is the ability to incorporate other people's perceptions and *see* an experience with their eyes."[87] Empathy fosters reconciliation: first, it recognizes each other's suffering, losses, and "woundedness"; second, it surfaces "common patterns" of a basic shared humanity;[88] third, it raises questions of each other's needs and rights;[89] fourth, it brings about by its very nature a connectedness with others. Empathy "reverses the process of dehumanization and returns humanity to the other.[90] Along with empathy, there is also a need, says Zembylas, for teachers and students to develop a "critical emotional literacy" that can analyze and critique "the ways in which the politics of trauma can encourage certain emotions and ideologies and prohibit others."[91]

(2) As a peace educator, H. B. Danesh observes: "We teach our children that the world is a jungle, that life is the process of survival in this jungle, and that power is the essential tool to emerge victori-

ous in this highly conflicted and violence-prone world."[92] What we need, says Danesh, is "a total reorientation and transformation of our approach to education."[93] We need to realize, that "conflict is the absence of unity and that peace is the process of creating unity in the context of diversity."[94] Peace is only possible within the context of a unity-based worldview.[95] It is important, therefore, to study the nature of peace and the nature of peacebuilding. As he says, "nothing short of a comprehensive, all-inclusive and sustained curriculum of education for peace could possibly alter the current attitudes and worldviews that contribute so greatly to conflict, violence and war affecting human societies worldwide."[96]

For Danesh, as individuals and collectively our development is meant to be from conflict to peace in terms of three worldviews that can be quite resistant to change:

- *A survivor-based worldview*: In this worldview—normal in childhood—the main purpose of life is survival; conflict and violence are inevitable, and authoritarianism is the main mode of leadership and governance. Power and conformity are foreground in this worldview, leading to injustice, poverty, physical threat, anarchy, and violence.
- *An identity-based worldview*: In this worldview—normal in adolescence—the main purpose of life is "to have" and "to win." Human nature is seen as greedy and selfish; conflict and power struggles are necessary for progress; and adversarial democracy is the main mode of leadership and governance. Individualism and group identities—ethnic, national, racial, religious—are foreground in this worldview, begetting competition and rivalry.
- *A unity-based worldview*: In this worldview—normal in adulthood—the main purpose of life is creating a culture of peace, celebrating equality, justice, diversity, and unity; conflict is the absence of unity, and a unity-based democracy is the main mode of leadership and governance. Oneness is foreground in this worldview, allowing for the care of all.[97]

FOUR EXCEPTIONAL EDUCATORS

We bring this chapter to a close by considering four educators who have also made outstanding contributions to our understanding of the self on the way to becoming adult, moral, and fully human. Not surprisingly, these educators are remarkable for the humanness they invite us to celebrate. Not surprisingly, these educators are all fostering a pedagogy of connection. We look briefly at the work of Nel Noddings, Jerry Starratt, Paulo Freire, and Parker Palmer.

NEL NODDINGS

Nel Noddings holds "that caring is the very bedrock of all successful education and that contemporary schooling can be revitalized in its light."[98] Caring, for her, is not a virtue of the carer but a relationship, "a connection or encounter between two human beings."[99] There is "a carer" and a recipient of care, "a cared-for." When we care, we are "feeling with" the cared for;[100] we have an "engrossment," an open receptivity which is accompanied by "motivational displacement" as we are "seized by the needs of the other."[101] As Noddings says: "When I attend in this way I become, in an important sense, a duality. I see through two pairs of eyes, hear with two sets of ears, feel the pain of the other self in addition to my own."[102] When the cared-for receives the carer's efforts, then both enter "a mutually satisfying relation." In fact, for Noddings: "Mature relationships are characterized by mutuality. They are made up of strings of encounters in which the parties exchange places; both members are carers and cared-fors as opportunities arise."[103]

Although violence, says Noddings, "has many roots," it seems clear that "people who feel cared for and who have learned to care for others will be less likely to engage in violent acts."[104] Teachers "not only have to create caring relations" but "they also have a responsibility to help their students develop the capacity to care."[105] For her, "learning to care and to be cared for is a major developmental task."[106] First, as teachers we *model* care; "we do not tell our students to care; we show them how to care."[107] Second, we engage in *dialogue*, in a search together "for understanding, empathy, or appreciation."[108] Third, we encourage our students to *practice* care in a way that is neither forced nor graded.[109] Fourth, we *confirm* their practice in a way that is honest.[110]

Nel Noddings sees care at the heart of education as a pedagogy of connection.

JERRY STARRATT

Robert J. (Jerry) Starratt, an educator and moral thinker, sees education as "a profoundly moral activity that should engage the full humanity of learners and their teachers."[111] Authentic learning enables learners to encounter "the natural, social, cultural worlds *they inhabit*" and "to *find themselves* in and through those very encounters."[112] Authentic learning is a mutuality that is "intrinsically moral."[113] "The knower and the known," says Starratt, "speak to each other, attract each other, puzzle each other, resist each other."[114] The knower and the known are "intertwined," and "implicated in each other's existence."[115] Without "a dialogue of mutual understanding at some minimal level, there is no knowledge"; we are left with "information or data" but "no meaning."[116] "Knowing is moral," says Starratt, "when the knower accepts the responsibility of coming to know the known carefully—that is, full of care for the meanings implied in the relationship with the known."[117]

Starratt speaks of three "foundational virtues" that capture of the essence of the human and that are "needed to infuse and energize the work of schools."[118] The virtue of responsibility allows educators "to put themselves in another's shoes, to feel what they feel, to look at situations from their perspective";[119] at the same time it allows them "to keep in mind the ultimate common good of the civic community."[120] The virtue of authenticity allows educators to "move beyond the surface impressions";[121] they are not afraid to "work from their insides"; they "tell the truth" and "live the truth as they see it."[122] The virtue of presence allows educators to have "an attitude of unconditional regard" for those they are with. "Affirming presence communicates the message that others have the right to be who they are."[123] For Starratt, schooling as a moral activity is a celebration of responsibility, authenticity and presence.

Jerry Starratt sees an ontology of relatedness at the heart of education as a pedagogy of connection.

PAULO FREIRE

Paulo Freire, an educator committed to human liberation, is interested in humanization as a "viable possibility" in the face of experienced dehumanization. For Freire, humanization is our "ontological vocation." It is a struggle for "the affirmation of men and women as persons," "the overcoming of alienation," and "the emancipation of labor."[124] Dehumanization, experienced as injustice, oppression, and the violence of the oppressors, thwarts our vocation, leading the oppressed "to struggle against those who made them so."[125] "In order for this struggle to have meaning, the oppressed must not, in seeking to regain their humanity (which is a way to create it), become in turn oppressor of the oppressors, but rather restorers of the humanity of both."[126] The violence and power of the oppressor, that is, whatever "prevents the oppressed from being fully human," is overcome by the "power that springs from the weakness of the oppressed."[127] For Freire, "No one can be authentically human while he prevents others from being so."[128]

Freire contrasts two opposing methods of education. In *the banking method* of education, the teacher, who is a fount of knowledge, gives that knowledge to the students. The teacher's role is to "deposit" information and the student's role is to "patiently receive, memorize, and repeat" it. This method is "lifeless and petrified." It perpetuates "a dichotomy between human beings and the world" that serves oppression and makes transformation impossible. In *the problem-posing method* of education, teachers and students, who are in a "quest for mutual humanization,"[129] confront reality directly in a "searching, questioning, probing, investigative, dialogical, critical approach to understanding and living in the world."[130] This method is realized through *conscientização* or "conscientization," a process of "learning to perceive social, political, and economic contradictions" and of taking action "against the oppressive elements of reality."[131] For Freire, liberation and education are together as a humanizing praxis, as "the action and reflection of men and women upon their world in order to transform it."[132]

Paulo Freire sees addressing oppression and violence at the heart of education as a pedagogy of connection.

PARKER PALMER

Parker Palmer, an educator and spiritual writer whom we saw in chapter 1, advocates for an *integrative pedagogy* in his chapters in *The Heart of Higher Education.* An integrative pedagogy aims to "think the world together" rather than "think it apart."[133] Higher education, says Palmer, is "notoriously slow to change."[134] Its conventional pedagogy "continues to occur within disciplinary silos."[135] It holds onto "an atomistic notion of the self and a competitive 'survival of the fittest' concept of human relations."[136] Its epistemology is "based on the myth that we must hold the world at arm's length in order to know it purely, untainted by subjectivity."[137] In fact, says Palmer, the outdated "philosophical foundations of conventional pedagogy are so weak" that no one even tries to defend them.[138] Palmer is convinced that we need much more in higher education than "the thin soup served up when data and logic are the only ingredients."[139]

Palmer wants a pedagogy in higher education that embraces "every dimension of what it means to be human."[140] He wants a knowing that "has paradoxical roots—mind and heart, hard data and soft intuition, individual insight and communal sifting and winnowing."[141] He wants a self that is not "atomic and competitive" but "interconnected and communal." He wants an epistemology that is not so "distanced" and "objectivist" that moral concerns cannot be raised. He wants conversations about the meaning, value, and purpose of life, about spirituality and religion, about "the cultivation of the fundamental human capacities for compassion and altruistic action."[142] In advocating for an integrative pedagogy in higher education, Palmer wants educated people skilled in "integration and synthesis" rather than "specialization and fragmentation."

Parker Palmer sees "collegial conversation" and community at the heart of education—especially higher education—as a pedagogy of connection.[143]

NOTES

1. *To Sir, with Love*, DVD, directed by James Clavell (1967; Culver City, CA: Columbia Tri-Star Home Video, 1999).

2. Tony Stigliano, "The Moral Construction of the Self," *Journal of Theoretical and Philosophical* Psychology 13, no. 1 (1993): 57, holds that being moral "implies being committed to reframing 'the traditions and institutions that form us.'"

3. *Merriam Webster*, 11th ed. s.v. "Moralism."

4. For a "move from fragmentation to connectedness" in education, see John P. Miller, *The Holistic Curriculum*, 2nd ed. (Toronto: University of Toronto Press, 2007), 13.

5. Tobin Hart, "From Category to Contact: Epistolary and the Enlivening and Deadening of Spirit in Education," *Journal of Humanistic Education and Development* 36 (September 1997): 27.

6. Roberta Loewy states: "The atomic individualized individual in the standard account of autonomy is simply a fiction and, when treated as reality, is capable of profoundly disrupting persons in their quest to meet their needs and interests." Roberta S. Loewy, *Integrity and Personhood: Looking at Patients from a Bio/Psycho/Social Perspective* (Boston: Kluwer Academic, 2000), 57.

7. Elli P. Schachter and Yisrael Rich, "Identity Education: A Conceptual Framework for Educational Researchers and Practitioners," *Educational Psychologist* 46, no. 4 (2011): 223–38.

8. Ibid., 223.

9. Ibid., 226. See also Tonia Bock and Peter L. Samuelson, "Educating for Moral Identity," *Journal of Character Education* 10, no. 2 (2014): 155–74.

10. See Zvi Lamm, *Conflicting Theories of Instruction: Conceptual Dimensions* (New York: McCutchan, 1976).

11. Schachter and Rich, "Identity Education," 227.

12. Ibid.

13. Ibid., 228.

14. Ibid., 227.

15. Nel Noddings, *The Challenge to Care in Schools: An Alternative Approach to Education*, 2nd ed. (New York: Teachers College Press, 2005), 74.

16. For an approach to embodied pedagogy, see Mary Dixon and Kim Senior, "Appearing Pedagogy: From Embodied Learning and Teaching to Embodied Pedagogy," *Pedagogy, Culture and Society* 19, no. 3 (2011): 473–84. See also Julia Lane, "Toward a Model of Embodied Environmental Education: Perspectives from Theatre and Indigenous Knowledges," *Journal of Experiential Education*, 35, no. 3 (2012): 395–411.

17. Michalinos Zembylas, "Pedagogies of Strategic Empathy: Navigating through the Emotional Complexities of Anti-racism in Higher Education," *Teaching in Higher Education* 17, no. 2 (April 2012): 120.

18. Nadine Dolby, *Rethinking Multicultural Education for the Next Generation: The New Empathy and Social Justice* (New York: Routledge, 2012).

19. For a reader-friendly understanding of neuroscience and empathy see Marco Iacoboni, *Mirroring People: The New Science of How We Connect with Others* (New York: Farrar, Straus and Giroux, 2008); see also Massimilano Aragona, Georgios D. Kotzalidis, and Antonella Puzella, "The Many Faces of Empathy, between Phenomenology and Neuroscience," *Archives of Psychiatry and Psychotherapy* 4 (2013): 5–12.; see also Jamil Zaki and Kevin Ochsner, "The Neuroscience of Empathy: Progress, Pitfalls and Promise," *Nature Neuroscience* 15, no. 5 (May 2012): 675–80.

20. See, for example, Stanley I. Olinick, "A Critique of Empathy and Sympathy," in *Empathy I*, ed. Joseph Lichtenberg, Melvin Bornstein, and Donald Silver (Hillsdale, NJ: The Analytic Press, 1984): 137–66.

21. *Merriam Webster*, 11th ed. s.v. "Empathy."

22. Ibid.

23. *Merriam Webster*, 11th ed. s.v. "Sympathy."

24. Ibid.

25. Arthur P. Ciaramicoli, *The Power of Empathy: A Practical Guide to Creating Intimacy, Self-Understanding, and Lasting Love* (New York: Plume, 2001), 80.

26. Ralph R. Greenson, "Empathy and its Vicissitudes, *International Journal of Psychoanalysis* 41 (1960): 418.

27. For a broad perspective on empathy see Jean Decety, *Empathy: From Bench to Bedside* (Cambridge, MA: The MIT Press, 2012).

28. Carl Rogers, "A Theory of Therapy, Personality, and Interpersonal Relationships as Developed in the Client-Centered Framework," in *Psychology: A Study of a Science*, Vol. III, ed. Sigmund Koch (New York: McGraw-Hill, 1959), 210.

29. Carl T. Rogers, "Empathic: An Unappreciated Way of Being," in *A Way of Being* (Boston: Houghton Mifflin, 1980), 142.

30. Ibid.

31. Ibid.

32. Ibid.

33. Ibid., 143.

34. Judith V. Jordan, "Relational Development Through Mutual Empathy," in *Empathy Reconsidered: New Directions in Psychotherapy*, ed. Arthur C. Bohart and Leslie S. Greenberg (Washington, DC: American Psychological Association, 1997), 344.

35. Ibid., 345.

36. Ibid., 343.

37. Beverly A. Musgrave, "The Ontogenesis of Empathy," in *In Search of Healing: Collected Papers from the Annual Conference of the Society for Pastoral Counselling Research,* ed. Augustine Meier (Ottawa, ON: The Society for Pastoral Counselling Research, 2003), 44.

38. Beverly A. Musgrave, "Empathy: The Caregiver Looks Both Ways," in *Partners in Healing: Bringing Compassion to People with Illness or Loss—A Handbook*, ed. Beverly A. Musgrave and John R. Bickle (New York: Paulist Press, 2003), 31–44.

39. Musgrave, "Ontogenesis of Empathy," 53.

40. Cornel West, "The Moral Obligations of Living in a Democratic Society," in *The Good Citizen*, ed. David B. Batstone and Eduardo Mendieta (New York: Routledge, 1999), 12.

41. Ibid.

42. Ciaramicoli, *Power of Empathy*, 4.

43. Ibid., 80.

44. Ibid., 153.

45. Ibid., 152.

46. Ibid.

47. George Lakoff, "Empathy, Sotomayor, and Democracy: The Conservative Stealth Strategy," in http://www.truth-out.org/, archive item 84347.

48. Ibid.

49. Ibid.

50. Deborah Meier, "Supposing That . . . ," *Phi Delta Kappan*, 78, no. 4 (December 1996): 272.

51. Ibid.

52. Ibid.

53. Ibid.

54. Ibid., 273.

55. Ibid.

56. Ibid., 274. See Gisela Labouvie-Vief, "Cognitive-Emotional Integration in Adulthood," in *Annual Review of Gerontology and Geriatrics* 17, ed. K. Warner Schaie and M. Powell Lawton (New York: Springer, 1998), 209. Her understanding of Piaget's theory of development is interesting. "His writings," she says, "show that he tends to equate development with a loss of organismic and imaginative relatedness, emphasizing instead the rise of objective, abstract structures of relating to the world." A few lines later she observes: "rather than adults struggling with issues of sexuality, love, and faith, we are left with visions of budding scientists exploring the world with objective detachment."

57. Mary Gordon, *Roots of Empathy: Changing the World Child by Child* (Toronto: Thomas Allen, 2005).

58. For examples of teaching empathy to children see Jessica Toulis, "Teaching Children Empathy," in *Educating from the Heart: Theoretical and Practical Approaches to Transforming Education*, ed. Aostre N. Johnson and Marilyn Webb Neagley (Lanham, MD: Rowman & Littlefield, 2011): 27–35. See also Tim Loreman, "Kindness and Empathy in Pedagogy," *Love as Pedagogy* (Rotterdam, The Netherlands: Sense Publishers, 2011), 15–31.

59. Gordon, *Roots of Empathy*, 30.

60. Ibid., 33.

61. Ibid., 30.

62. Ibid.

63. Ibid. See also Karen E. Gerdes, Elizabeth A. Segal, Kelly F. Jackson, and Jennifer L. Mullins, "Teaching Empathy: A Framework Rooted in Social Cognitive Neuroscience and Social Justice," *Journal of Social Work Education* 47, no. 1 (Winter 2011): 109–31.

64. For a discussion of the relation of care and justice in education, see *Justice and Caring: The Search for Common Ground in Education*, ed. Michael S. Katz, Nel Noddings, and Kenneth A. Strike (New York: Teachers College Press, 1999). See also John P. Miller, *Educating for Wisdom and Compassion: Creating Conditions for Timeless Learning* (Thousand Oaks, CA: Corwin Press, 2006). See also Darcia Narvaez and Daniel K. Lapsley, "Teaching Moral Character: Two Alternatives for Teacher Education," *The Teacher Educator* 43 (2008): 156–72.

65. Brenda E. Morrison and Dorothy Vaandering, "Restorative Justice: Pedagogy, Praxis, and Discipline," *Journal of School Violence* 11 (2012): 139.

66. Ibid.

67. Ibid. See also Catherine Bargen, *Educating for Peacebuilding: Implementing Restorative Justice Principles and Practices into a School System* (Langley, BC: Fraser Region Community Justice Initiatives, 2010).

68. Morrison and Vaandering, "Restorative Justice," 140.

69. Ibid., 147.

70. Ibid.

71. F. Clark Power, "The Just Community Approach to Moral Education," *Journal of Moral Education* 17, no. 3 (October 1988), 199.

72. F. Clark Power and Ann Marie Power, "A Raft of Hope: Democratic Education and the Challenge of Pluralism," *Journal of Moral Education* 21, no. 3 (1992): 194.

73. Ibid.

74. Power, "Just Community Approach," 200.

75. Ann Higgins-D'Alessandro and F. Clark Power, "Character, Responsibility, and the Moral Self," in *Character Psychology and Character Education*, ed. Daniel K. Lapsley and F. Clark Power (Notre Dame, IN: University of Notre Dame Press, 2005), 105.

76. Power, "Just Community Approach," 198–99.

77. Ibid., 199.

78. Ibid., 206.

79. S. Fountain, "Peace Education in UNICEF." Working Paper (New York UNICEF, 1999), 1.

80. For a history of his own experience as a Greek Cypriot in a divided Cyprus, see Michalinos Zembylas, *The Politics of Trauma in Education* (New York: Palgrave Macmillan, 2008), 6–11.

81. Michalinos Zembylas, "The Politics of Trauma: Empathy, Reconciliation and Peace Education," *Journal of Peace Education* 4, no. 2 (September 2007): 208.

82. Michalinos Zembylas, "Critical Emotional Praxis for Reconciliation Education: Emerging Evidence and Pedagogical Implications," *Irish Educational Studies* 31, no. 1 (March 2012): 21.

83. Michalinos Zembylas, "The Emotional Complexities of 'Our' and 'Their' Loss: The Vicissitudes of Teaching about/for Empathy in a Conflicting Society," *Anthropology and Education Quarterly* 44, no. 1 (2013): 20.

84. Michalinos Zembylas, "Critical Emotional Praxis," 28.

85. Ibid., 20.

86. Zembylas, "Politics of Trauma," 214.

87. Zembylas, *Politics of Trauma in Education*, 46.

88. Zembylas, "Emotional Complexities," 25.

89. Ibid.

90. Zembylas, *Politics of Trauma in Education*, 45–46.

91. Zembylas, "Politics of Trauma," 218.

92. H. B. Danesh, "Toward an Integrative Theory of Peace Education," *Journal of Peace Education* 3, no. 1 (March 2006): 58. See also H. B. Danesh, *Fever in the World of the Mind: On Causes and Prevention of Violence* (Victoria, BC: EFP Press, 2013).

93. Ibid., 62.

94. H. B. Danesh, "Introduction: Educating for a Civilization of Peace," *Education for Peace Reader* (Victoria, BC: EFP Press, 2011), xi.

95. See H. B. Danesh, "Unity-Based Peace Education," *Education for Peace Reader* (Victoria, BC: EFP Press, 2011), 55–61. See also "Human Need Theory,

Conflict, and Peace: In Search of an Integrated Model," *Education for Peace Reader* (Victoria, BC: EFP Press, 2011), 63–67.

96. Danesh, "Towards an Integrative Theory," 58.

97. H. B. Danesh, "Conceptual Foundations of Education for Peace: A Summary," *Education for Peace Reader* (Victoria, BC: EFP Press, 2011), 69–77.

98. Nel Noddings, *The Challenge to Care in Schools*, 27.

99. Ibid., 15.

100. Nel Noddings, *Caring: A Feminine Approach to Ethics and Moral Education*, 2nd ed. (Berkeley: University of California Press, 2003), 30.

101. Ibid., 16. See also Nel Noddings, "Identifying and Responding to Needs in Education," *Cambridge Journal of Education* 35, no. 2 (June 2005): 147–59.

102. Nel Noddings, *Starting at Home: Caring and Social Policy* (Berkeley: University of California Press, 2002), 15.

103. Ibid., 17.

104. Nel Noddings, "Learning to Care and to Be Cared For," in *Schools, Violence, and Society*, ed. Allan M. Hoffman (Westport, CT: Praeger, 1996), 196–97.

105. Noddings, *Challenge to Care in Schools*, 18.

106. Noddings, "Learning to Care and to Be Cared For," 185.

107. Noddings, *Challenge to Care in Schools*, 22.

108. Ibid., 23.

109. Ibid., 24–25.

110. Ibid., 25. See also Nel Noddings, "The Caring Relation in Teaching, *Oxford Review of Education* 38, no. 6 (December 2012): 771–81.

111. Robert J. Starratt, *Ethical Leadership* (San Francisco: Jossey-Bass, 2004), 9.

112. Robert J. Starratt, "The Moral Character of Academic Learning: Challenging the Exclusivity of the Reigning Paradigm of School Learning," in *Second International Handbook of Educational Change*, ed. Andy Hargreaves et al. (New York: Springer, 2010), 631.

113. Ibid.

114. Starratt, *Ethical Leadership*, 76.

115. Starratt, "Moral Character of Academic Learning," 640.

116. Ibid.

117. Ibid.

118. Starratt, *Ethical Leadership*, 9.

119. Ibid., 49–50.

120. Ibid., 51.

121. Ibid., 73.

122. Ibid., 72.

123. Ibid. 93.

124. Paulo Freire, *Pedagogy of the Oppressed*, 30th Anniversary Edition (New York: Continuum, 2009), 44.

125. Ibid.

126. Ibid.

127. Ibid.

128. Ibid.

129. Ibid.

130. Peter Roberts, *Paulo Freire in the 21st Century: Education, Dialogue and Transformation* (London: Paradigm Publishers, 2010), 136.

131. Freire, *Pedagogy of the Oppressed*, 35, note 1.

132. Ibid., 79.

133. Parker J. Palmer, "Toward a Philosophy of Integrative Education," in *The Heart of Higher Education: A Call to Renewal: Transforming the Academy Through Collegial Conversations*, ed. Parker J. Palmer and Arthur Zajonc, with Megan Scribner (San Francisco: Jossey-Bass, 2010), 22.

134. Ibid., 20.

135. Ibid., 24.

136. Ibid., 25.

137. Ibid., 31.

138. Ibid., 24.

139. Ibid., 21.

140. Ibid., 20.

141. Ibid., 22.

142. Interview with Parker J. Palmer and Arthur Zajonc in "Inside Higher Ed" February 8, 2011. https://www.insidehighered.com/news/2011/02/08/interview_with_authors_of_the_heart_of_higher_education, 2.

143. For a practical approach to peace education, see Rebecca Spence and Jonathan Makuwira, "Do We Make a Difference? Teaching and Researching Peace at Tertiary Level," *Journal of Peace Education* 2, no. 1 (March 2005): 17–31.

Chapter Six

Psychotherapy and the Fully Human

In the movie, *Good Will Hunting*, Will is a young mathematical genius in therapy with Sean, a seasoned therapist engaged to help Will with his delinquent behavior and his incredible promise. Expert at fending off Sean's care and concern, Will attacks him with flip responses and amazingly hurtful comments, doing everything possible not to talk about himself, about his being abused as an orphan, about his fears and his future. As a later session is about to begin, Will sees an evaluation file Sean has prepared for the judge, leading to a dialogue about counseling and the traumatic childhood they both had. Then, with file in hand, Sean quietly says: "It's not your fault." Will replies: "I know." Sean says again: "It's not your fault." Will replies: "I know." Moving close to where Will is standing, Sean repeats again and again: "It's not your fault." Tears are forming each time Will says: "I know." Then, Will sobs uncontrollably into Sean's arms. If the scene is one of compelling drama, it is as well one of therapeutic expertise and the power of empathy.[1]

In this chapter, we look at psychotherapy from an adult-moral perspective to see its role in helping us become an integral and mutual self, a caring and just self, a self of peace—the three-in-one of the fully human. Seen from this perspective, psychotherapy is a mutual relationship that offers a second line of approach to becoming fully human, a line of approach that is often invaluable, especially when early childhood and normal education, for whatever reasons, are not able to foster that kind of growth. The kind of change psychotherapy is able to bring about—through care, justice, and empathy—speaks to its being an essential practice of human development shared by a number of the helping professions.

Looking at psychotherapy as a mutual relationship that helps the client to become an integral and mutual self, means, of course, that psychotherapy is a way of becoming a fully moral person as well as becoming an adult. Yet—and this is the fascinating historical irony—a positive connection between psychotherapy and morality was often seriously opposed, especially in the psychoanalytic and behavioral traditions that were so influential in defining the profession. In its beginnings, psychotherapy was meant to be scientific and value-free. The last thing it could tolerate is any contamination by cultural belief systems and time-worn moral traditions—systems and traditions that not only have no scientific basis in reality but that also may be responsible for causing us to be neurotic or maladjusted in the first place.

Today, psychotherapy is usually seen as a process in which the therapist helps one or more clients resolve personal difficulties or alter thinking and behavior that is problematic in some way. A person typically goes into therapy because he or she is stuck or is in some kind of pain because life is not working out the way it is supposed to. Over time, however, therapy tends to facilitate the growth and development of the client, usually having the client's adult functioning as its implicit goal. Within the many different approaches and theoretical underpinnings in which it functions, psychotherapy—from a developmental perspective—is a process that wants the client's own experience to become the basis upon which values are chosen, decisions are made, the self is accepted, relationships are lived, and the world is understood—all of which is a good description of how we function when we are mature.

PSYCHOTHERAPY: A RESPONSE TO FIVE PRACTICAL QUESTIONS

This chapter responds practically to five questions. The first question is: Can psychotherapy be measured in light of the fully human, in light of becoming an adult-moral self, a fully human self, an integral self-in-mutuality? The second question is: Traditionally, why has psychotherapy been so adamantly opposed to morality? The third question is: If psychotherapy and morality cannot exist in separation—if psychotherapy is actually a moral as well as a human practice—what does this mean? The fourth question is: Is there a practice of psychotherapy—one that fosters integrity and mutuality—that gives us a snapshot of how this mutual process works? The last question is: If we consider the psychotherapy of those who have been traumatized by personal violence, what do we find in light of the fully human?

PSYCHOTHERAPY AND AN INTEGRAL AND MUTUAL SELF

The first question: Can psychotherapy be measured in light of the fully human, in light of becoming an adult and moral self, an integral self-in-mutuality? Rarely is this question asked so directly—in part because the culture's mosaic of the fully human is difficult to find, in part because therapeutic psychology and developmental psychology are often not on the same page, and in part because there are so many different psychotherapies with so many different approaches and goals. Yet, this question of human development is one that is extremely important. As it turns out, the fully human is able to measure psychotherapy in its fullness, while psychotherapy in its fullness returns the favor, confirming the process of becoming fully human in ways that are quite clarifying.

The ultimate goal of psychotherapy, at least from an adult-moral perspective, is for the client—whether that client is an individual person, or in a marriage, family, or group—to become an integral and mutual self. Interestingly enough, while it is not common to talk about psychotherapy and adulthood together, it is not at all unusual to talk about psychotherapy in relation to integrity and mutuality. Donald Ford and Hugh Urban find that the goal of most therapies is that "an individual can function as a unified whole in coherent transactional relationship with his or her contexts."[2] For Sidney Blatt and Richard Ford, the goal of psychotherapy is to help the client have a "unique identity" in relationships that are "mutually engaged."[3] Ruthellen Josselson says that psychotherapy is for "independent, differentiated selfhood" that is also capable of "healthy interpersonal relationships."[4] Integrity and mutuality together is seen as the goal of psychotherapy by a great many therapists.

Most often adulthood and morality surface together in the professional code of ethics that the psychotherapist is expected to adhere to. The *Code of Ethics and Conduct* of The British Psychological Society, for example, describes at length four ethical principles in terms of: *respect*, for "the dignity and worth of all persons"; *competence*, with the "development and maintenance of high standards"; *responsibility* "to clients, to the general public, and to the profession and science of Psychology"; and *integrity,* valuing the "honesty, accuracy, clarity, and fairness in their interactions with all persons."[5] In fact, most professional organizations of psychotherapists (and most other professional groups) mandate as a matter of course that the members of the profession pay attention to the demands of integrity and mutuality.

For the psychotherapist, being enough of an integral and mutual self is seen as essential for the therapeutic process. One way to put this is to say that the therapist needs to own her or his "pieces," enough at least, if he or she hopes to help the client to own his or her "pieces." The therapist has to welcome "the loved and the unloved, the comfortable and the uncomfortable, the good and the bad" in herself or himself if she or he wants the client to be able to do the same. A whole-enough psychotherapist needs to relate fully to his or her client: taking care of the actual needs of the client without his or her own needs getting in the way, being just in respecting the client, respecting confidentiality and all the other particulars of the therapeutic relationship that need to be safeguarded.[6] In other words, the integrity and mutuality of the therapist is essential for fostering the integrity and mutuality of the client.

Seeing psychotherapy as a process that fosters the becoming of an integral self-in-mutuality lets us see how the six characteristics of this self are at play as the therapeutic process unfolds. If the culture often has a hard time understanding and appreciating the characteristics that make us integral and mutual, perhaps it is because many of us often have a hard time realizing these characteristics as well. In therapy, how we struggle as a client with these characteristics is often the focus of the relationship. In fact, these characteristics of the fully human are a good description of a favorable outcome of the struggle.

Owning the body-self with its memories, its sexuality, its strivings, and its limits can be very hard to do. Much of psychotherapy is concerned with issues that keep us, one way or another, from becoming a body-self. These issues range from the addictions, to personality disorders, to sexual problems, to anxiety, to depression, to trauma, and to feeling unreal or disconnected. Psychotherapy, from an adult-moral perspective, is in the service of healing the mind-body dichotomy as well as its ever-present companion, the self-other dichotomy. In psychotherapy, disembodied rationality gets challenged in a practical way. Over time, the client often becomes comfortable enough as a body-self to be able "to love and to work"—Freud's definition of maturity and Erikson's definition of adult morality.[7]

As a client, for example, I might say: "It is taking a long time, but I feel like slowly I am coming together; it's not just how horribly he violated me, but it's that I can't believe anyone could be so hateful to another human being." Or as a client, I might say: "I can see now that taking drugs all those years was mostly to hide the emptiness I felt, that I was nothing inside; I have a lot more empathy now, for myself and for everyone else." Or as a client, I might say: "The things that are important for me to do I need to own; it's funny, but now it's like sometimes my body knows what they are before I do."

Psychotherapy as the quest for an adult-moral self is also in the service of becoming a feeling self. "Feeling, says Eugene Gendlin, is how we are alive in the environment, and therefore we feel, in a bodily way, the whole context of our living."[8] But "when there are parts of ourselves we still disown, the path to wholeness is obstructed."[9] Psychotherapy involves a therapist in touch enough with his or her feeling to help the client to be the same. Being in touch with feeling helps the "emotionally tinged" and the "rationally grasped" come together even as it helps heal the splits we have between the self and the other. Feeling, as John Heron reminds us, "celebrates unity in diversity and identification with what is different without loss of personal distinctness."[10]

As a client, for example, I might say: "I was never allowed to be angry growing up; I realize now I have a lot of anger and it's pretty self-protective, keeping me from relating to others and keeping me from really being me." Or as a client, I might say: "Getting in touch with all this personal stuff these past few months has been extremely painful, but as I was going home the other night—and this was powerful—it came to me: not feeling anything at all was far worse." Or as a client, I might say: "I am more accepting of how I feel inside; it's who I am—the good, the bad, and the ugly; I'm more at peace now, not at war all the time."

In psychotherapy, especially over time, the client often begins to feel more and more a sense of inner depth along with a respect for the depth of the other.[11] In the depth, images and metaphors that are healing often begin to surface. Over time, some of the dichotomies that keep us stuck may be gradually transformed into paradox. Over time, the depth often begins to reveal a sense of coherence and direction. Over time, if the process goes well enough, care for one's own needs and the needs of the other grow together. Over time, respect, fairness, and equity for the self and the other grow as well. Depth is the "place" where care, justice, and peace are struggled with and hopefully become more real.

As a client, for example, I might say: "I feel some openness now, there's an inner space; there's a kind of freedom and there's a good part of me; it's nice to think that that's there and that I can even find it in others." Or as a client, I might say: "What was inside was just a twisted mess; when my boyfriend said he forgave me and that he loved me, I felt myself breathe; I need to keep breathing." Or as a client, I might say: "I'm not so empty now inside; something is stirring; I feel more real, more connected, it's like I am beginning to find out who I am."

Psychotherapy is all about the self finding its own clear boundaries. Over time, things may begin to become clearer: who I am and who I am not; who I am and who you are; what I need to own and what I do not need to own; what I am responsible for and what I am not responsible for. Clear boundaries are, of course, crucial for the mutuality of the therapeutic relationship itself. "Boundaries—of space, time, financial structure, and limits on personal sharing—help to secure the 'safe space' within which mutual respect can take place."[12] Quite simply, psychotherapy is *in* and *for* clear boundaries.

As a client, for example, I might say: "Owning all the expectations that I have in the family is killing me; it's going to take some time but I know now that I don't have to do that." Or as a client, I might say: "It's just that I am a human being; no one has the right to treat me as if I have no feelings of my own." Or as a client, I might say: "I am grateful for how evenly you listen to me, and I feel your concern and respect for me; things are clearer; I am starting to trust and own myself, but it is still very hard."

Psychotherapy, over time, is also for the realization of an intimate self. It is a "respectful intimacy in which the integrity of the other is fully perceived, understood, and embraced."[13] Therapy is *in* and *for* intimacy. In therapy, clear boundaries and intimacy go together. As Kenneth Bragan observes, "increasing mutuality is the goal of the relationship."[14] Feldman and Blatt say the goals of psychotherapy are "an essentially positive, realistic, well-differentiated, and integrated sense of self," and "the capacity for reciprocal, mutually satisfying, intimate interpersonal relationships."[15] Psychotherapy is often about relationship issues, about how and to what extent to be intimate, about all the things that keep us from intimacy.

As a client, for example, I might say: "Being loved for who I am is still frightening, but it is also kind of nice; big parts of me are responding to that." Or as a client, I might say: "After the betrayal of my best friend, I thought I would never be open with anyone; but here I am, vulnerable again; it's scary but I'm alive." Or as a client, I might say: "We have to negotiate it and not take it for granted, but what I have with her is the best thing that has ever happened to me."

Perhaps the main goal of psychotherapy—acknowledged in nearly every therapeutic approach—is for the client to become a responsible self. It is for accepting normal responsibilities and for being able to respond as oneself to the other. Writing from a psychoanalytic point of view, Nancy Sherman says: "Put simply, the analytic project is ultimately a chance to take responsibility for one's character, where the conception of what that responsibility consists of has become expanded rather than diminished."[16] In the beginning of therapy, clients often blame others for their difficulties, but as they become more aware of their own feeling, depth, and boundaries, blaming often gives way to taking responsibility. In actual fact, taking responsibility is the healing of the split between the mind and the body and between the self and the other.

As a client, for example, I might say: "So much of the fear and anxiety is gone; I feel much freer now to do what I need to do; there's a lot more energy there to honestly face life." Or as a client, I might say: "Our daughter's disease still overwhelms both of us, but I feel more whole now and I find that somehow I can handle it better than before." Or as a client, I might say: "As a social worker, I have to make sure, especially with difficult clients, that I don't keep getting overinvolved, but there is nothing else in the world that is more important to me and nothing that could be more rewarding."

What allows the client to move toward his or her own integrity and mutuality is, of course, the unique care and justice offered by a therapist who is whole and mutual enough. Psychotherapy, at least from an adult-moral perspective, is inherently a process made possible by the therapist's caring for the needs of the client—the overall as well as the moment-to-moment needs—and by the therapist's respect for the client without condition, no matter who the client is or what the client has done. To be sure, learning to care and to be just in this therapeutic way requires a lot of training and supervision. But also, to be sure, as an artful and creative skill, psychotherapy is invaluable for some of us in becoming an integral and mutual self, invaluable for us as clients but also invaluable for us as therapists as well.

Just as empathy is at the heart of a pedagogy of connection, it is also at the heart of the therapeutic relationship.[17] In fact, much of the description of empathy in the last chapter comes from practicing psychotherapists. "One of the earliest and most consistent findings in the psychotherapy research literature is the importance of the therapist's empathy for the patient."[18] In the film, *Good Will Hunting*, Sean is very human, very practiced, very patient, and very empathic. He has a good sense of what Will is experiencing. He is exceptional in his attending and in his respect. He knows how to wait, how to let things go, how to challenge, how to engage. He knows just the right time to address the inner, to say quietly to Will again and again—and seemingly out of the blue—"It's not your fault, it's not your fault; it's not your fault."

Empathy is at the heart of dialogue, and psychotherapy is often one of the most profound adult and moral dialogues we ever have. William Doherty sees this dialogue as a conversation "in which the therapist listens, reflects, acknowledges, questions, probes, and challenges—and in which the client is free to do the same and to develop a more integrated sense of moral sensibilities."[19] Alan Tjeltveit sees dialogue in psychotherapy in a similar way. It is a moral discourse that promotes "collaboration, negotiation, open-mindedness, serious attempts to listen to and understand one another, open-ended exchanges, a willingness to reconsider one's position, give and take, and respect for one another."[20] If dialogue—in essence the feeling and inner depth of the self engaging the feeling and depth of the other—is the official language of adulthood and adult morality, it is the official language of psychotherapy as well.

PSYCHOTHERAPY AND MORALITY: IN OPPOSITION

The second question: Traditionally, why has psychotherapy been so seriously opposed to morality? Three explanations—all related—help to answer this question. The first is more historical; the second more developmental; and the third more therapeutic.

A Historical Explanation

Two very influential traditions go into our understanding of how psychotherapy is presently understood in the culture: the psychoanalytic tradition with its founder, Sigmund Freud (1856–1939) and the behaviorist tradition with one of its founders, J. B. Watson (1878–1958). Although Freud and Watson had no respect for each other's theories, both men were brilliant, courageous in their own ways, and accomplished in empirical (animal) research. Noteworthy also, both men had a pronounced antipathy toward religion. For them, religion simply *is* morality; controlling us with shame, guilt, and shunning while imposing demands and teachings on us that are completely irrational and unscientific. The new scientific psychotherapy was designed to liberate us from morality and especially from moralistic religion.

SIGMUND FREUD

Sigmund Freud thought of psychoanalysis as science, as biological science, as medical science. In his early research with eels and crayfish, for example, he was trying "to make hidden structures reliably and stably observable."[21] In psychoanalysis, he was interested in a healing technique, but he was also interested in "the right method to reveal the structure of what was to be treated," what he called "the psychical apparatus": the id, the ego, and the superego.[22] In this apparatus, the superego, which represses instinctual desire, *is* morality. On the one hand, as a pure scientist Freud can say that "psycho-analysis has no concern whatever" in making judgments of value.[23] On the other hand, as a practicing analyst he can be "acerbically critical" of traditional morality.[24] This morality—coming from religious ancestors "far more ignorant than we are"—he saw as the major cause of the repressed sexuality of so many of his neurotic patients.

Freud describes the relating of the id, the ego, and the superego.[25] The id, the foundation of the structure, is our "untamed passions" seeking pleasure without constraint.[26] Acting unconsciously, it "knows no values, no good and evil, no morality."[27] The superego, the internalized demands of our parents, is "the origin of conscience" and the structure of religion.[28] Working unconsciously, it controls the id by threatening the ego with anxiety and guilt, often in ways quite harsh and punitive. The ego, as "reason and circumspection," relates us to reality.[29] It serves, says Freud, "three tyrants": "the external world, the super-ego, and the id."[30] Interesting enough, rather than being an ego function, morality is seen by Freud as the task of the superego—an unconscious and irrational inner voice, controlling and demanding, that represses instinct and punishes us with requisite amounts of anxiety and guilt.[31]

JOHN BROADUS WATSON

In "Psychology as the Behaviorist Views It," J. B. Watson, writing in 1913, sets out his program for behaviorism: "Psychology as the behaviorist views it is a purely objective experimental branch of natural science. Its theoretical goal is the prediction and control of behavior."[32] Any organism, whether it is an animal or a human, can be understood in terms of stimulus and response. There is no need to talk about "experience" or "introspection" as most psychologists were fond of doing.[33] For him, there is "no observable separate entity called mind," and there are "no such things as consciousness or its substratum, the unconscious."[34] There is no inner at all. Since all behavior is controlled by the environment, it is important to observe behavior and habit formation.[35] As a science of the directly observable, behaviorism is—much like "chemistry and physics"—not concerned with morality.[36] If the environment can be controlled, then behavior can be controlled. Psychology is a science of that control. Morality is not involved.

Watson was named after John Broadus, a well-known fundamentalist preacher of his time. Raised by a deeply religious mother who wanted him to study for the ministry, Watson came to reject religion as an imposed system of unquestioned concepts—steeped in "fear stimuli" and in the service of control—which conditioned people to live in society.[37] Religion and morality are two sides of the same coin. "In the larger group," he says, "God or Jehovah takes the place of the family father. Thus even the modern child is confronted by the dicta of medicine men—be they the father, the soothsayer of the village, the God or Jehovah." Watson wants to replace the dogmatic and paternalistic morality of religion with "better ways of living and thinking" offered by behaviorism so that "the world finally becomes a place fit for human habitation."[38]

For both Freud and Watson, morality is primitive, alien, moralistic, irrational, and religious. Although they had radically different understandings of psychotherapy, they saw this new therapy as not only in opposition to what they understood morality to be but also as a rational alternative that would help us to reclaim our humanness. Both theorists—especially in their framing of morality—have had a deep and lasting effect on our understanding of psychotherapy.

A Developmental Explanation

If we look at the thinking of Freud and Watson from a developmental perspective, it is clear that they understand morality as anything but adult. Morality is in terms of early childhood and then of adolescence. From a developmental perspective, however, we can distinguish two moralities that are markedly different: a preadult morality and an adult morality. Preadult morality, the morality most often found in the culture, comes in different forms. It often has its beginnings as a morality of shame, guilt, and humiliation in our early years. As we begin to become more socialized, it moves to a morality that is conventional, a morality of rules and norms that are codified in law and celebrated in the culture. Later, preadult morality may develop into a rational and abstract morality based on principles, but these principles are usually held to be quite objective.[39]

If there is one hallmark of this preadult morality, it is that it is *something external to the self,* something from the outside. Seen in terms of the subject-object dichotomy of reality—which is also preadult—this morality is *objective* and not subjective at all, not at all connected to the experiencing subject. If there is a second hallmark of preadult morality, a hallmark based on its external quality, it is that it is a morality of *control* and *constraint*, mandating certain rules and norms—often because of our selfishness and our inherently asocial tendencies—and demanding punishment when we do not conform. If there is a third hallmark of preadult morality—an overarching hallmark—it is that, with its external and controlling qualities, it functions as a *superego* morality, a punitive, guilt-evoking morality we take in from significant others as well as from the culture.[40]

Not surprisingly, the belief that so many of us in so many cultures have about the nature of justice reveals a preadult or superego notion of morality. The belief that "Justice must be objective, rational, abstract, and impersonal" goes hand-in-hand with the subject-object thinking that makes morality external to the self rather than a part of it. The belief that "To be just is to follow the law," which defines conventional thinking, is the epitome of external morality. The belief that "Justice is punishment" is fully in harmony with all the hallmarks of a preadult morality: it is meant to be external and objective; it is meant to control and constrain; and it is a superego morality having as much shame and guilt—if not outright dehumanization—as seems to be warranted.

If we ask again: "Traditionally, why has psychotherapy been so seriously opposed to morality?" the answer we can give is: "If by psychotherapy we mean a transforming process that can help us to become whole and mutual, and if by morality we mean a preadult superego morality, then if we are to become fully human *this pre-*

adult superego morality is the very thing to be transformed." In this transformation, morality moves from being something external to the self, from something objective in a *subject-object* split, to being something intrinsic to an integral self-in-mutuality, a self that is *inner* and *relational* together. Although neither Freud nor Watson spent much time talking about adulthood, let alone about adult morality, both of them were thoroughly convinced that psychotherapy at least had to free the person from the external constraints of the superego morality of the culture.

A Therapeutic Explanation

If psychotherapy is understood in an adult and moral perspective, and if clients are on their way toward becoming adult and moral, the critical question is: How is morality part of the therapeutic process? How are psychotherapy and morality related? Does morality have any place in psychotherapy? Can the client bring up explicitly moral concerns? The answer to this question has to be: Of course, the client needs to be free to discuss whatever concerns he or she may have so they can be explored and understood in a way that is helpful. Morality is inherent in the process of psychotherapy. It is meant, however, to be discovered in the psychotherapeutic dialogue as it unfolds. It is meant to come from within the therapeutic process itself and not be determined by already-decided values coming either from the psychotherapist or from the culture. The therapist's presence in this exploration is often pivotal, if not crucial, precisely because of the boundaries of the psychotherapeutic relationship and because of the trust and respect that both parties have for the process itself.

The role of the psychotherapist is to help the client pay attention to his or her own feeling and inner depth. This *paying attention* is the essence of the therapeutic process. If I am the client, I may need my therapist to help me in doing this attending and to make the process safe enough to engage in, but what is not helpful at all is for my therapist to put something from the outside onto what I am trying to find inside. As a client, I may be lost, or even desperate. I may say: "Please tell me what I should do!" And if I say this to my therapist, I hope my therapist will say: "It might seem helpful if I could do that, but—no matter how much experience I have—I cannot decide for you what you should do. In fact, the work we are doing together is just *the opposite* of that: the essence of the work is to help you to decide what it is that you want to do, to decide how it is that you need to be going forward."

On the one hand, human development is inherently moral; human development and moral development are inseparable. In psychotherapy, we are always dealing with both together. On the other hand, if I am the client, the last thing I need is for my therapist to act as my moralist. If I am suffering from my own version of superego morality, I do not need my therapist to compound my confusion by giving me his or her version as well. I need my therapist to be very present to me as I struggle to put my own "pieces" together in a way that might help me become a responsible self, to help me find my own integrity and mutuality. In psychotherapy—and in the other helping professions—we need a caring, respectful, empathic person who will let us listen to our own inner voice telling us how to be and act. If psychotherapy is meant to go beyond the superego—and it may be exceptionally helpful in doing this—it is not meant to go beyond morality. "Psychotherapy," as Mark Bickhard puts it, "is a very special kind of intrinsically ethical relating to another person."[41]

PSYCHOTHERAPY AND ADULT MORALITY: IN CONNECTION

The third question: If psychotherapy and morality cannot exist in separation—if psychotherapy is actually a moral as well as a human practice—what does this mean? The preliminary answer to this question we already know: it means that psychotherapy is able to foster a morality that is adult. If we consider the columns in chapter 2 of preadult morality compared with a morality of inner depth, psychotherapy can be seen as bringing about the transformation of the one to the other. It allows for the transformation of a voice that is "the internalized values of others" to a voice "that is my own way of valuing self and other." It allows for the transformation of a voice that is "in the service of control and social conformity" to a voice that is "in service of integrity and mutuality."

A Superego Morality	**A Morality of Depth**
• a voice that is the internalized values of others	• a voice that is my own way of valuing self and other
• a voice that comes from "the mind" or "the head"	• a voice that comes from feeling, from the body-self
• a voice that is often loud, harsh, critical, and judgmental	• a voice that is gentle and friendly, with caring and respect
• a voice that is usually a direct command	• a voice of dialogue that is self-reflective
• a voice that is "at me" to make me guilty or to punish me	• a voice that is "from me," from "the inner" to call me forward
• a voice that tends to freeze me in some bad way that I am	• a voice of inner prompting that brings change and development
• a voice of self-concern, asking "Am I good or bad?"	• a voice of empathy, asking "Are we all OK?"
• A voice that is in the service of control and social conformity	• a voice that is in the service of integrity and mutuality

The voice of column two, the voice of inner depth, is heard in psychotherapy—usually gradually and haltingly at first—as it continues over time. It is the client's voice: a voice from inside calling the client forward, a voice coming from feeling, from the body-self; it is a voice of the client's own valuing, a voice of conscience that is often gentle, caring, open, and respectful; it is a voice of self-reflection inviting dialogue; and above all, it is a voice of empathy for self and other. The voice of a morality of depth—the voice that psychotherapy and the other helping professions are able to foster—is in the service of the client's integrity and mutuality. With the exception of helping clients who had initially acquired little or no superego, if it is hard to see what psychotherapy and preadult morality have in common, it is easy to see that psychotherapy and adult morality are intimately connected.

Most important to note in the transformation from preadult to adult morality is that the transformation may be a seachange. Psychotherapy is able to foster an adult morality that is radically different from preadult morality. Preadult morality is an external, controlling, superego morality, an objective morality firmly under the aegis of the subject-object dichotomy. As a transformation of preadult morality, adult morality is a *paradigm shift*. Its roots are in the self-in-relation. If it is not objective, neither is it subjective; if not found "outside," neither is it found "inside"—if, of course, the inside is who we are as dichotomized subjects. Rather, adult morality is the voice of an integral self-in-mutually. *Adult morality is a morality that is both inner and relational*, a morality of both *depth* and *connection*, a dialectical morality, a morality of living paradox. Adult morality *is* integrity and mutuality. Perhaps the clearest and most practical way to describe it is to say, as we have been saying: it is a morality of care and justice together. It is a morality of peace.

Psychotherapy is a relationship that allows us to move from preadult morality to a morality of care and justice, the morality of a fully human self. When seen in adult-moral perspective, psychotherapy shows us not only the fullness of morality, but also it offers us one very practical way of coming to embody it, especially when early upbringing and education have not been able to do that. Morality—not the external version, not the preadult version, not the shame and guilt version so presumed in the culture, but the inner and relational version, the adult version, the care and justice version—returns the favor. It tells us what psychotherapy is for in its fullness.

PSYCHOTHERAPY AND THE ORGANISMIC TRADITION

The fourth question is: Is there a tradition in psychotherapy—one that fosters integrity and mutuality—that gives us a snapshot of how this mutual process works? In the organismic approach to psychotherapy there is an understanding of the self that is very much in harmony with an adult-moral self as an integral self-in-mutuality and its characteristics. The hallmark of the organismic approach is that the self is an organism-environment reality. In this tradition, the stand-alone, separate, particle self is an abstraction; it makes no actual sense at all. The embodied self is a living organism, and there is no such thing as a living organism that does not interact with its environment.

In the organismic tradition, we look very briefly at: Andras Angyal (1902–1960), a holistic thinker with a "bird's eye view" of how the self functions; Carl Rogers (1902–1987), a humanistic psychotherapist known for his person-centered approach to psychotherapy; and Eugene Gendlin (1926–2017) who is known for his approach to psychotherapy called "focusing." Angyal influenced Rogers in major ways, and Rogers influenced Gendlin in major ways. All three had a great deal in common—especially a profound respect for the embodied self, a very relational understanding of the person, and a unique way of describing psychotherapy as an interpersonal dialogue of therapeutic change.

ANDRAS ANGYAL

Angyal's holistic insight is: "the life process does not take place *within* the organism, but *between the organism and the environment*."[42] Looking down "from above" at this process, Angyal sees that it has two basic trends or tendencies: autonomy and homonomy.[43] On the one hand, every organism, every living body whether human or not, of its very nature tends to be autonomous. It wants to increase in self-government, self-determination, and freedom; it wants to use and master the environment in pursuit of its own becoming.[44] On the other hand, every organism also tends to be homonomous (homonomy is, "the law of likes," a concept he makes up). Every organism wants to be with others as part of a larger whole of "likes." Homonomy is the need for connection, and for us humans it is the need for community. Most pointedly, it is the need "to love and to be loved."[45] Quite simply, we are meant to develop as autonomous selves participating in a larger whole of likes, a larger whole of likes which nurtures and depends on us.

As a path of human wholeness and relatedness, autonomy and homonomy is the healthy organization of the self. We can, however, suffer from neurosis, from an impaired organization. Growing up, we may have had neither enough experience of mastery nor have had enough experience of being loved and loving others. Later, our autonomy and homonomy may be seriously weakened, perhaps by addiction, or illness, or trauma of some kind. Neurosis is simply "an impairment of self-determination" and an "impairment of the capacity to love."[46] For Angyal, neurosis is simply a narrowed-in life, a life lived in isolation. If we are neurotic, we are "small, weak, and inadequate" in an "alien" world.[47]

What is psychotherapy for Angyal? It is a process of moving from neurosis to health. Typically, it has four steps, with the last step, the loving care and respect of the therapist, allowing the process to unfold. If I am the neurotic client, typically in the process of therapy I come to experience:

1. *recognition*—I begin to see that the way I am acting, or perhaps even my entire life, is unsound or distorted; this step may take time because it seems that usually I want to "feel better" before I want to "be better."
2. *responsibility*—I begin to "recognize realistically" the part I am playing in my self-destructive mode of living; rather than blaming others or even blaming myself, "I decide to take responsibility for what I am doing."
3. *regret*—I am not just sorrowful but I realize that the unsound way I have been living is completely bankrupt; "I have to change."
4. *therapist attitude of acceptance*—throughout the process, *the unconditional love of the therapist* for me as a person—the care and respect of the therapist—in spite of the unhealthy and destructive way I have been acting, is the "fulcrum" that allows for therapeutic change; it lets me move from neurotic isolation to living life fully again as an autonomous and homonomous person.[48]

CARL R. ROGERS

Influenced by Angyal's understanding of autonomy, Carl Rogers points out that human motivation lies in the tendency of the organism to actualize itself in its environment in valued ways.[49] We find this actualizing tendency in a *flow of feeling*, and this feeling is "emotion and cognition as they are experienced inseparably in the moment."[50] For Rogers, if we could always be in touch with our flow of feeling, if our actual feeling could be "available to awareness," then we would be healthy and "fully open to our experience," then no matter what experiences we might have we would always be "in touch with our feeling" and so be engaged in "full existential living."[51]

Our problem, says Rogers, is that growing up we usually experience some "conditions of worth." We are loved, but usually loved *conditionally*. Unfortunately, we take those conditions of worth into our self-concept. Because the love from significant others is so important for us we *deny* or *distort* our actual experiencing in order to be worthy of that love. For example, "I deeply value and love biology. I have, however, flunked it twice. But my father and my grandfather are doctors and ever since I can remember I am going to be a doctor." Or as a woman born with a physical deformity says: "The implicit demand from my parents was that in order to maintain their attachment to me, I had to privilege their misfortune over mine."[52] Because we experience conditional love from significant others, we become incongruent; we develop a self-concept that is no longer in harmony with what our organism actually feels.

What is psychotherapy? It is simply a process of moving from incongruence to congruence; it is a process of allowing our self-concept to come into harmony with what our organism is actually experiencing; it is a process of letting into awareness all the "pieces" that the organism is feeling, of accepting our actual feeling that we have been denying or distorting. It is not a mystery why Rogerian therapists often ask: "And how do you *feel* about that?"

Rogers finds that three "necessary and sufficient" conditions *in the therapist* allow the therapeutic process to happen:

1. *empathy*—the therapist senses "the client's inner world of private personal meanings" as if it were his or her own, yet never losing the "as if."[53] Rogers finds "a high degree of empathy in a relationship is possibly *the* most potent factor in bringing about change and learning."[54] He also finds: "*The*

better integrated the therapist is, the higher the degree of empathy he or she exhibits."[55]

2. *congruence*—the therapist owns all of her or his "pieces." He or she is whole enough not to deny or distort her or his experiencing during the therapeutic process. Rogers finds that the more "the therapist is able to listen acceptantly to what is going on within, and the more the therapist is able to *be* the complexity of his or her feelings, the higher the degree of congruence."[56]
3. *unconditional positive regard*—the therapist loves and prizes the client unconditionally; the therapist has no "conditions of worth" for accepting the client. With no conditions of worth coming from the therapist, the client is free to get in touch with what he or she is actually feeling; organismic experiencing surfaces more and more in awareness; the self-concept is becoming more and more in line with actual experiencing; and the client engages more and more in "full existential living."[57]

EUGENE T. GENDLIN

Reflecting Angyal's thinking, Eugene Gendlin says: "A person is a bodily interaction with others and the environment, much as breathing is a bodily interaction with an environment."[58] This bodily interaction is available to us in *feeling*. "Feeling is how we are alive in the environment," says Gendlin, "and therefore we feel, in a bodily way, the whole context of our living."[59] Gendlin often uses the phrases "felt sense," and "body sense" as synonyms for feeling because for him, as it is for Rogers, feeling is both meaningful and bodily. Even more, feeling is primary in us; feeling is our organism-environment awareness *before* it is abstracted by the subject-object or reason-emotion thinking we are used to. As it turns out, feeling is at the heart of the relational self that Oliver describes in the first chapter.

What is psychotherapy? A number of years ago, Gendlin and others working with him studied thousands of counseling sessions, and they found that *how* the client spoke about problems in therapy was a reliable predictor of a favorable outcome of the process. Clients who were able to speak from the felt sense or body sense of their problem—able to speak *from feeling*—were the ones who later were found to have experienced therapeutic change.[60] Gendlin began developing and teaching a way to engage this feeling process, a way he called "focusing."

Focusing is paying direct attention to the feeling, or felt sense, or body sense of a situation or problem long enough for it to form and be there (usually in the middle of the body); if we pay attention to feeling this way—giving it enough time and not trying to analyze it or fix it—then it may shift and open up. Meaning comes from the feeling, and the body's living of the situation changes. Focusing is a patient, caring, and respectful self-empathy or empathy for the other that brings organism-environment change. In Angyal's terms, focusing brings an increase in autonomy and homonomy. In Rogers' terms, focusing brings an increase in congruence, in existential living. In terms of an adult-moral self, focusing brings an increase in integrity and mutuality. It is a process, often in small steps, of allowing us to become an integral and mutual self.

The following is a focusing dialogue in which the client, a man not familiar with the process of focusing, enters into it, staying with the feeling and not trying to figure it out.

CL: It's the same old thing, the responsibility, the over responsibility. I know I kind of got it from my father. He left us when I and my little sister were little. I became the responsible one. But I still have it in spades. I am super responsible at work, with my son, in the marriage, as a coach, with everything. I know it is way too much but I just can't help myself.

TH: I hear it. Right now, it's your super responsibly in everything. . . . I wonder what it feels like to have that? Is it like frustration or exhaustion? I get the sense that it is a huge burden you are carrying.

CL: It is. I know it is.

TH: Can you go into your body and let yourself feel inside what this whole thing about having to be responsible feels like right now?

CL: I know it's a burden. I know that—

TH: (interrupting) Can you let what you know go by for a moment, and if you can, just let yourself feel what having all this responsibility is like for you? . . . Can you let the feeling of the whole of it come and be there inside, maybe in the middle of your body? . . . (30 seconds) . . . There's no hurry . . . wait and see what comes, the felt sense . . . of all this responsibility.

CL: (after a minute and a half) . . . I can feel it. . . . (20 seconds) . . . It's heavy . . . like a huge weight.

TH: Be with that, the feeling, the felt sense . . . heavy and like a huge weight.

CL: (maybe 30 seconds) . . . umph! It's *so* heavy.

TH: It's there, and it's *so* heavy.

CL: Yes . . . (after a long silence) . . . It's easing, just a bit . . . the heavy feeling . . . but now it's like . . . You have to carry it, it's your *job*.

TH: Um, hmm. It's your *job* to carry it, you have to do it. That's how it feels now?

CL: It's shifting a bit. . . . (30 seconds) . . . Oh, it's the blame. . . . (20 seconds) . . . That's what comes there . . . it's the blame, but . . .

TH: Can you welcome that? . . . It's the blame . . . be with that.

CL: (slowly smiling and much less tense) . . . That's it . . . it's the blame . . . I don't want the blame. And I do it to myself. It's not so much that others will blame. It's that I just don't ever want to blame myself. . . . (20 seconds) . . . It feels OK now. It's OK now. I don't need to do that. I don't have to carry all that responsibility. . . . Wow!

TH: It's a huge relief.

CL: Yeah. Isn't that something! That's what it was all about. I think now I can be less crazy.[61]

PSYCHOTHERAPY, TRAUMA, AND MUTUALITY

The fifth question: If we consider the psychotherapy of those traumatized by the violence of others, what do we find in light of the fully human? Surprisingly, perhaps, considering psychotherapy, trauma, and mutuality together reveals not only that all three throw light on each other but also that all three end up revealing each other's contours.

What is trauma? In Greek, trauma means "a wound." It is a serious wound to the self and therefore to the self's integrity and mutuality.[62] As a human-moral injury, it is a direct assault on caring and justice and a direct assault on peace. It is an insult to the human that deconstructs the stages of development described by Erik Erikson. "Developmental conflicts," as Judith Herman observes, "of childhood and adolescence, long since resolved, are suddenly reopened."[63] Along with basic trust, the survivor may have to relive "all her earlier struggles over autonomy, initiative, competence, identity, and intimacy."[64]

In suffering trauma, integrity may simply disintegrate; the "pieces" that go to make the self are torn apart, much like a house after a hurricane or typhoon. The self lies in fragments with walls, furniture, and mementoes randomly strewn about. At the same time, mutuality with the other may dissolve; relationships that give meaning to life—my partner, my children, my friends, my work, my favorite activities and places—become shadowlike, or meaningless, or are no longer felt as real.[65]

In suffering trauma, I may experience my body-self as split with mind and body disconnected in fearful and horrible ways, perhaps inviting me to escape in fantasy. My empathy may simply vanish, leaving the feeling self completely numb or disconnected. In suffering trauma, I may find "a vacuous inner world," with spirit gone, heart broken, and soul departed."[66] My violated boundaries may simply disappear, leaving me overwhelmed and utterly vulnerable. Intimacy—either far too threatening or compulsively sought—may fail to provide closeness. Being a responsible self—the very core of my humanness—may be taken from me, leaving me powerless, anxious, depressed, and terrified. In short, trauma is a devastating disconnection of the self, a severing within and without.

What might psychotherapy with a client who has suffered trauma look like? The challenge for the client may be a number of things: it may be to muster enough courage to trust a therapist who is "supposed to be nurturant."[67] It may be the fear of shame, or guilt, or humiliation; it may be self-loathing, or the fear of rejection, or of not being believed or taken seriously; it may be the fear that talking about it will make it real. In all of this, there may be profound ambivalence—desperately needing to trust and needing not to; desperately needing to talk and not wanting to; desperately needing to attend to the pain but needing to escape from it; desperately needing to rely on the therapist yet fearing further betrayal.

The challenge for the therapist may be: to provide a very safe therapeutic space for the client; to accept and believe the client; to be empathic, especially when the details of the trauma are painfully real, raw, and heart-wrenching; to hold therapeutic boundaries and yet be authentic, transparent, and perhaps even self-revealing. Often, the challenge for the therapist lies in possible "vicarious traumatization": being invaded or overwhelmed; haunted by the client's fear, or flashbacks, or numbness, or anxiety, or depression.[68] The challenge is: to be with the client's vulnerability without succumbing to it; to be fully and skillfully empathic without letting the client's fragmented "pieces" become one's own; to be completely open and mutual and yet hold one's own integrity.

If we consider the therapy of someone who is traumatized by the traumatization of others, the moral dimension of trauma surfaces clearly. Peter Marin introduces the notion of "moral pain" in understanding the suffering of some of the veterans who returned home after the Vietnam War. This pain is "a profound moral distress arising from what they saw and sometimes did in the war."[69] Some therapists talk about "moral injury" suffered by veterans in any war, an injury defined as: "*Perpetrating, failing to prevent, bearing witness to, or learning about acts that transgress deeply held moral beliefs and expectations*."[70]

In light of the challenges that arise in trauma therapy—and perhaps because of these challenges—the relationship between client and therapist is often one of deep mutuality.[71] This mutuality is asymmetrical to be sure: the client and the therapist have different "roles, functions, power, and responsibilities."[72] Yet, the stakes could not be higher. The client is struggling mightily to get back some semblance of his or her life, and the therapist is trying to facilitate that often long and difficult process. At some point, the therapist may fail in empathy as his or her "unfinished pieces, shortcomings, and blind spots" inevitably show themselves. In empathy, the client may need to forgive the therapist as their shared humanity and vulnerability touch and intermingle and their mutuality becomes even more focal.

What does the profoundly human, intimate, vulnerable, and mutual psychotherapy of trauma reveal? It reveals integrity and mutuality. For the client, if all goes well, the devastating disconnection in the self and from the other gradually moves toward connection. The "pieces" of the self begin to cohere or to cohere again and mutuality begins to be possible.[73] Mind and body start to come together. Feeling—the inner and the relational—is felt. Inner depth starts to appear, with the heart, the soul, and the spirit gradually coming to life. Boundaries begin to form or reform, bringing some definition and safety. Intimacy becomes possible again and is welcome. The self that was immobilized, suspended, or nearly dead responds to the other more and more as itself. If all goes well enough in the therapy, there is a gradual birth or rebirth of a self that is integral and mutual—all thanks to the mutuality of the therapeutic process.

For the therapist, the mutuality of this process often makes for more connection as well. The client's human-moral courage often encourages the therapist in facing parts of his or her own life. Touched by the client's vulnerability, the therapist understands that vulnerability touches us all, that what happened to the client or to the perpetrator—given different events and circumstances—could have happened to the therapist. "One significant reward of doing trauma therapy," Pearlman and Saakvitne say, "has been our increased sense of connection with people who suffer everywhere, across time and across cultures."[74] The therapist may see that the "us and them" of the culture is not real and begin "to live as if we are all *us*."[75] In fact, the effect on the therapist is often a sense of presence, acceptance, hope, and wisdom.[76] Providing trauma therapy," say Pearlman and Saakvitne, "deepens our humanity in increasing our awareness of all aspects of life."[77]

If it is true that the more mutual we become the more whole we are, then the psychotherapy of trauma is an excellent example. Trauma therapy is a profound human-moral response. As best it can, it helps to reconstruct human and moral development. In this reconstruction, it is important to notice that trauma, psychotherapy, and a self that is mutual and whole are all together and yet each is seen in very clear relief. It is important to realize that this therapy is at the heart of the fully human

NOTES

1. *Good Will Hunting*, DVD, directed by Gus Van Sant (1997; Burbank, CA: Buena Vista Home Entertainment, 2000).

2. Donald H. Ford and Hugh B. Urban, *Contemporary Models of Psychotherapy: A Comparative Analysis*, 2nd ed. (New York: John Wiley & Sons, 1998), 586.

3. Sidney J. Blatt and Richard Q. Ford, *Therapeutic Change: An Object Relations Perspective* (New York: Plenum, 1994), 267.

4. Ruthellen Josselson, "The Embedded Self: I and Thou Revisited," in *Self, Ego, and Identity: Integrative Approaches*, ed. Daniel K. Lapsley and F. Clark Power (New York: Springer-Verlag, 1988), 91.

5. The British Psychological Society, *Code of Ethics and Conduct: Guidance Published by the Ethics Committee of The British Psychological Society* (Leicester, UK: The British Psychological Society, 2009), 10–24.

6. See Seymour Sarason, *Caring and Compassion in Clinical Practice: Issues in the Selection, Training, and Behavior of Helping Professionals* (Northvale, NJ: Jason Aronson, 1995).

7. See Erik H. Erikson, "Eight Ages of Man," in *Childhood and Society*, 2nd ed. (New York: Norton, 1963), 265. Erikson reports that Freud, when asked "what he thought a normal person should be able to do well," was "reported to have said: Lieben und arbeiten (to love and to work)." Also Erikson sees adult morality as about "intimate relationships and work associations." Erik H. Erikson, *Insight and Responsibility: Lectures on the Ethical Implications of Psychoanalytic Insight* (New York: Norton, 1964), 226.

8. Eugene T. Gendlin, "Experiential Explication and Truth," *Journal of Existentialism* 6 (1965–1966): 131.

9. Kenneth Bragan, *Self and Spirit in the Therapeutic Relationship* (London: Routledge, 1996), 62.

10. John Heron, *Feeling and Personhood: Psychology in another Key* (London: Sage, 1992), 93.

11. See Ton Jorna, "The Longing for Human Contact: Why it is Crucial That We Foster Awareness for the Inner Self in Ourselves and in Others," *Journal of Spirituality in Mental Health* 14 (2012): 23–37.

12. Karen Labacqz and Ronald G. Barton, "Boundaries, Mutuality, and Professional Ethics," in *Boundary Wars: Intimacy and Distance in Healing Relationships,* ed. Katherine H. Ragsdale (Cleveland, OH: Pilgrim, 1996), 103.

13. Peter Marin, *Freedom and Its Discontents: Reflections on Four Decades of American Moral Experience* (South Royalton, VT: Steerforth Press, 1995), 135.

14. Bragan, *Self and Spirit* , 77.

15. Ruth Feldman and Sidney J. Blatt, "Precursors of Relatedness and Self-definition in Mother-infant Interaction," in *Psychoanalytic Perspectives on Developmental Psychology: Empirical Studies of Psychoanalytic Theories*, ed. Jo-

seph M. Masling and Robert F. Bornstein (Washington, DC: American Psychological Association, 1996), 3.

16. Nancy Sherman, “The Moral Perspective and the Psychoanalytic Quest,” *Journal of the American Academy of Psychoanalysis* 23, no. 2 (1995): 223.

17. For an understanding of the role of empathy in psychotherapy, see Arthur C. Bohart and Leslie S. Greenberg, “Empathy and Psychotherapy: An Introductory Overview,” in *Empathy Reconsidered: New Directions in Psychotherapy*, ed. Arthur C. Bohart and Leslie S. Greenberg (Washington, DC: American Psychological Association, 1997), 3–31.

18. Lewis Aron, *A Meeting of Minds: Mutuality in Psychoanalysis* (Hillsdale, NJ: Analytic Press, 1996), 129.

19. William J. Doherty, *Soul Searching: Why Psychotherapy Must Promote Moral Responsibility* (New York: Basic Books, 1995), 37.

20. Alan C. Tjeltveit, *Ethics and Values in Psychotherapy* (New York: Routledge, 1999), 172.

21. Martin Wieser, “From the Eel to the Ego: Psychoanalysis and the Remnants of Freud’s Early Scientific Practice,” *Journal of the History of the Behavioral Sciences* 49, no. 3 (Summer 2013): 271.

22. Ibid.

23. Sigmund Freud, *An Autobiographical Study*, trans. James Strachey (New York: Norton, 1952), 72.

24. Edwin R. Wallace, IV, “Freud as Ethicist,” in *Freud, Appraisals and Reappraisals*, ed. Paul E. Stepansky (Hillsdale, NJ: The Analytic Press, 1985), 87.

25. See for example, Sigmund Freud, *New Introductory Lectures on Psycho-Analysis*, trans. J. H. Sprott (New York: Norton, 1933). See also Sigmund Freud, *The Ego and the Id*, trans. Joan Riviere (New York, Norton, 1962).

26. Freud, *New Introductory Lectures*, 107.

27. Ibid., 105.

28. Ibid., 88.

29. Ibid., 107.

30. Ibid., 108.

31. For an understanding of morality with an ego focus, see E. Mansell Pattison, “Ego Morality: An Emerging Psychotherapeutic Concept,” *The Psychoanalytic Review* 55 (1968): 187–222.

32. John B. Watson, “Psychology as the Behaviorist Views It,” *Psychological Review* 20 (1913): 158. See also John B. Watson, “What Is Behaviorism?” *Harper’s Magazine* 152 (1926): 723–29.

33. Watson, “Psychology as the Behaviorist Views It,” 163.

34. John B. Watson, “The Myth of the Unconscious,” *Harper’s Magazine* 155 (1927): 503.

35. Watson, “Psychology as the Behaviorist Views It,” 163.

36. Ibid. 176.

37. John B. Watson, *Behaviorism* (New Brunswick, NJ: Transaction Publishers, 1998), 3.

38. Ibid., 248.

39. Reflecting this point, Jonathan Krieger, "The Concept of the Object Scale and Cognitive Styles: Measures of Differentiation and Their Relationship to Empathy" (PhD diss., Fordham University, 1988), 20, observes: "According to Piaget, a mature concept of the object requires the perception that the object exist in its own right and that it continues to exist separate and independent of the activity of the perceiving subject."

40. These three hallmarks of preadult morality seem to be a fairly accurate description of how morality is so often characterized in the culture.

41. Mark H. Bickhard, "Ethical Psychotherapy and Psychotherapy as Ethics: A Reply to Perrez," *New Ideas in Psychology* 7, no. 2 (1989): 163.

42. Andras Angyal, *Foundations for a Science of Personality* (New York: Viking, 1972), 31–32.

43. Andras Angyal, "A Theoretical Model for Personality Studies," in *The Self: Explorations in Personal Growth*, ed. Clark Moustakas (New York: Harper Colophon, 1974), 45.

44. Ibid.

45. Ibid., 46.

46. Ibid., 53.

47. Andras Angyal, *Neurosis and Treatment: A Holistic Theory* (New York: Viking, 1965), 77.

48. Andras Angyal, "The Convergence of Psychotherapy and Religion," *Journal of Pastoral Care* 5, no. 4 (1951): 13.

49. Carl R. Rogers, "A Theory of Therapy, Personality, and Interpersonal Relationships as Developed in the Client-Centered Framework," in *Psychology: A Study of a Science*, Vol. III, ed. Sigmund Koch (New York: McGraw-Hill, 1959), 196.

50. Ibid., 198.

51. Ibid.

52. Johanna M. Tiemann, "The Survivor-Analyst as Analysand: An Autobiographical Account of An Analytic Treatment of Complex Trauma," *International Journal of Psychoanalytic Self Psychology* 7 (2012): 538.

53. Carl R. Rogers, "The Interpersonal Relationship: The Core of Guidance," *Harvard Educational Review* 32, no. 4 (Fall 1962): 417.

54. Carl T. Rogers, "Empathic: An Unappreciated Way of Being," in *A Way of Being* (Boston: Houghton Mifflin, 1980), 139.

55. Ibid., 148.

56. Rogers, "Interpersonal Relationship," 417.

57. For an understanding of Rogers's theory in terms of mutuality, see David Murphy, Duncan Cramer, and Stephen Joseph, "Mutuality in Person-Centered Therapy: A New Agenda for Research and Practice," *Person-Centered and Experiential Psychotherapies* 11, no. 2 (June 2012): 109–23.

58. Eugene T. Gendlin, "Focusing," *Psychotherapy: Theory, Research and Practice* 6, no. 1 (Winter 1969): 8.

59. Eugene T. Gendlin, "Experiential Explication and Truth," *Journal of Existentialism* 6 (1965–1966): 135.

60. See Eugene T. Gendlin, John Beebe III, James Cassens, Marjorie Klein, and Mark Oberlander, "Focusing Ability in Psychotherapy, Personality, and Creativity," in *Research in Psychotherapy*, Vol. 3, ed. John M. Schlien (Washington, DC: American Psychological Association, 1967): 217–38. See also Eugene T. Gendlin, "What Comes after Traditional Psychotherapy Research," *American Psychologist* 41, no. 2 (February 1986): 131–36.

61. For a thorough understanding of focusing in psychotherapy, see Eugene T. Gendlin, *Focusing-Oriented Psychotherapy: A Manual of the Experiential Method* (New York: Guilford, 1996). For information about learning focusing, go to The International Focusing Institute, http://www.focusing.org/.

62. See Laurie Anne Pearlman, "Moral Dimensions of Trauma Therapies," in *The Social Psychology of Morality: Exploring the Causes of Good and Evil,* ed. Mario Mikulincer and Phillip Shaver (Washington, DC, American Psychological Association, 2012), 311–26.

63. Judith L. Herman, *Trauma and Recovery* (New York: Basic Books, 1992), 52.

64. Ibid.

65. Ibid., 107. The author observes: "Fragmentation in the inner representations of the self prevents the integration of identity. Fragmentation in the inner representations of others prevents the development of a reliable sense of independence within connection."

66. Laurie Anne Pearlman, "Trauma and the Self: A Theoretical and Clinical Perspective," *Journal of Emotional Abuse* 1, no. 1 (1998): 14. See also Taiwo Afuape, *Power, Resistance and Liberation in Therapy with Survivors of Trauma: To Have Our Hearts Broken* (New York: Routledge, 2011).

67. Ibid., 15.

68. See Laurie Anne Pearlman and Karen W. Saakvitne, *Trauma and the Therapist: Countertransference and Vicarious Traumatization in Psychotherapy with Incest Survivors* (New York: Norton, 1995). See also Carolyn Knight, "Indirect Trauma: Implications for Self-Care, Supervision, the Organization, and the Academic Institution," *The Clinical Supervisor* 32 (2013), 224–43.

69. Marin, *Freedom and Its Discontents*, 120.

70. Brett T. Litz, Nathan Stein, Eileen Delaney, et al., "Moral Injury and Moral Repair in War Veterans: A Preliminary Model and Intervention Strategy," *Clinical Psychology Review* 29, no. 8 (2009): 700.

71. See Jeffrey A. Kottler and Sally V. Hunter, "Clients as Teachers: Reciprocal Influences in Therapy Relationships," *The Australian and New Zealand Journal of Family Therapy* 31, no. 1 (2010): 4–12.

72. Aron, *A Meeting of Minds*, 124.

73. See Herman, "Chapter 10: Reconnection," *Trauma and Recovery*, 196–213.

74. Pearlman and Saakvitne, *Trauma and the Therapist*, 405.

75. Laurie Anne Pearlman, "Moral Dimensions of Trauma Therapies," 324.

76. George E. Vaillant, *Triumphs of Experience: The Men of the Harvard Grant Study* (Cambridge, MA: Harvard University Press, 2012), 155, makes an interesting observation: "It is possible to imagine care without wisdom, but not wisdom without care—and indeed, in adult development, the capacity to care does precede wisdom. Wisdom requires not only concern, but also the appreciation of irony and ambiguity, and enough perspective and dispassion not to take sides." Later, on page 186, Vaillant quotes a seventy-five-year-old man in the human development study. Asked his definition of wisdom, the man said: "Empathy through which one must synthesize both care and justice."

77. Pearlman and Saakvitne, *Trauma and the Therapist*, 406.

Chapter Seven

Spirituality and the Fully Human

In the movie, *Babette's Feast*, on a bleak night on the coast of Denmark, a terrorized woman, Babette Hersant, knocks at the door of Martine and Filippa, aging sisters continuing the ministry founded by their father to an austere, fractious, and dwindling band of believers. Babette presents a letter from a former suitor of Filippa asking for shelter. Her husband and son are killed in a Paris insurrection, and she is fleeing for her life. "I'll work for nothing," she says, and for the next fourteen years she serves them as their live-in maid and cook.

The sisters decide to have a simple dinner honoring the hundredth anniversary of their father's birth. Babette, having won 10,000 francs in a lottery renewed each year by a friend, asks to prepare the dinner and procures the finest ingredients from Paris. A former suitor of Martine, General Löwenhielm, joins the small band for the evening. As the feast is served, the General cannot believe how wonderful it is. The other guests, who have no experience of such exotic fare, look to his example as each course is presented. He compares the feast with an exquisite dinner he once had years before at the *Café Anglais* in Paris.

The effect of the feast is extraordinary. Gradually, all present begin to talk more freely with each other in an honest and caring way, asking pardon for wrongs done over the years and expressing affection for each other. The General gives a wise and self-revealing speech, and among all there is a profound sense of acceptance and communion. After the feast, Babette reveals to the sisters that she was once the head chef at the *Café Anglais*. If the feast initiated an exceptional transformation in all the participants, it was that for Babette as well as she reclaims and honors all the pieces of herself in her incredibly compassionate and generous act.[1]

In this final chapter, we consider spirituality—religious or not—in light of the fully human. We approach spirituality this way not only because by definition spirituality is meant to enliven our humanness but also because understanding the fully human gives us a unique perspective on what spirituality might be. If full humanness is captured by being an integral and mutual self, we could not have a better template for understanding spirituality in its fullness.[2] If being caring and just is how we act when we are fully human, then we can see that mature spirituality is about motivating, encouraging, embodying, and animating the care and justice that allows us to be peace. In other words, whatever else our spirituality is and whatever meaning, or power, or strength, or hope, or conviction our spirituality may give us, if it is mature it is about being whole and mutual, about being caring and just, and about being peace. Mature spirituality is revealed in the three-in-one of the fully human.

As a dimension of the human, spirituality is a process with its own developmental continuum.[3] If the self, as Robert Kegan holds, is "evolving" in how it goes about making meaning of reality, then spirituality—the meaning that helps us to understand our life as a whole—is able to evolve as well.[4] Precisely how spirituality evolves can be, however, quite difficult to predict or control. It may or may not develop with the normal growth of the self. It may or may not develop in light of lifeshaping events such as "deep illness," or exceptional love, or unbearable loss, or profound awakening, or terrible inequity, or devastating trauma.[5] But when mature spirituality appears, it does so as a *wholing* and *connecting* power. Whatever the seeds of spirituality and however unique, complex, and unfathomable our spirituality may be, it affects and furthers the fully human.

This chapter addresses six practical questions. The first question is: If mature spirituality is actually an adult-moral phenomenon, is there a good-enough definition of what it is? The second question is: If seeing spirituality in light of integrity and mutuality captures its fullness, what is spirituality when described in this light? The third question is: What does spirituality tend to look like before it is mature, before it is in harmony with integrity and mutuality and its characteristics? The fourth question is: Can we critique a spirituality that has little or nothing to do with the three-in-one of the fully human? The fifth question is: How does compassion as a common denominator of the world religions relate to mature spirituality? The sixth question is: If mature spirituality and recovery from trauma go together so well, what does that tell us?

As we introduce the notion of spirituality in this chapter, it is important to say at the outset that this notion has many understandings and is often thought of in ways that are very different. Some of us may experience it marginally, if at all, because finding over-all meaning for life is not an issue or does not seem either important or possible. Some of us see spirituality as practices that are simply too strange or esoteric. Some of us see spirituality as unwarranted by anyone who would take science seriously. Some of us see spirituality as a form of ideology, offering us a system of ideas and a set of values that feel forced or foreign. Some of us keep spirituality at arm's length because it is too connected with religious beliefs or mythology. For some of us, spirituality—religious or not—can seem too precious, or too controlled, or too judgmental, or too steeped in shame and guilt, or too marketed, or too hypocritical, or too rooted in denial, illusion, sentimentality, infantilism, irrationality, or irresponsibility. For some of us, spirituality may have been imposed on us as children in ways that were terrorizing, or that made no sense, or that did not leave us free to be ourselves.

Yet, for some of us spirituality may be experienced as something "that can give grounding and strength" to us as human beings.[6] For some of us, our spirituality is lifegiving and world-affirming. For some of us, our spiritual practice may be what supports and motivates us. For some of us, our spirituality may be profoundly meaningful and transformative, perhaps the most important thing in life. Spirituality may be something that nourishes self-empathy and empathy for the other, something that encourages care and justice, something that renews hope and love, something that heals our hearts and our relationships, something that challenges us to go beyond our places of comfort to find a deeper reality, something amazingly generous that reveals who we are and gives us purpose in life.

It is also important to say at the outset that while spirituality may be religious it need not be religious in any way. For some of us, spirituality is a living relationship with God, but for some of us it involves little or no relating to a God at all. While it may be found in any number of the different religions throughout the world, spirituality may be quasi-religious, or vaguely religious, or have no connection at all with religion. We may, for example, be inspired by our sense of being one with all humanity, and that inspiration may be religious, or partly religious, or not religious. We may find meaning and the larger whole in oneness with nature or the cosmos, and that meaning may be religious, or partly religious, or not religious. We may find our life's purpose in genuine compassion for the other's suffering, and again that compassion may be religious, or partly religious, or not religious at all.

Seeing spirituality as part of our humanness may seem strange at first. Often the spiritual is understood—perhaps to honor the sense of the sublime or the divine—as something so profoundly different that it transcends the human rather than expands, or deepens, or heightens it. But sublime, or divine, or neither, spirituality breaks open human imagination, allowing us "to think of things as possibly being so."[7] In its different incarnations, it offers us a kaleidoscopic vision of what full humanness might uniquely come to mean for us. Paradoxically, the fully human returns the favor. Not only does it measure spirituality in its fullness but it also allows us to critique aspects of spirituality in ourselves, in the culture, and in the organized religions of the world that would negate that fullness. For those of us who identify as being spiritual, a powerful dialogue takes place between the fully human and the spiritual—one influencing, testing, challenging, and furthering the other.[8] Paradoxically, our spirituality measures us even as we come to measure it.

A PRACTICAL DEFINITION OF MATURE SPIRITUALITY

The first question: If mature spirituality is actually an adult-moral phenomenon, is there a good-enough definition of what it is? While there is any number of definitions of spirituality that try to convey its nature, still the meaning of the term usually remains somewhat elusive. Three basic things we can say about spirituality if it is alive in us: first, it is something that is personally meaningful; second, it affects the "whole person"; and third, it seems to connect us to a reality greater than the self. With these three things in mind, and taking the experiential and the practical into account, we can offer a definition of spirituality in its fullness:

> Spirituality is a felt power, or energy, or force that animates the body-self as a whole, as a "time-gestalt," offering us overall meaning, purpose, value, or vision for life; drawing us deeper into full humanness; overcoming disconnection, violence, and evil; bringing connection, healing, and wholeness; and inviting us in openness, compassion, love, and peace to be part of a larger whole or oneness that we are drawn to yet do not control.[9]

Six aspects are immediately important to highlight in this definition of adult-moral spirituality:

- This spirituality is of the fully human. As such it is *felt*. No matter how spirituality comes to be described, no matter how transcendent its referent may be, no matter that it may in relation to God, the Goddess, the Sacred, the Higher Power, the cosmos, the universe, the environment, or ultimate reality there is no such thing as beyond-the-human spirituality.[10]
- This spirituality, as fully human, *integrates* and *connects*.[11] It transforms separation and disconnection. It honors integrity and mutuality together. It honors care and justice together. It is of peace and not of violence. It is of felt meaning, of felt union, and of felt healing. It is quite at home in human vulnerability, especially as a response to the "tragic triad" of "pain, death, and guilt."[12]
- This spirituality, as fully human—searched for, found, or welcomed by us—is ours as we can accept and appropriate it. It is, paradoxically, an ideal and a reality, a call and a gift, an attraction and a response, a quest and a commitment. Although it may be in one or more spiritual traditions, it is not forced. Even if we need to probe it, to challenge it, or to test it, ultimately it is ours to freely claim or not.
- This spirituality, as fully human, is felt as a generous mutuality—a sacred space, a welcoming place, a milieu, a presence, a deep resonance, a nurturing community, a common cause, a higher calling, a worthy ideal, an inviting mystery, the Unknown, a loving God.[13] This mutuality is a "more" that makes us more. It is a "beyond" that nourishes inner depth.[14] We may cultivate, or evoke, or enter into this "more" or "beyond," yet paradoxically, although definitely felt it is not ours to control.[15]
- This spirituality, as fully human, animates us, informs us, inspires us, challenges us, guides us, encourages us, and sustains us

in feeling and in depth as embodied selves. It is care and respect for us, even as it calls us to care and respect the other.

- This spirituality, as fully human, is a felt connection or a felt oneness. It is at once *inner* and *relational*. As inclusive, it is about "us" and not about "us vs. them." It is the "within us" and the "other-than-us" together. In some traditions, this felt connection or felt oneness is mystical awareness, or mystical consciousness, or a unity of ultimate meaning.
- This spirituality, as fully human, may be cosmic, or numinous, or mystical, or divine; it may be in "nature, the ancestors, and the community";[16] it may be in a deep and meaningful sense of love, care, justice, and hope.[17] The uniting power of this spirituality weds the ideal with the real. The belonging power of this spirituality allows the responsible self to flourish. The transforming power of this spirituality—at times felt in wonder and awe—penetrates the heart, enlivens the spirit, and allows the soul to come alive.

At this point, we may be saying: "This definition of mature spirituality is not an imagining of what is possible. It is pure projection, pure fantasy."[18] The obvious question is: How can we define adult-moral spirituality as we are doing? Is our definition anything more than wishful thinking or a wonderful idealization? How can we say with any confidence that this spirituality is a felt power, or force, or energy or living truth that animates our lives as a whole, offering us an over-all meaning, purpose, and vision for life? What allows us to say that it is a power drawing us forward in our humanness, bringing healing, wholeness, and relatedness? How do we know that spirituality is a power that overcomes disconnection, violence, and evil, and that invites us in compassion, love, and peace to participate in a larger reality or oneness which we do not control?

The answer to these questions is that—in addition to spirituality actually being experienced this way by some of us—the reason we can define it as we have is that, even though spirituality is a power, or energy, or force that we are not in charge of, it is still inherently human and developmental. Although just how or why spirituality develops can be hard to specify or predict, the structure of mature spirituality is, as it turns out, the same as the structure of an adult and moral self. Even though it is easy to idealize spirituality, our definition of mature spirituality with its highlighted aspects is not an idealization. It is *spirituality as it is able to be experienced in its adult-moral fullness.*[19] It is a spirituality of the fully human, and as such it is a possible spirituality for all of us who are living on the planet.[20]

By understanding the adult-moral self as we have, we can understand spirituality in its *humanness*, in its *wholeness*, in its *connectedness*, and in its *transforming power* in a way that is warranted and that, perhaps, little else allows us to do. Four simple examples may be helpful in indicating some of its contours.

(1) My boundaries are fairly clear. I am a well-known politician, and in my country I have opportunities all the time to engage in good old-fashioned corruption. After all, they say: "Everyone does it in order to survive and get ahead." Even if being caring and just were not a central part of my religion, I know that engaging in corruption is something I cannot do. Neither my wife nor I condone it. Even if no one else ever knew, I would know. Corruption devalues me and it devalues everyone else. I love being involved in the community; nothing is more important than that. Being an intimate part of the day-to-day lives of others is the meaning of my life. Strangely, the more important the community is for me, the more being just is simply not negotiable. Corruption breaks down fairness and trust; it leaves us using each other; it lessens us all.

(2) I am faithful to the recovery program that my drinking and drugging led me to. I am divorced, and now I am working as hard as I can to connect with my adult children and to be the kind of grandmother that their children could love and respect—and they actually do respect and love me. I have been in Alcoholics Anony-

mous for almost twenty years. It has saved my life. Some people say the spirituality of AA is the community. That works for me. At the meetings, after I am there for awhile with the stories and the brokenness, I begin to feel right inside myself and I know who I am. But there's more. I feel the presence of God. Who is God? For me, that's simple. God is a whole that makes everything else whole.

(3) I believe "To err is human, to forgive is divine." I think this is true intuitively because I cannot force myself to forgive the person at work for how he has been trying to ruin my reputation. Yet, my anger is eating me up. My best friend says to me: "You have to let it go, you have to forgive this miserable bastard. If you don't, you won't be able to live with yourself, let alone anyone else." Somehow—and I don't really know how—I decide to forgive him. In my heart, it's the right thing to do. As I let the forgiveness come, my feeling about him changes. The anger is no longer inside. Soon, I am myself again and fit to be with. Curiously, a few weeks after that, our son was caught stealing at school. I asked myself: "Is he still not worthy of my love and respect?" And I realized it was something more, something about me and him together. I thought back to the man at work, and I asked myself a question I didn't know I could: "Was the man who did his best to ruin my reputation still not entitled to care and respect?"

(4) I know I am a caring person. I have been living for almost three years in this refugee camp a few kilometers from the border of Syria. My second daughter is alive; she is with me. But I lost my husband, his father, my two sons, and my other two daughters in the bombing of our village that would not end. I teach at a school for the children, many of them orphans, here at the camp in the desert. We have practically nothing, not even some of the basic things. At first, I was in shock, utterly distraught by the killing, the bombing, the destruction of our village. But now nothing is more important than the care of the children. I am responsible for them. I don't know if there can be a God. But I look into the faces of the

children, and along with the suffering I see goodness and hope. It melts my heart. Their goodness is my goodness; their hope is my hope.

A FULLY HUMAN SPIRITUALITY

The second question: If seeing spirituality in light of integrity and mutuality captures its fullness, what is spirituality when described in this light? Before we look at spirituality on a template of integrity and mutuality and its characteristics to see what it is "of," we consider three reasons why looking at spirituality this way is a clarifying thing to do.

First, in stark contrast to how morality is seen so often in the culture, spirituality is often described in the literature as a phenomenon that is both adult and moral. It seems that when we talk about spirituality it is not at all unusual to talk about it in a way that reflects its fully human character. As Edward Canda says, spirituality is "the wholeness of what it is to be human."[21] Although there is, as we will see, ample evidence of a spirituality that is preadult, there is perhaps an equal amount of evidence to show that spirituality is easily understood as a power that nourishes integrity and mutuality and that is in turn nourished by it. As it turns out, spirituality reflects the fully human with uncanny precision, even as the fully human proves to be an excellent structure for describing how spirituality impacts us.

Second, as we describe spirituality in relation to being an adult-moral self, the nature of this self is confirmed and clarified. Mature spirituality supports and augments our understanding of the fully human in ways that are quite normalizing. For example, mature spirituality takes for granted that the human and the moral are connected, that integrity and mutuality are connected, that mind and body, along with reason and emotion, are connected. It takes for granted, for example, that the separate, stand-alone self of disembodied rationality is a fiction and that human embodied vulnerability is very real. Conversely—and this connection is invaluable—an adult-moral self returns the favor. It supports and clarifies the nature of spirituality in its fullness in ways that are defining, honest, and sorely needed in the culture. In fact, the way of relating between an adult-moral self and adult spirituality can be an amazingly powerful dialectic, one that shows the integrity of both even as it reveals a wonderfully creative mutuality.

Third, seeing that spirituality clearly mirrors the structure of an integral and mutual self with its characteristics lets us also understand that spirituality is about something "more" or "beyond" the otherwise normal fullness of the self. A paradox—and this is what it is—calls for our attention. On the one hand, spirituality fits our human confines and categories; it is clearly and eminently "of" the fully human in its connectedness within and without. On the other hand, spirituality is a "more" or a "beyond" that breaks into the self with inviting meaning and unique connecting that each of us may reach for, find, and enter into. Spirituality is a caring milieu we become part of; we enter into this milieu but we do not create it and we do not control it. Depending on the nature of the "more" or the "beyond," spirituality—as we have seen in the four examples—runs the gamut from being self-and-other enhancing to being self-and-other transformative. In short, while being "of" the fully human, spirituality is also "of" something "beyond" the self, expanding the self and allowing the self to become something "more" by participating in it.[22]

Spirituality Is "of" an Integral and Mutual Self

The structure of an integral and mutual self is a fitting template for seeing what mature spirituality is "of." Spirituality suffuses this adult-moral self with fullness of life. Spirituality, says Barbara Kimes Myers, "surrounds us and is in us and in our relationships."[23] It "encompasses the wholeness of what it is to be human."[24] It "permeates all human activities and experiences rather than being additional to them."[25] In spirituality, "all of reality is active and interactive, a vast web of mutual relationships."[26] Spirituality is about "wholeness and connectedness."[27] It lets us "integrate different parts of 'self' into a harmonious whole," and it allows us to "deepen connection with humankind and the universe."[28] Spirituality, says Edward Canda, lies "*in relationship* with oneself, other people, other beings, the universe, and ultimate reality however understood."[29] Clearly, spirituality—mature spirituality—is "of" wholeness and mutuality seamlessly together.

If mature spirituality is about wholeness and mutuality together, it is essentially understood as a *connectedness.* At heart, it is, says Froma Walsh, about "connectedness with oneself and with all others."[30] It is about "a commitment to choose, as a primary context for understanding and acting, one's relatedness with all that is."[31] But if spirituality is essentially connectedness, it is equally well understood as *oneness*. It is about unifying, about a bringing together, about integration. In different spiritual traditions, this oneness is often described as mystical consciousness, but that need not mean it is esoteric or extremely rare. In mature spirituality, oneness is simply experienced; it is awareness, often deeply felt, that we are part of the whole, that we are intimately connected with the other—be that fellow human beings, the cosmos, the universe, or a God of wholeness and mutuality. In other words, an awareness of oneness is profoundly spiritual, even as it is profoundly human and moral, even as it is the profound connection at the heart of a person of peace.

Spirituality Is "of" the Body-Self

A mature spirituality is "of" the body-self. It is "grounded in the body."[32] It is "a discipline of the whole person."[33] It is the wholeness of the body-self—the "mind" and "body" together—that makes adult spirituality possible. It is in our meaningfully embodied spirituality that we act in care and justice. A "sense of compassionate mutuality with nature," for example, is possible only in and through a body-self.[34] Love, hope, oneness, and peace are only possible when "the mind is centered in the heart." Each of these qualities is mind and body *wholeness*; each of these qualities is organism-environment *relatedness*. Love, hope, oneness, and peace do not know disconnection. Perhaps this is what Ludwig Wittgenstein means when he says: "The human body is the best picture of the human soul."[35]

Spirituality Is "of" the Feeling Self

A mature spirituality is "of" the feeling self. If feeling is "the wholeness of human response to reality," if feeling "celebrates unity in diversity," and if feeling is the emotionally tinged and the rationally grasped, then *it is in feeling where the wholeness and relatedness of spirituality is found.* This spirituality is reason (an idea and an ideal) and emotion (a moving toward, a being drawn, an affirming) together. It "involves subtle feelings, a bodily sense, and not simply a cognitive belief system."[36] It has "emotional and physical aspects of human experience," says Homer Jernigan, "as well as cognitive aspects."[37] It is a *felt connection*, a *felt rightness* that draws us forward as ourselves; it is a *felt relating* in generous mutuality that envelops us. Mature spirituality is inner and relational, felt and meaningful at the same time.

Spirituality Is "of" the Inner Depth

A mature spirituality is "of" the inner depth. The word "spirituality" is, in fact, a "highly useful code word for the depth dimension of human experience."[38] "It is in the depths of the soul," says David Elkins, "that one discovers the essential and universal dimensions of spirituality."[39] As inner and relational at the same time, spirituality involves "a deep sense of wholeness"[40] and "a deep sense of connectedness with others."[41] This wholeness and connectedness may be very comforting and affirming and it may be quite unsettling and challenging. Spirituality that touches the inner depth reminds us "that life cannot be encompassed by rationality but extends into an unknown."[42] A spirituality of depth is another way of speaking about a spirituality of the "more" or the "beyond." It invites "the willingness and the courage to open oneself to mystery."[43] It often "touches us deeply and can transform suffering into learning, enmity into collaboration, and indifference into love."[44]

Spirituality Is "of" Clear Boundaries

A mature spirituality is "of" clear boundaries. It does not violate our boundaries; it does not impose something "outside" on something "inside." In the words of a Zen master, "a borrowed plumage never grows."[45] Rather, a mature spirituality permeates, expands, and transforms our boundaries. It speaks to the whole of our experience; it accepts all the "pieces" of the self; it honors human possibilities; it draws us forward with meaning for life that is uniquely ours. It knows pain, death, and guilt, the "tragic triad" of the human; it responds to our experiences of disconnection, violence, and trauma. "No spirituality," says Kenneth Leech, "can be of lasting value or provide adequate nourishment which has not faced the realities of despair and dereliction."[46] "Much of spiritual life," says Jack Kornfield, "is self-acceptance, maybe all of it. Indeed, in accepting the songs of our life, we can begin to create for ourselves a much deeper and greater identity in which our heart holds all within a space of boundless compassion."[47]

Spirituality Is "of" Intimacy

A mature spirituality is "of" intimacy. Just as there can be no integral adulthood without the experience of intimacy, there also can be no mature spirituality without the feeling and depth of the self relating to the feeling and depth of the other. Intimacy is about empathy, openness, vulnerability, and unconditional love—the four qualities that are the relational power at the heart of any mature spirituality. Empathy, openness, vulnerability, and unconditional love are the heart of compassion, and without a living compassion there is no real spirituality. In spirituality, says James Olthuis, we know with "the eye of love and the ear of compassion."[48] A spirituality that does not embody love and compassion remains sterile and lifeless. "Loveless spirituality," says David Elkins "is an oxymoron and an ontological impossibility."[49]

Often, spirituality and sexuality come together in intimacy. Lynn Rhodes describes one way this can happen:

> Our love is embodied in our feelings, our passion, and our care. If spirituality loses touch with its roots in sexuality, it loses power to form and influence our deepest selves. When sexuality is separated from spiritual development, it becomes something we use to manipulate, control, and harm what we profess to love. When spirituality is separated from our sexuality, it loses the power of personal connection and becomes lifeless—it cannot move us to passionate care for the world.[50]

Spirituality Is "of" Responsibility

Finally, a mature spirituality is "of" a responsible self. Any integral or whole spirituality is its own path, its own call, its own justification, and its own unique response. In responding to our own needs and to the needs of the other, meaning is actually found. In responding to the "more" or the "beyond," our spirituality honors, deepens, and transforms the self as it relates in mutuality to that larger reality. A mature spirituality cannot be justified by something outside of itself—by fear, by force, by promises, by the glowing testament of others. At the same time, a mature spirituality is always a response of empathy, of self-empathy and empathy for the other. It is not just inner, but inner and relational together as it responds—as we can see in the four examples—in an adult and moral way to the needs of the self and the other. Being a responsible self—the fullness of the human in response—is always the measure of the fullness of spirituality.

THE DIFFERENCE BETWEEN PREADULT AND MATURE SPIRITUALITY

The third question: What does spirituality tend to look like before it is mature, before it is in harmony with integrity and mutuality and its characteristics? This spirituality can be thought of as preadult. No matter what it is about and no matter that *in description it may be exactly like mature spirituality*, preadult spirituality is not yet the wholing and connecting power or energy it may later be. Preadult spirituality is normal in human development just as adult spirituality reflects the fullness of that development. In preadult spirituality, the two overarching disconnections we suffer from growing up—between integrity and mutuality and between care and justice—have a definite influence. These disconnections, so prominent in the culture and in psychological and religious writings, visit us in "the subject-object dichotomy," in "us vs. them thinking," and in "the reason-emotion dichotomy."

First, "the subject-object dichotomy" invites us to see spirituality as either something I have as a personal value or something that is an objective fact. For example: "I may feel that my spirituality is unique to me as an individual; it is about the things that inspire me; it is completely subjective; there is nothing objective about it at all." Or: "My spirituality is objectively fact; it is captured in the clear statements of my faith tradition, and it can be proven; who I am and how I feel about it as a subject are not involved." In this dichotomy—so endemic and pervasive in so many of us and in so many cultures—spirituality is either my personal feeling or it is a formal "thing" that I ascribe to. It is an "either-or" and not yet *inner* and *relational*, not yet empathic, and often not yet a wholing and connecting energy.

Second, "us vs. them thinking" easily makes spirituality something "we" are right about and "others" who do not share our spirituality are wrong about. For example, we might say with conviction: "My spirituality is the truth; we have the right beliefs and are on the right path. What others believe, therefore, is wrong. Their spirituality is false." In this thinking—so endemic and pervasive in so many of us and in so many cultures—spirituality presents itself as immediately partisan, making it a locus of contradiction, making it *a deposit of conflicting beliefs* that—quite ironically—has us arguing strenuously and at the mercy of disconnection.

Third, "the reason-emotion dichotomy" easily supports the split in us and in the culture between justice and care. Spiritually defined by reason might allow us to say, for example: "Spirituality consists in holding right beliefs and just principles of action; it is purely rational and not contaminated by our emotions." Spirituality defined by emotion, on the other hand, might allow us to say: "Caring for others is all that is important; all reason does—a reason that prides itself on being disembodied—is that it excuses us from the need to care." In this dichotomy—so endemic and pervasive in so many of us and in so many cultures—the meaning of spirituality is lost in confusing ambiguity, if not internal contradiction, and we are left floating, again ironically, in *a quarrelsome sea of disconnection.*

The question is: What is missing in preadult spirituality? The answer is clear. In preadult spirituality, an integral and mutual self is often missing. The body-self is often missing; feeling that reveals the inner and the relational together may be missing; felt depth may not be seriously touched or evoked; clear boundaries and intimacy may not be in play together; and the responsible self—our fullness of human response—may be engaged little if at all. Not surprisingly, preadult spirituality is as different from adult spirituality as preadult morality is different from adult morality. Although it makes too stark and too clear a contrast to see preadult and adult or mature spirituality in side-by-side columns—after all we are talking about a developmental process along a continuum and not about an either-or contradiction—still some sense of how different these two spiritualities actually function is very important to understand.

A Preadult Spirituality	**An Adult Spirituality**
• a spirituality that is "of" some disconnection	• a spirituality that is "of" connection
• a spirituality of "us vs. them"	• a spirituality of "us"
• a spirituality that is either subjective or objective	• a spirituality that is felt as inner and relational
• a spirituality that is either rational or emotional	• a spirituality that is alive in feeling, in empathy
• a spirituality thought to be "the more" or "the beyond"	• a spirituality felt as "the more" or "the beyond"
• a spirituality that often can be understood in clear concepts	• a spirituality of inner depth often in metaphor
• a spirituality "transcending" the human and the moral	• a spirituality enlivening the human and the moral
• a spirituality of control—something "we have"	• a spirituality of surrender—something that "has us"
• a spirituality that may or may not foster the responsible self	• a spirituality that flows fully from the responsible self
• a spirituality that may or may not serve care and justice	• a spirituality that serves care and justice
• a spirituality that may or may not serve full humanness	• a spirituality that reflects and enhances full humanness

Our spirituality tends to be understood by us according to where we are along the continuum of its development. In its explicit concepts and beliefs, preadult spirituality may be the same as adult spirituality, but because of the way it lives in us, in the culture, and in the world religions it may be disconnected from the human in ways that leave it incomplete, unfinished, and at the mercy of ambiguities, contradictions, and negations. Unfortunately, instead of helping in our quest for full humanness, preadult spirituality—as long as it remains preadult—can be a powerful source of motivation but one that may have little if anything to do with being adult and moral, little if anything to do with being fully human. In fact, as a transformation of preadult spirituality, mature spirituality rightly can be thought of as a kind of paradigm shift.

When we see spirituality as a "thing in itself," as a power or force that radically transcends the human—even when we do this to honor its sublime nature—it is easy to make it whatever we want it to be. In organized religion, for example, when the Higher Power or the Supreme Being is seen as completely other than our humanness, it can easily take on some of our worst characteristics, justifying and abetting all kinds of violence and evil. It is a serious mistake to think that religion—understood as spirituality—is simply about a transcendent reality to be understood or accepted in a subject-object framework. *Mature religion is inner and relational*; it is about the human and the divine together; it is about the self and the other together. Only then is it clearly seen as a spirituality of compassion, a spirituality of care, justice, and peace.

LESS-THAN-HUMAN SPIRITUALITY

The fourth question: Can we critique a spirituality that has little or nothing to do with becoming or being fully human?[51] We are making the case that adult-moral spirituality is the full measure of spirituality—religious or not. Understanding spirituality as intrinsic to the human and to human development lets us make a much-needed and very practical critique. It not only lets us understand the nature of mature spirituality but it also allows us to see that *spirituality cannot be whatever anyone wants to say it is*. We can see that if connection is the hallmark of mature spirituality as well as to some extent of preadult spirituality, it is meant to affect and further the fully human. Any spirituality that cannot do that—if it can be called a spiritually—serves disconnection and ends up supporting dehumanization and violence.

If being adult, being moral, and being spiritual go together, then a less-than-human spirituality, a dehumanizing spirituality, is neither adult nor moral. This criterion is critical for assessing any spirituality that we accept or take part in. Likewise, it is critical for assessing the world religions. Different kinds of inequality, discrimination, or violence—in terms of class, ethnicity, or gender—have no place in religion as authentic spirituality. Unfortunately, in some world religions as lived, inequality, discrimination, or violence are far too prominent. In most of the world religions as lived, the dominance of patriarchal practice—supported either by the founders or by the culture—is longstanding and it is clearly one of the causes of violence against women. The inequality, discrimination, and violence that exists in different world religions as practiced keeps them from embodying compassion, keeps them from being mature spiritualities of peace.

A SPIRITUALITY OF COMPASSION

The fifth question: How does compassion as a common denominator of the world religions relate to mature spirituality? Surprisingly, perhaps, the compassion of the world religions and the compassion of a mature spirituality—a spirituality "of" an integral and mutual self—are clearly in harmony. The compassionate self expressed uniquely in the different religious traditions down through the ages is in essence the compassionate self that lies in the mature spirituality we are describing in this chapter. The spirituality celebrated for centuries as compassion by our ancestors is the same as the spirituality we celebrate today as part of our full humanness. The compassion of the world religions and the compassion of the fully human—seemingly mirror images of each other in practice—are mutually validating, mutually clarifying, and mutually affirming. In other words, *religion and the human—in their fullness—are one in compassion.*

"The practice of compassion," says Karen Armstrong, "is central to every one of the major world religions—but sometimes you would never know it. Instead, religion is associated with violence, intolerance and seems more preoccupied by dogmatic and sexual orthodoxy."[52] Armstrong looks back to the Axial Age, the period in history roughly from 800 to 200 BCE, when "not what you believed but how you behaved" was central to the religious sages.[53] "The only way you could encounter what they called 'God,' 'Nirvana,' 'Brahman,' or the 'Way' was to live a compassionate life."[54] "Indeed," she says with wonderful clarity, "religion *was* compassion."[55] In all the major world religions—we can include Zoroastrianism, Confucianism, Taoism, Jainism, Sikhism, Hinduism, Buddhism, Shinto, Judaism, Christianity, Islam, and Baha'i—compassion is a common denominator. In these religions, compassion is the way of being and relating that best characterizes them as a whole.[56]

In the different world religions, we find that compassion is our response to human weakness, vulnerability, and suffering. Compassion extends to all living things. Compassion is concern for the other's pain and misery. Compassion is empathy, altruism, and unconditional love. Compassion is neither self-centered nor self-concerned and often involves paying a price. Compassion is not only nonviolent but is a conscious antidote to violence. Compassion goes hand in hand with wisdom as the pinnacle of humanness. Compassion binds us together in a way that is inescapably necessary. Compassion is the Golden Rule in action. Compassion is a name for God or it *is* God. And, of course, compassion is the way of peace.

Unfortunately, however, in the world religions as practiced there are two quite different strands. There is the mature religious strand we are describing—championed by any number of sages, saints, and scholars in each tradition—in which religion clearly *is* compassion. But there is also an immature religious strand, a preadult strand—championed by any number of religious leaders and followers in each tradition—that sees religion primarily in terms of describing the right teachings, beliefs, and rituals. In this strand, religion is more about orthodoxy or right belief than about orthopraxy or the practice of compassion. "Centuries of institutional, political, and intellectual development," says Armstrong, "have tended to obscure the importance of compassion in religion. All too often the religion that dominates the public discourse seems to express an institutional egoism: *my faith is better than yours!*"[57]

In the adult-moral self, we find that compassion is the traditional way of describing the care, justice, and empathy that make peace possible. Attending to the needs, rights, and freedoms of the self and the other for wholeness *is* compassion. Respect, fairness, and equity in caring for the needs, rights, and freedoms of the self and the other for wholeness *is* compassion. Compassion is especially concerned for human suffering, for those whose lack of the needed care and justice is causing great pain or serious harm, be that another person, oneself, families, institutions, animals, the environment, or the planet. Compassion is, of course, only possible in empathy and in peace. In fact, empathy and peace are perhaps the synonyms we use the most to describe compassion.

In religion and in the self, compassion is connection within and without. Compassion leads to peace even as it is a guarantee of peace. Unquestionably, the compassion that is a common denominator of the world religions is also the compassion of mature spirituality, a spirituality "of" the fully human. "Compassion has always been," as Elkins says, "the hallmark of authentic spirituality and the highest teaching of religion."[58]

SPIRITUALITY AND TRAUMA

The sixth question: If mature spirituality and recovery from trauma go together so well, what does that tell us? In responding to this question, we look first at our definition of mature spirituality and at a few examples from the literature on recovery in order to see their commonalities. As we do this, some of the central notions of this book come together.

(1) Mature spirituality and recovery from trauma are both about the *vulnerability* and *suffering* of the self that cry out for *transformation.*

Mature spirituality is at home in human vulnerability, especially as a response to the "tragic triad" of "pain, death, and guilt."[59] It animates us, informs us, inspires us, challenges us, guides us, encourages us, and sustains us. The transforming power of this spirituality—at times felt in wonder and awe—penetrates the heart, enlivens the spirit, and lets the soul come alive.

In *The Way of the Wound: A Spirituality of Trauma and Transformation*, Robert Grant finds that trauma reveals us as "vulnerable and incapable of protecting ourselves."[60] But he also finds that trauma is a call, an opening for a "reconstitution of the self to a new and higher order."[61] While the ego may want to return to the safety of how things were and to a God of safety, trauma's losses may "touch one's inner being" and be experienced as an invitation to the self to experience "life's deeper mysteries" and "the Spirit."[62] "It is easy in the contemporary world to avoid both the call of the Spirit and the truth contained in one's wounds."[63] The suffering of trauma, however, is "a call to live in accord with the Spirit's will and not exclusively one's own."[64] In other words, the way of the wound is an opening to a spirituality of transformation.

In *Man's Search for Meaning*, Viktor Frankl, a prisoner at Auschwitz, says: "In spite of all the physical and mental primitiveness of the life in a concentration camp, it was possible for spiritual life to deepen."[65] His analysis of what makes us both human and spiritual, reveals three things: (1) *freedom* ("I make my own choices"); (2) *responsibility* ("I am responsible for my life"); and flowing from these two, a *will-to-meaning* ("I alone can determine the meaning of my life").[66] While in life there are different meanings I create and experience, the most important kind of meaning—the meaning in which I face human vulnerability and suffering—is attitudinal meaning. It is in the attitude I take to the "tragic triad" of pain, death, and guilt that meaning is often most at stake. When searched for and found, this meaning can transform the whole of one's life.[67]

(2) Mature spirituality and recovery from trauma are both about the *connection* and *wholeness* of the self that reveal *transformation.*

Mature spirituality draws us deeper into full humanness. It overcomes disconnection, violence, and evil. It brings connection, healing, and wholeness. It invites us in openness, trust, empathy and compassion, and peace to be part of a larger whole or oneness that we are drawn to yet do not control.

Judith Herman, in her classic *Trauma and Recovery*, speaks to the central role of connection in recovery: "A mature sense of connection is the foundation of personality development. When this connection is shattered, the traumatized person loses her basic sense of self."[68] If the "core experiences of psychological trauma are disempowerment and disconnection from others," then recovery "is based upon the empowerment of the survivor and the creation of new connections."[69] In the "renewed connections with other people, the survivor re-creates the psychological faculties that were damaged or deformed by the traumatic experience."[70]

In his *Trauma and the Soul: A Psycho-Spiritual Approach to Human Development and Its Interruption*, Donald Kalsched has a chapter on "Wholeness and Anti-Wholeness Defenses."[71] As he begins this chapter, Kalsched says that trauma can leave us with defenses, with "deforming mirrors" that give us with a sense of ourselves as "less than, and different from, the real person we are."[72] Then, he says: "To glimpse the possibility of our wholeness the deforming mirrors created by these defenses must be transformed so that we can 'see through' the dissociative barriers to our authentic selfhood—to the soul-life that wants to unfold its pattern of wholeness in our developing lives."[73] The task of recovery in *Trauma and the Soul* is finding wholeness.

One thing that the going together of mature spirituality and trauma recovery tell us is that they reflect each other: the meaning of the former invites and gives space in the human for the meaning of the latter. In preadult spirituality the intimate connection with trauma recovery may be much harder to see or may not be present at all. But a mature spirituality, a spirituality of connection and wholeness—religious or not—that provides overall meaning, purpose, value, or vision for life, could not be more congruent with the needs of a person recovering from trauma, a person who is often desperate to find connection and wholeness.

A second thing that the going together of mature spirituality and trauma recovery tells us is that they are both about a search for a meaning in life that is profound. As we have seen, trauma can devastate the inner depth; it can wipe out the connection between the inner and the relational; it can leave us "with the spirit gone, the heart broken, and the soul departed." A mature spirituality—religious or not—may invite us to a "more" or a "beyond" that offers us a sacred space, a welcoming place, a milieu, a presence, a deep resonance, a nurturing community, a common cause, a worthy ideal, an inviting mystery, the Unknown, a loving God. The "more" or the "beyond" of this mutuality is a transforming space that can nourish inner depth, that can penetrate the heart, enliven the spirit, and allow the soul to come alive again.

A third thing that the going together of mature spirituality and trauma recovery tells us is that they both involve a spirituality of compassion. This spirituality—religious or not—is a way of life always in service of connection and wholeness and always concerned with vulnerability, suffering, and transformation. A spirituality of compassion, as a generous mutuality offering us meaning, purpose, and vision for life, can, of course, greatly enhance all aspects of life, but it often seems especially significant when our full humanness is most severely tested.

In recovering from trauma—in fact, in recovering from vulnerability and suffering of any kind—the compassion that is available in the world's religions can be extremely helpful. There is an acceptance and wisdom in the experience of the divine and in the believing community that provides a place of safety and the promise of personal transformation. The presence of God, or the Higher Power, or the Prevailing Wisdom—however found, experienced, or articulated—is often quite restorative of the meaning of life, especially over time. In other words, compassion can be found as palpable and nurturing in a religious community steeped in care and respect.[74]

A spirituality of compassion may also be found in ways somewhat religious or not religious at all. Some cultures are so cohesive that they almost naturally embody the "more" or the "beyond." The continuity we may have with those who have gone before us can be felt as compassion. Sensing oneness with the universe, feeling a connection with all living things, appreciating the interconnectedness and order in the cosmos, and experiencing unconditional love can be experiences of compassion. In the care and respect of our families, in deep personal sharing, in personal therapy, in rap-groups, in Zen sitting, in witnessing the courage of others, in the random kindness we or others show, in the laughter of young children—in all of these things the "more" or the "beyond" may be felt breaking in. Compassion can be found in caring for animals, being with pets, and tending a garden. Fortunately, the caring and respect of only a few others or of a simple experience can be felt as the compassion of the world.

Witnessing the stars at night, climbing in the mountains in the late afternoon, resting beside a powerful waterfall, basking in a sunlit meadow of freshly mown hay, standing safely on a beach after a terrible storm, viewing incredibly honest or exquisite art, listening to inspiring music—these and other unique experiences of oneness may be felt by us as the compassion of nature or culture. With its "more" or "beyond," a spirituality of compassion—which we may find ourselves naturally drawn to—heals and furthers the fully human with its added measure of wholing and connecting, of caring and respect, of empathy and peace.

Mature spirituality gives us hope for our humanness. It responds to violence and trauma and to vulnerability and suffering in a way that nothing else in the human can—in a way that is generous, caring and full of respect, in a way of nonviolence that is transforming and the advent of peace.

NOTES

1. *Babette's Feast*, DVD, directed by Gabriel Axel (1987; Irvington, NY: The Criterion Collection, 2013).

2. It is interesting to note in relation to spiritual development that Polly Young-Eisendrath and Melvin Miller, eds., *The Psychology of Mature Spirituality: Integrity, Wisdom, Transcendence* (London: Routledge, 2000), 3, state: "*Integrity*—referring as it does to both an ethical commitment and an integration of diverse states—was the easiest and the first quality that came to mind as 'mature spirituality.'" See also John Beebe, "The Place of Integrity in Spirituality," in *The Psychology of Mature Spirituality: Integrity, Wisdom, Transcendence*, ed. Polly Young-Eisendrath and Melvin Miller, eds. (London: Routledge, 2000), 11–20.

3. David N. Elkins, "A Humanistic Approach to Spiritually Oriented Psychotherapy," in *Spiritually Oriented Psychotherapy*, ed. Len Sperry and Edward P. Shafranske (Washington, DC: American Psychological Association, 2005), 138.

4. See Robert Kegan, *The Evolving Self: Problem and Process in Human Development* (Cambridge, MA: Harvard University Press, 1982).

5. See Arthur W. Frank, "Just Listening: Narrative and Deep Illness," *Families, Systems and Health* 16, no. 3 (1998): 197, where he says: "illness is 'deep' when perceived as lasting, as affecting virtually all life choices and decisions, and as altering identity."

6. It can be noted that Elkins, "A Humanistic Approach," 131, affirms that "human personality and spirituality exist on the same continuum."

7. Kieran Egan, *Imagination in Teaching and Learning* (Chicago: University of Chicago Press, 1992), 3.

8. William James, who focused on spirituality much as we understand it today in *The Varieties of Religious Experience* (Cambridge, MA: Harvard University Press, 1985), 210, says: "the best fruits of religious experience are the best things that history has to show." James was deeply interested in understanding how the human and the spiritual go together.

9. The idea of the self as a "time-gestalt," a living, ongoing whole that composes itself in and through time, comes from Andras Angyal, "Personality as a Time Gestalt," in *Neurosis and Treatment: A Holistic Theory*, Eugenia Hanfmann and Richard M. Jones, eds. (New York: Viking, 1965), 62–68.

10. David N. Elkins, L. James Hedstrom, Lori L. Hughes, J. Andrew Leaf, and Cheryl Saunders, "Toward a Humanistic-Phenomenological Spirituality: Definition, Description, and Measurement," *Journal of Humanistic Psychology* 28, no. 4 (Fall 1988): 8, state: "Spirituality is a human phenomenon and exists, at least potentially, in all persons."

11. Kenneth Bragan, *Self and Spirit in the Therapeutic Relationship* (London: Routledge, 1996), 9, sees that the very nature of spirituality is to respond to our "yearning for authentic being and wholeness." Jane Bone, "Exploring Trauma, Loss and Healing: Spirituality, *Te Whāriki* and Early Childhood Education," *International Journal of Children's Spirituality* 13, no. 3 (August 2008): 266, sees spirituality as "a means of connecting people to each other, to all living things, to nature and the universe."

12. Viktor E. Frankl, *The Will to Meaning: Foundations and Applications of Logotherapy* (New York: New American Library, 1969), ix.

13. David R. Brown, Jamie S. Carney, Mark S. Parrish, and John L. Klem, "Assessing Spirituality: The Relationship between Spirituality and Mental Health," *Journal of Spirituality and Mental Health* 15 (2013): 110, define spirituality as "a sense of connectedness to a higher power."

14. In speaking of "generous mutuality" as a "more" or a "beyond," we are describing what is often called "transcendence." Young-Eisendrath and Miller, *The Psychology of Mature Spirituality*, 4, define transcendence as "extending or expanding the limits of our ordinary consciousness or experience in ways that connect us with a symbolic or phenomenal reality beyond the ordinary."

15. Pamela J. Birrell and Jennifer J. Freyd, "Betrayal Trauma: Relational Models of Harm and Healing," *Journal of Trauma Practice* 5, no. 1 (2006): 49–63.

16. Evangeline A. Wheeler, Lena M. Ampadu, and Ester Wangari, " Lifespan Development Revisited: African-Centered Spirituality throughout the Life Cycle," *Journal of Adult Development* 9, no. 1 (January 2002): 73.

17. The "b-values" that Abraham Maslow finds in persons who are self-actualizing are often experienced as spiritual values. See Abraham H. Maslow, *The Farther Reaches of Human Nature* (New York: Viking, 1972), 126–48.

18. Sharon Daloz Parks, *Big Questions, Worthy Dreams* (San Francisco: Jossey-Bass, 2000), 106, says that "the task of the imagination, and particularly of the religious imagination, is *to compose the real*."

19. In relation to integrated spirituality, Kenneth Pargament, *Spiritually Integrated Psychotherapy: Understanding and Addressing the Sacred* (New York: Guilford Press, 2007), 136, observes: "At its best, spirituality is defined by pathways that are broad and deep, responsive to life's situations, nurtured by the larger social context, capable of flexibility and continuity, and oriented toward a sacred destination that is large enough to encompass the full range of human potential and luminous enough to provide the individual with a powerful guiding vision."

20. For models of mature spiritual development that have some resonance with what is presented here, see Jared D. Kass and Susan Lennox, "Emerging Models of Spiritual Development: A Foundation for Mature, Moral, and Health-Promoting Behavior," in *Judeo-Christian Perspectives on Psychology: Human Nature, Motivation, and Change*, ed. William R. Miller and Harold D. Delaney (Washington, DC: American Psychological Association, 2005), 185–204.

21. Edward R. Canda, "Spirituality, Religious Diversity, and Social Work Practice," *Social Casework* 69, 4 (1988): 243.

22. The "more" or the "beyond" of spirituality allows the different world religions to be seen as spiritual, and it also allows to see spirituality as not about the parts of our humanness we are most proud of but about *connection*, about a larger whole or reality we are involved in.

23. Barbara K. Myers, *Young Children and Spirituality* (London: Routledge, 1997), 62.

24. Canda, "Spirituality, Religious Diversity," 245.

25. Wheeler et al., "Lifespan Development Revisited," 77.

26. Parker Palmer, *The Active Life: A Spirituality of Work, Creativity, and Caring* (San Francisco: Jossey-Bass, 1990), 52.

27. Eugene W. Kelly, Jr., *Spirituality and Religion in Counseling and Psychotherapy: Diversity in Theory and Practice* (Alexandria, VA: American Counseling Association, 1995), 89. Philip Sheldrake, *Spirituality: A Guide for the Perplexed* (London: Bloomsbury, 2014), 8, says that spirituality "is best understood not so much as one element among many in human existence but as the integrating factor—treating 'life-as-a-whole.'"

28. Mo Y. Lee, Siu-man Ng, Pamela P. Leung, Cecilia L. Chan, *Integrative Body-Mind-Spirit Social Work: An Empirically Based Approach to Assessment and Treatment* (New York: Oxford University Press, 2009), 173.

29. Edward L. Canda and Leola D. Furman, *Spiritual Diversity in Social Work Practice: The Heart of Helping*, 2nd ed. (New York: Oxford University Press, 2010), 75.

30. Froma Walsh, "Spirituality, Healing and Resilience," in *Re-Visioning Family Therapy: Race, Culture, and Gender in Clinical Practice*, 2nd ed., ed. Monica McGoldrick and Kenneth V. Hardy (New York: Guilford, 2008), 63.

31. James L. Griffith and Melissa E. Griffith, *Encountering the Sacred in Psychotherapy: How to Talk with People about Their Spiritual Lives* (New York: Guilford, 2002), 15.

32. David N. Elkins, *Beyond Religion: A Personal Program for Building a Spiritual Life outside the Walls of Traditional Religion* (Wheaton, IL: Quest Books, 1998), 142.

33. Constance Leean, "Spiritual and Psychological Life Cycle Tapestry," *Religious Education* 83, no. 1 (Winter 1988): 49.

34. Drew Leder, *The Absent Body* (Chicago: University of Chicago Press, 1990), 164.

35. Ludwig Wittgenstein, *Philosophical Investigations*, trans. G. E. M. Anscombe (Oxford: Blackwell, 1968), 178.

36. Elfie Hinterkopf, *Integrating Spirituality in Counseling: A Manuel for Using the Experiential Focusing Method* (Alexandria, VA: American Counseling Association, 1998), 11.

37. Homer L. Jernigan, "Spirituality in Older Adults: A Cross-Cultural and Interfaith Perspective," *Pastoral Psychology* 49 (2001): 417.

38. William H. Becker, "Spiritual Struggle in Contemporary America," *Theology Today*, 51 (July 1994): 257.

39. Elkins, *Beyond Religion*, 33.

40. Kelly, Jr., *Spirituality and Religion*, 89.

41. Ibid., 92.

42. Bragan, *Self and Spirit in the Therapeutic Relationship*, 11.

43. Gerald G. May, *Will and Spirit: A Contemplative Psychology* (San Francisco: Harper & Row, 1982), 32.

44. Christopher Faiver, et al., *Explorations in Counseling and Spirituality: Philosophical, Practical, and Personal Reflections* (Belmont, CA: Brooks/Cole, 2001), 1.

45. D. T. Suzuki, *Zen Buddhism* (New York: Doubleday, 1956), 97.

46. Kenneth Leech, *Experiencing God: Theology as Spirituality* (San Francisco, Harper & Row, 1985), 193.

47. Jack Kornfield, *A Path with Heart: A Guide through the Perils and Promises of Spiritual Life* (New York: Bantam, 1993) 47–48.

48. James H. Olthuis, "Introduction: Love/Knowledge: Sojourning with Others, Meeting with Differences," in *Knowing Other-wise: Philosophy at the Threshold of Spirituality,* ed. James H. Olthuis (New York: Fordham University Press, 1997), 7.

49. Elkins, *Beyond Religion*, 33.

50. Lynn Rhodes, *Co-Creating: A Feminist Vision of Ministry* (Philadelphia: Westminster, 1987), 64–65.

51. In raising this question we are making a distinction between humanizing and dehumanizing spirituality, or between positive and negative spirituality, or between authentic and inauthentic spirituality, or between healthy and unhealthy spirituality.

52. Karen Armstrong, "Do unto Others," https://www.theguardian.com/commentisfree/2008/nov/14/religion.

53. Karen Armstrong, Introduction to *The Great Transformation: The Beginning of Our Religious Traditions* (New York: Alfred Knopf, 2006), xiii.

54. Ibid.

55. Ibid.

56. Michael Cavanagh, "Rediscovering Compassion," *Journal of Religion and Health* 34, no. 4 (Winter 1995): 320, observes: "Compassion is such an intricate part of most religions that one can reasonably state that to be religious and to be compassionate should be synonymous, although one should not have to be religious to be compassionate." See James E. Gilman, "Whose God? Which Religion? Compassion as the Heart of Interreligious Cooperation," *Journal of Ecumenical Studies* 40, no. 3 (Summer 2003): 267–95.

57. Armstrong, *The Great Transformation*, 393.

58. Elkins, *Beyond Religion*, 33.

59. Frankl, *Will to Meaning*, ix.

60. Robert Grant, *The Way of the Wound: A Spirituality of Trauma and Transformation* (Oakland: CA: Robert Grant, 1996), 11.

61. Ibid., 55.

62. Ibid., 56.

63. Ibid., 233.

64. Ibid., 130.

65. Viktor E. Frankl, *Man's Search for Meaning: An Introduction to Logotherapy* (New York: Pocket Books, 1963), 56.

66. Viktor Frankl, "Dynamics, Existence, and Values," *Journal of Existential Psychiatry* 2 (1961): 9. See also Frankl, *Will to Meaning.*

67. Viktor Frankl, "The Philosophical Foundations of Logotherapy" in *Phenomenology: Pure and Applied*, ed. Erwin Straus (Pittsburgh, PA: Duquesne University Press, 1964), 56.

68. Judith L. Herman, *Trauma and Recovery* (New York: Basic Books, 1992), 33.

69. Ibid., 133.

70. Ibid.

71. Donald Kalsched, *Trauma and the Soul: A Psycho-Spiritual Approach to Human Development and Its Interruption* (New York: Routledge, 2013), 159–86.

72. Ibid., 159.

73. Ibid.

74. See Barbara Glasson, *A Spirituality of Survival: Enabling a Response to Trauma and Abuse* (London: Continuum, 2009). See also Teresa Rhodes McGee, *Transforming Trauma: A Path toward Wholeness* (Maryknoll, NY: Orbis, 2005).

Conclusion

THE HUMAN GOING FORWARD

Knowing how important connection is for being fully human, there are things to remember that are helpful for us going forward.

First, we cannot do without a mosaic of the fully human. We need to see an integral and mutual self, a caring and just self, and a peaceful self as the three-in-one of the fully human. We need to allow the separate, static, non-developing, stand-alone, particle, self—the enabler of subject-object thinking and still the norm in the culture and in academia—to find the dustbin of history. We need to accept that there are no overarching disconnections in the fully human. We need to know, for example, there is no "us" and "them." There is only connection. There is only "us."

Second, we need to address the overarching disconnections that keep us from taking human development seriously: the disconnection between the human and the moral, the disconnection between subject and object, the disconnection between self and other, the disconnection between integrity and mutuality, the disconnection between clear boundaries and intimacy, the disconnection between the inner and the relational, the disconnection between care and justice, the disconnection between mind and body, the disconnection between reason and emotion. In all of this, we always need to keep in mind the connection to be found between disconnection and violence.

Third, we need to acknowledge and embrace empathy—feeling as the emotionally tinged and the rationally grasped—as the human ability most intrinsic to human connection, to being fully human, to being adult and moral, to being integral and mutual, to being caring and just, and to being peace. We need to remember that empathy does not mean *agreeing* with the self or the other; it means being with *the inner* of the self or the other. We need creative ways to teach empathy and to further its practice. We need to know from the inside that to be human and to be empathic go together.

Fourth, we need to see that there is nothing more humanly powerful—and nothing more indispensable—than the care and justice that are the practice of integrity and mutuality flowing from empathy. We need to see that care and justice together leads to the fully human and comes from the fully human. We need to honor care and justice, recognizing that in its fullness it is the only way we have as human beings to foster, to become, to be, and to live in peace.

Fifth, we need to celebrate peace—an "an at-oneness within and without"—as the pinnacle of human development in action. We need to see that peace is who we are as fully human. We need to understand peace not as an external requirement but as our ultimate human need and our crowning human achievement. We also need to keep in mind that peace is an ongoing dialectic with violence that defines who we are. We need to keep a clear, honest, and steady focus on violence and peace, understanding that they remain the two major trajectories of human development.

Sixth, if education is our most foundational human endeavor, we need to approach it at every level through a pedagogy of connection that addresses three main goals: first, to help the self to become integral and mutual, caring and just, and at peace within and without; second, to monitor and challenge as a critical pedagogy the disconnection, the violence, and the evil that we find in ourselves and in the culture; third, to always see the learner as a whole self in living connection with whatever surfaces as other in the world. We need to see education as learning to attend to and respect the needs, rights, and freedoms of the self and the other.

Seventh, we need to see psychotherapy—and all the helping professions—as a dedicated and informed process of connection or reconnection allowing us to become humanly and morally adult, allowing us to own all of our "pieces" and to relate mutuality to the other. We need to see psychotherapy as a skillful exercise of care and justice that lets the client's experience become the basis on which values are chosen, decisions are made, the self is accepted, relationships are lived, and the world is understood. We need to see psychotherapy—and the other helping professions—as directly in service of human development and therefore as directly in service of a morality of depth.

Eighth, we need to realize that the culture and many religious institutions are often hopelessly stuck in preadult morality. In fact, they often seem unaware that there even is such a thing as a morality of depth. We need to recognize that this preadult morality—so normalized and taken-for-granted yet so truncated, incomplete, and impoverished—is a creation of the particle self and the result of subject-object thinking. We need to understand that this morality is not nearly human enough, not nearly personal enough, not nearly mature enough, not nearly intimate enough, not nearly moral enough, not nearly connecting enough. Most importantly, we need to understand that this preadult morality—structurally static and easily self-justifying—is *not nearly adequate enough to bring us and the culture into the future.*

Ninth, we need to see that preadult and mature spirituality lie on a developmental continuum. We need to see adult or mature spirituality as a profoundly human power of connection, a life-enhancing and often transformative power that allows us to deepen our integrity and mutuality, to enliven our care and justice, to enrich and vitalize all of our meaningful ventures, and especially to find peace, even if peace must be grasped in the face of vulnerability and violence.

Tenth, we need to think of the three-in-one of the fully human as a kind of paradigm shift—in how we understand human nature, in how we understand the body, in how we understand rationality, in how we understand knowing, in how we understand morality, in how we understand care, in how we understand justice, in how we understand peace, in how we understand education, in how we understand psychotherapy, and in how we understand spirituality.

This paradigm shift takes human development seriously, when otherwise we might not know how important that is. It directly challenges the inadequacy of subject-object thinking, when otherwise we might not even suspect that the inner and relational go together. It takes the disconnections and partial pictures of the human seriously, when otherwise the culture might have the last word. It takes care and justice seriously, when otherwise they might not recognize themselves or speak to each other. It takes violence seriously, when otherwise we might not acknowledge it as inherently human. It takes peace seriously, when otherwise we might not be able to see it as defining our innermost and as the one thing that we and the world must rely on going forward.

Appendix

PRACTICAL QUESTIONS FOR REFLECTION AND DIALOGUE

Chapter 1

1. If being an integral and mutual self captures the meaning of being adult and moral, why is this understanding of the fully human so countercultural? Why is it so hard to put the human and the moral together? Do challenges and difficulties in embodying integrity and mutuality mean that these two notions are not correlative? Do I know anyone I consider to be imperfect but fully human?
2. Is there any experience in my own life that lets me believe that owning all my own pieces and relating to the other as other are intimately connected? What tends to foster the development of integrity and mutuality? What evidence do I have—humanly and morally—that integrity and mutuality do not exist in disconnection? What stands out for me in Palmer's, Erikson's, and Noam's framing of integrity? What stands out for me in Jordan's, Nothwehr's, and Oliver's framing of mutuality?

3. Does it make sense that the stand-alone, one-dimensional, nondeveloping particle self, described as "autonomy," or "freedom," or "rationality," skews our human nature? Does it lead to a skewed morality? Am I a mutual interaction *before* I am an individual self? How do I understand why a stand-alone self is held so tenaciously in the culture?
4. Are there other questions about integrity and mutuality that are important to raise and discuss?

Chapter 2

1. Is empathy at the heart of the human? What do I find when I reflect on my experience of empathy growing up? If feeling is the language of the body-self that captures the *inner* and the *relational* together, what does this mean in how I relate to others and to what is meant by objective morality? What is the price to be paid by functioning within the mind-body and subject-object dichotomies? What does "objective morality" actually mean to me?
2. As I look at the columns that compare a superego morality with a morality of depth, what questions come to mind about my own development? What questions come to mind about how adult development and moral development are considered in the culture? If we automatically understand morality in the culture as superego morality, what would explain that? What would allow that understanding to be challenged or changed?
3. If being adult and moral is not primarily about external rules and norms, is that ultimately a problem? How are boundaries and intimacy inherent in how I see morality? Do I find it hard to talk about responsibility? Does the culture find it hard to talk about responsibility? Is it strange to see being responsible and being fully human together? How do the first five characteristics influence the meaning of responsibility? Is it

surprising to see a mosaic of the "whole person" that is so countercultural?

4. Are there other questions about the six characteristics that are important to raise and discuss?

Chapter 3

1. How important do I find the critique of care and justice in the culture? Are the mature definitions of care and justice comprehensive enough? Are there any ways I could suggest for introducing these mature understandings into the culture? Do I have good reasons to appreciate a mature understanding of care and justice and to appreciate their mutuality?
2. As mature and connected, are care and justice how we act when we are fully human? What examples of this connection do I find in my own experience? Is it sexist to see care as feminine and justice as masculine? Do I find that being caring and acting justly—together as one—leads to and flows from the fully human?
3. What do I make of the belief that "justice is punishment?" If I were in charge of a prison, what would be some of my major concerns? Is it possible for care and justice to work together in a prison setting? If I separate care and justice, what are the consequences?
4. Are there other questions that about care and justice that are important to raise and discuss?

Chapter 4

1. Is it accurate to think of violence and peace not just as intimately human but also as the two major trajectories of human development? If disconnection is the right hand of violence, what does that say about the politics of separation in different societies? Is shame as powerful as it is described in this chap-

ter? Are there ways that could make it easier to talk about shame, or disconnection, or violence? If violence and peace were not seen as abstractions, would it be easier to talk about them together?

2. Do I find it true that there is nothing more powerful in the human than care and justice, that there is nothing more powerfully human than peace? Is it helpful to see peace not just as personal but also as the pinnacle of human development? What usually comes to mind for me when I find myself yearning for peace? What is my normal response to violence? Do I find I am becoming a violent person or becoming a person of peace?
3. Is seeing peace as distributive care and justice a good basic definition? Does restorative care and justice seem to be a viable way of working with victims and perpetrators of crime? Have I ever been in a situation in which nonviolence was a response? What do I personally think about being a nonviolent person? Are empathy and peace necessarily intertwined?
4. Are there other questions about violence and peace that are important to raise and discuss?

Chapter 5

1. How much sense does it make to see education as the human and the moral together? How do I feel about seeing integrity and mutuality, care and justice, and peace as the foundation and ultimate goal of education? If education is about the *inner* and the *relational* together, what ways could I find for making that real in whatever educating I might do?
2. If I am an educator, what specific strategies are most natural for me in providing a pedagogy of connection? If I am not an educator, what elements of my own education come to mind as I contemplate the unique place of care and justice in educa-

tion? If I were going to teach empathy, or care and justice, or peace, how would I go about preparing to do it?

3. What strikes me in the extraordinary work of Michalinos Zembylas and H. B. Danesh, especially as related to empathy and connection? What aspects of the thinking of Nel Noddings, Jerry Starratt, Paulo Freire, or Parker Palmer especially caught my attention? In what ways, did any of these exceptional educators remind me of some of my own teachers or of how I would like to be as a teacher?
4. Are there other questions about education and the fully human that are important to raise and discuss?

Chapter 6

1. Does it make sense to me to consider psychotherapy in an adult-moral lens, to see it from a perspective of integrity and mutuality, a perspective of care and justice, a perspective of peace? In what ways is it helpful to see psychotherapy as developmental, as inherently human and inherently moral? What is my personal attitude toward psychotherapy? What do I take away from the thinking of Sigmund Freud and J. B. Watson?
2. As I look at the columns that compare a superego morality with a morality of depth, what does it say to me to see psychotherapy as one way we move from the first column to the second? Does the organism-environment thinking of Angyal, Rogers, and Gendlin make sense? Is unconditional positive regard at the heart of psychotherapy? Can paying attention to feeling be therapeutic?
3. Does a description of trauma therapy evoke anything in me? Could there be a number of people in the culture or cultures I know who suffer from trauma? Do I know anyone who might be affected by trauma or moral injury and might not be aware of it?

4. Are there other questions about psychotherapy and the fully human that are important to raise and discuss?

Chapter 7

1. Does the notion of mature spirituality make sense? If spirituality is unique for each person, can we still talk in general terms about mature spirituality? Does it make sense to see spirituality as inherently human and yet—paradoxically—as a "more" or a "beyond" breaking into the human? Is spirituality essentially about a broader connection or is it basically a way of talking about the best parts of our humanness?
2. If disembodied rationality and mature spirituality were to have a debate, what would the central issues be? Would they oppose each other? Would compassion be discussed? On which side do I think I would find myself? What makes any spirituality credible for me or what keeps it from being credible? Is the notion of mature spirituality an antidote to steely rationality or is it simply irrational fantasy or wishful thinking?
3. From my own experience, what sense do I make of the distinction between preadult and adult spirituality? Does it make sense to see spirituality on a developmental continuum? Do I know anyone who has mature or adult spirituality? Does it make sense to talk about a violent or disconnecting or inhuman spirituality? Is compassion the missing link between mature spirituality and the world religions? What might make it possible to find a mature spirituality of connection?
4. Are there other questions about spirituality and the fully human that are important to raise and discuss?

Bibliography

A Few Good Men. DVD. Directed by Rob Reiner. 1992. Culver City, CA: Columbia Tri-Star Home Video, 2001.

Aertsen, Ivo, Jana Arsovska, Holger-C. Rohne, Marta Valiñas, Kris Vanspauwen, eds. *Restoring Justice after Large-scale Violent Conflicts: Kosovo. DR Congo and the Israeli-Palestinian Case*. Devon, UK: Willan, 2008.

Afuape, Taiwo. *Power, Resistance and Liberation in Therapy with Survivors of Trauma: To Have Our Hearts Broken*. New York: Routledge, 2011.

American Psychiatric Association. *Diagnostic and Statistical Manual of Mental Disorders* (DSM-5). Washington, DC: American Psychiatric Association, 2013.

Anderson, Herbert, Edward Foley, Bonnie Miller-McLemore, and Robert Schreiter, eds. *Mutuality Matters*. Lanham, MD: Rowman & Littlefield, 2004.

Angyal, Andras. "The Convergence of Psychotherapy and Religion." *Journal of Pastoral Care* 5, no. 4 (1951): 4–14.

———. "Personality as a Time Gestalt." *Neurosis and Treatment: A Holistic Theory*, edited by Eugenia Hanfmann and Richard M. Jones, 62–68. New York: Viking, 1965.

———. *Neurosis and Treatment: A Holistic Theory*, edited by Eugenia Hanfmann and Richard M. Jones. New York: Viking, 1965.

———. *Foundations for a Science of Personality*. New York: Viking Press, 1972.

———. "A Theoretical Model for Personality Studies." In *The Self: Explorations in Personal Growth*, edited by Clark Moustakas, 44–57. New York: Harper Colophon, 1974.

Aragona, Massimilano, Georgios D. Kotzalidis, and Antonella Puzella. "The Many Faces of Empathy between Phenomenology and Neuroscience." *Archives of Psychiatry and Psychotherapy* 4 (2013): 5–12.

Armstrong, Karen. *The Great Transformation: The Beginning of Our Religious Traditions*. New York: Alfred Knopf, 2006

———. "Do unto Others." https://www.theguardian.com/commentisfree/2008/nov/14/religion.

Aron, Lewis. *A Meeting of Minds: Mutuality in Psychoanalysis*. Hillsdale, NJ: The Analytic Press, 1996.

———. "The Clinical Body and the Reflexive Mind." In *Relational Perspectives on the Body*, edited by Lewis Aron and Frances S. Anderson, 3–37. Hillsdale, NJ: Analytic Press, 1998.

——— and Frances Sommer Anderson, eds. *Relational Perspectives on the Body*. Hillsdale, NJ: The Analytic Press, 1998.

Babette's Feast. DVD. directed by Gabriel Axel (1987; Irvington, NY: The Criterion Collection), 2013.

Bargen, Catherine. *Educating for Peacebuilding: Implementing Restorative Justice Principles and Practices into a School System*. Langley. BC: Fraser Region Community Justice Initiatives, 2010.

Barsalou, Lawrence W. "Grounded Cognition: Past. Present. and Future." *Topics in Cognitive Science* 2 (2010): 716–24.

Becker, Christina. *The Heart of the Matter: Individuation as an Ethical Process*. Wilmette. IL: Chiron Publications, 2004.

Becker, William H. "Spiritual Struggle in Contemporary America." *Theology Today* 51 (July 1994): 256–69.

Beebe, John. *Integrity in Depth*. College Station: Texas A&M University Press, 1992.

———. "Integrity in the Analytic Situation." *The Psychoanalytic Review* 86 (1999): 607–25.

———. "The Place of Integrity in Spirituality." In *The Psychology of Mature Spirituality: Integrity, Wisdom, Transcendence*, edited by Polly Young-Eisendrath and Melvin E. Miller, 11–20. London: Routledge, 2000.

Belenky, Mary F., Blythe M. Clinchy, Nancy R. Goldberger, and Jill M. Tarule, eds. *Women's Ways of Knowing: The Development of Self, Voice, and Mind*. New York: Basic Books, 1986.

Benhabib, Selya. "The Generalized and the Concrete Other: The Kohlberg-Gilligan Controversy and Feminist Theory." In *Feminism as Critique: On the Politics of Gender*, edited by Selya Benhabib and Drucilla Cornell, 77–93. Minneapolis: University of Minnesota Press, 1987.

Bickhard, Mark H. "Ethical Psychotherapy and Psychotherapy as Ethics: A Reply to Perrez." *New Ideas In Psychology* 7, no. 2 (1989): 159–64.

Bigwood, Carol. "Renaturalizing the Body (With the Help of Merleau-Ponty)." *Hypatia* 6, no. 3 (1991): 54–73.

Birrell, Pamela J., and Jennifer J. Freyd. "Betrayal Trauma: Relational Models of Harm and Healing." *Journal of Trauma Practice* 5, no. 1 (2006): 49–63.

Blasi, Augusto. "Identity and the Development of the Self." In *Self, Ego, and Identity: Integrative Approaches*, edited by Daniel K. Lapsley and F. Clark Power, 226–42. New York: Springer-Verlag, 1988.

———. "Neither Personality nor Cognition: An Alternative Approach to the Nature of the Self." In *Changing Conceptions of Psychological Life*, edited by Cynthia Lightfoot, Chris Lalonde, and Michael Chandler, 3–25. Mahwah, NJ: Lawrence Erlbaum Associates, 2004.

———. "Moral Character: A Psychological Approach." In *Character Psychology and Character Education,* edited by Daniel K. Lapsley and F. Clark Power, 67–100. Notre Dame, IN: University of Notre Dame Press, 2005.

Blatt, Sidney J., and Richard Q. Ford. *Therapeutic Change: An Object Relations Perspective*. New York: Plenum, 1994.

Bloom, Katya. *The Embodied Self: Movement and Psychoanalysis*. London: Karnac, 2006.

Blum, Lawrence A. "Gilligan and Kohlberg: Implications for Moral Theory." *Ethics* 98, no. 3 (April 1988): 472–91.

Bock, Tonia, and Peter L. Samuelson. "Educating for Moral Identity." *Journal of Character Education* 10, no. 2 (2014): 155–74.

Boff, Leonardo. *Essential Care: An Ethics of Human Nature*. Waco, TX: Baylor University Press, 2007.

Bohart, Arthur C., and Leslie S. Greenberg, eds. *Empathy Reconsidered: New Directions in Psychotherapy*. Washington, DC: American Psychological Association, 1997.

———. "Empathy and Psychotherapy: An Introductory Overview." In *Empathy Reconsidered: New Directions in Psychotherapy*, edited by Arthur C. Bohart and Leslie S. Greenberg, 3–31. Washington, DC: American Psychological Association, 1997.

Bone, Jane. "Exploring Trauma, Loss and Healing: Spirituality, Te Whāriki and Early Childhood Education." *International Journal of Children's Spirituality* 13, no. 3 (August 2008): 265–76.

Bordo, Susan. *Unbearable Weight: Feminism, Western Culture, and the Body*. Berkeley: University of California Press, 1993.

Bouson, J. Brooks. *Embodied Shame: Uncovering Female Shame in Contemporary Women's Writings*. Albany: State University of New York Press, 2009.

Bozarth, Jerold D. "Empathy From the Framework of Client-Centered Theory and the Rogerian Hypothesis." In *Empathy Reconsidered: New Directions in Psychotherapy*, edited by Arthur C. Bohart and Leslie S. Greenberg, 81–102. Washington, DC: American Psychological Association, 1997.

Bragan, Kenneth. *Self and Spirit in the Therapeutic Relationship*. London: Routledge, 1996.

Braman, Brian. *Meaning and Authenticity: Bernard Lonergan and Charles Taylor on the Drama of Authentic Human Existence*. Toronto: University of Toronto Press, 2008.

The British Psychological Society. *Code of Ethics and Conduct: Guidance Published by the Ethics Committee of The British Psychological Society*. Leicester, UK: The British Psychological Society, 2009.

Brown, Brené. *Daring Greatly: How the Courage to Be Vulnerable Transforms the Way We Live, Love, Parent, and Lead*. New York: Gotham Books, 2012.

Brown, David R., Jamie S. Carney, Mark S. Parrish, and John L. Klem. "Assessing Spirituality: The Relationship Between Spirituality and Mental Health." *Journal of Spirituality and Mental Health* 15 (2013): 107–22.

Bubeck, Diemut E. *Care, Gender, and Justice*. Oxford: Clarendon, 1995.

Buchbinder, Eli, and Zvi Eisikovits. "Battered Women's Entrapment in Shame: A Phenomenological Study." *American Journal of Orthopsychiatry* 73, no. 4 (2003): 355–66.

Butler, Judith. *Undoing Gender*. New York: Routledge, 2004.

———. *Frames of War: When Is Life Grievable*? New York: Verso, 2009.

Calhoun, Cheshire. "Standing for Something." *The Journal of Philosophy* 92, no. 5 (May 1995): 235–60.

Canda, Edward R. "Spirituality, Religious Diversity, and Social Work Practice." *Social Casework* 69, no. 4 (1988): 238–47.

Canda, Edward R. and Leola D. Furman. *Spiritual Diversity in Social Work Practice: The Heart of Helping*, 2nd ed. New York: Oxford University Press, 2010.

Caputo, John D. *Against Ethics: Contributions to a Poetics of Obligation with Constant Reference to Deconstruction*. Bloomington: Indiana University Press, 1993.

Card, Claudia. *Confronting Evils: Terrorism, Torture, and Genocide*. New York: Cambridge University Press, 2010.

Carter, Stephen L. *Integrity*. New York: HarperCollins, 1996.

Casey, Edward S. *Spirit and Soul: Essays in Philosophical Psychology*. Dallas, TX: Spring, 1991.

Cavanagh, Michael. "Rediscovering Compassion." *Journal of Religion and Health* 34, no. 4 (Winter 1995): 317–28.

Chernus, Ira. *American Nonviolence: The History of an Idea*. New York: Orbis, 2004.

Ciaramicoli, Arthur P. *The Power of Empathy: A Practical Guide to Creating Intimacy, Self-Understanding, and Lasting Love*. New York: Plume, 2001.

Code, Lorraine. *Epistemic Responsibility*. Hanover, NH: University Press of New England, 1987.

Cohen, Dov, and Angela K.-y Leung. "Violence and Character: A CuPS (Culture x Person x Situation Perspective)." In *Human Aggression and Violence: Causes, Manifestations, and Consequences*, edited by Phillip R. Shaver and Mario Mikulincer, 187–200. Washington, DC: American Psychological Association, 2011.

Corbin, Juliet M. "The Body in Health and Illness." *Qualitative Health Research* 13, no. 2 (February 2003): 256–67.

Cragg, Wesley. *The Practice of Punishment: Towards a Theory of Restorative Justice*. New York: Routledge, 1992.

Crotty, Kevin. "Democracy, Tragedy, and Responsibility." In *Taking Responsibility: Comparative Perspectives*, edited by Winston Davis, 106–20. Charlottesville: University of Virginia Press, 2001.

Csordas, Thomas J. "Embodiment as a Paradigm for Anthropology." *Ethos* 18, no. 1 (March 1990): 5–47.

Dalal, Farhad. "Specialists without Spirit: Sensualists without Heart: Psychotherapy as a Moral Endeavour." 36th S. H. Foulkes Annual Lecture. *Group Analysis* 45, no. 4 (2012): 405–29.

Damasio, Antonio. *Descartes' Error: Emotion, Reason, and the Human Brain*. New York: Putnam, 1994.

———. *The Feeling of What Happens: Body and Emotion in the Making of Consciousness*. New York: Harcourt, Inc., 1999.

Danesh, H. B. "Toward an Integrative Theory of Peace Education." *Journal of Peace Education* 3, no. 1 (March 2006): 55–78.

———. "Introduction: Educating for a Civilization of Peace." In *Education for Peace Reader*, ix–xii. Victoria, BC: EFP Press, 2011.

———. "Human Need Theory, Conflict, and Peace: In Search of an Integrated Model." In *Education for Peace Reader*, 63–67. Victoria, BC: EFP Press, 2011.

———. "Unity-Based Peace Education." In *Education for Peace Reader*, 55–61. Victoria, BC: EFP Press, 2011.

———. "Conceptual Foundations of Education for Peace: A Summary." In *Education for Peace Reader*, 69–77. Victoria, BC: EFP Press, 2011.

———. *Fever in the World of the Mind: On Causes and Prevention of Violence*. Victoria, BC: EFP Press, 2013.

Davis, Charles. *Body as Spirit: The Nature of Religious Feeling*. New York: Crossroad, 1976.

Dead Man Walking. DVD. Directed by Tim Robbins. 1995. Santa Monica, CA: MGM Home Entertainment, 2005.

Decety, Jean. *Empathy: From Bench to Bedside*. Cambridge, MA: The MIT Press, 2012.

Deming, Barbara. "New Men, New Women: Some Notes on Nonviolence" in *We Cannot Live Without Our Lives*, 3–13. New York: Grossman, 1974.

———. "On Revolution and Equilibrium." In *Nonviolence in America: A Documentary History*, edited by Staughton Lynd and Alice Lynd, 405–27. Maryknoll, NY: Orbis Books, 1995.

Desmond, William. *Perplexity and Ultimacy: Metaphysical Thoughts from the Middle*. Albany: State University of New York Press, 1995.

Dixon, Mary, and Kim Senior. "Appearing Pedagogy: From Embodied Learning and Teaching to Embodied Pedagogy." *Pedagogy, Culture and Society* 19, no. 3 (2011): 473–84.

Doherty, William J. *Soul Searching: Why Psychotherapy Must Promote Moral Responsibility*. New York: Basic Books, 1995.

Dolby, Nadine. *Rethinking Multicultural Education for the Next Generation: The New Empathy and Social Justice*. New York: Routledge, 2012.

Dominian, Jack. *The Capacity to Love*. London: Darton Longman & Todd, 1985.

Dowrick, Stephanie. *Intimacy and Solitude*. New York: Norton & Company, 1994.

Egan, Kieran. *Imagination in Teaching and Learning*. Chicago: University of Chicago Press, 1992.

Ehinger, Darlene. “Toward an Ethic of Mutuality: An Integrated Concept of Justice.” *Sewanee Theological Review* 36, no. 3 (1993): 396–415.

Elkins, David N. *Beyond Religion: A Personal Program For Building A Spiritual Life Outside the Walls of Traditional Religion*. Wheaton, IL: Quest Books, 1998.

———. “A Humanistic Approach to Spiritually Oriented Psychotherapy.” In *Spiritually Oriented Psychotherapy*, edited by Len Sperry and Edward P. Shafranske, 131–51. Washington, DC: American Psychological Association, 2005.

———, James Hedstrom, Lori L. Hughes, J. Andrew Leaf, and Cheryl Saunders. “Toward a Humanistic-Phenomenological Spirituality: Definition, Description, and Measurement.” *Journal of Humanistic Psychology* 28, no. 4 (Fall 1988): 5–18.

Elliott, Liz. “Security, Without Care: Challenges for Restorative Values in Prison.” *Contemporary Justice Review* 10, no. 2 (June 2007): 193–208.

Erikson, Erik H. “The Roots of Virtue.” In *The Humanist Frame*, edited by Julian Huxley, 145–65. New York: Harper & Brothers, 1962.

———. “Eight Ages of Man.” In *Childhood and Society*, 2nd ed., 247–74. New York: Norton, 1963.

———. *Insight and Responsibility: Lectures on the Ethical Implications of Psychoanalytic Insight*. New York: Norton, 1964.

———. *Identity: Youth and Crisis*. New York: Norton, 1968.

———. “Reflections on the Dissent of Contemporary Youth.” *Daedalus* 99, no. 1 (Winter 1970): 154–76.

———. “Autobiographic Notes on the Identity Crisis.” *Daedalus* 99, no. 4 (Fall 1970): 730–59.

Evans, Donald. *Spirituality and Human Nature*. Albany: State University of New York Press, 1993.

Evans, Richard I. *Dialogue with Erik Erikson*. New York: Praeger, 1981.

Faiver, Christopher, R. Elliott Ingersoll, Eugene M. O’Brien, and Christopher McNally. *Explorations in Counseling and Spirituality: Philosophical, Practical, and Personal Reflections*. Belmont, CA: Brooks/Cole, 2001 .

Falk, Richard. “Comparative Protection of Human Rights in Capitalist and Socialist Third World Countries.” *Universal Human Rights* 1, no. 2 (April–June 1979): 3–29.

Feldman, R uth, and Sidney J. Blatt. “Precursors of Relatedness and Self-definition in Mother-infant Interaction.” In *Psychoanalytic erspectives on Developmental Psychology: Empirical Studies of Psychoanalytic Theories*, edited by Joseph M. Masling and Robert F. Bornstein, 1–42. Washington, DC: American Psychological Association, 1996.

Fischer, Kathleen R. *Reclaiming the Connection: A Contemporary Spirituality*. Kansas City, MO: Sheed & Ward, 1990.

Fitterer, Robert J. *Love and Objectivity in Virtue Ethics: Aristotle, Lonergan, and Nussbaum on Emotions and Moral Insight*. Toronto: University of Toronto Press, 2008.

Fonagy, Peter. "Toward a Developmental Understanding of Violence." *British Journal of Psychiatry* 183, no. 3 (August 2003): 190–92.

Ford, Donald H., and Hugh B. Urban. *Contemporary Models of Psychotherapy: A Comparative Analysis*, 2nd ed. New York: John Wiley, 1998.

Fountain, S. "Peace Education in UNICEF." *Working Paper*. New York: UNICEF, 1999.

Frank, Arthur W. "Just Listening: Narrative and Deep Illness." *Families, Systems and Health* 16, no. 3 (1998): 197–212.

Frankl, Viktor E. "Dynamics, Existence, and Values." *Journal of Existential Psychiatry* 2 (1961): 5–16.

———. *Man's Search for Meaning: An Introduction to Logotherapy*. New York: Pocket Books, 1963.

———. "The Philosophical Foundations of Logotherapy" in *Phenomenology: Pure and Applied*, edited by Erwin E. Straus, 43–59. Pittsburgh, PA: Duquesne University Press, 1964.

———. *The Will to Meaning: Foundations and Applications of Logotherapy*. New York: New American Library, 1969.

Freire, Paulo. *Pedagogy of the Oppressed*. 30th Anniversary Edition. New York: Continuum, 2009.

Freud, Sigmund. *New Introductory Lectures on Psycho-Analysis*. Translated by J. H. Sprott. New York: Norton, 1933.

———. *An Autobiographical Study*. Translated by James Strachey. New York: Norton 1952.

———. *The Ego and the Id*. Translated by Joan Riviere. New York: Norton, 1962.

Galtung, Johan. "Violence, Peace, and Peace Research." *Journal of Peace Research* 6, no. 3 (1969): 167–91.

———. "Cultural Violence." *Journal of Peace Research* 27, no. 3 (1990): 291–305.

———. *Peace by Peaceful Means: Peace and Conflict, Development and Civilization*. London: Sage, 1996.

———. "Peace Studies and Conflict Resolution: The Need for Transdisciplinarity." *Transcultural Psychiatry* 47, no. 1 (February 2010): 20–32.

Gandhi, Mahatma. *Non-Violent Resistance (Satyagraha)*. New York: Schocken Books, 1961.

Gardner, Howard. "Introduction." In *Responsibility at Work: How Leading Professionals Act (or Don't Act) Responsibly*, 1–18. San Francisco: John Wiley & Sons, 2007.

Garvin, Lucius. "Retributive and Distributive Justice." *The Journal of Philosophy* 42, no. 10 (1945): 270–77.

Gendlin, Eugene T. "Experiential Explication and Truth." *Journal of Existentialism* 6 (1965–1966): 131–46.

———. "Focusing." *Psychotherapy: Theory, Research and Practice* 6, no. 1 (Winter 1969): 4–15.

———. *Focusing*. New York: Bantam, 1981.

———. "What Comes after Traditional Psychotherapy Research?" *American Psychologist* 41, no. 2 (February 1986): 131–36.

———. "The Primacy of the Body, Not the Primacy of Perception." *Man and World* 25, no. 3–4 (1992): 341–53.

———. *Focusing-Oriented Psychotherapy: A Manual of the Experiential Method*. New York: Guilford, 1996.

———, John Beebe III, James Cassens, Marjorie Klein, and Mark Oberlander. "Focusing Ability in Psychotherapy, Personality, and Creativity." In *Research in Psychotherapy*. Vol. 3, edited by John M. Schlien, 217–38. Washington, DC: American Psychological Association, 1967.

Gerdes, Karen E., Elizabeth A. Segal, Kelly F. Jackson, and Jennifer L. Mullins. "Teaching Empathy: A Framework Rooted in Social Cognitive Neuroscience and Social Justice." *Journal of Social Work Education* 47, no. 1 (Winter 2011): 109–31.

Gibbs, Raymond W., Jr. *Embodiment and Cognitive Science*. New York: Cambridge University Press, 2006.

Gilligan, Carol. *In a Different Voice: Psychological Theory and Women's Development*. Cambridge, MA: Harvard University Press, 1982.

———. "The Conquistador and the Dark Continent: Reflections of the Psychology of Love." *Deadalus* 113, no. 3 (Summer 1984): 75–95.

Gilligan, James. "Exploring Shame in Special Settings: A Psychotherapeutic Study." In *Forensic Psychotherapy: Crime, Psychodynamics and the Offender Patient*. Vol. 2: Mainly Practice, edited by Christopher Cordess and Murray Cox, 475–89. London: Jessica Kingsley, 1996.

———. *Violence: Reflections on a National Epidemic*. New York: Putnam, 1996.

———. *Preventing Violence*. New York: Thames & Hudson, 2001.

———. "Shame, Guilt, and Violence." *Social Research: An International Quarterly* 70, no. 4 (2003): 1149–80.

———. "Sex, Gender and Violence: Estela Welldon's Contribution to Our Understanding of the Psychopathology of Violence." *British Journal of Psychotherapy* 25, no. 2 (2009): 239–56.

Gilman, James E. "Whose God? Which Religion? Compassion as the Heart of Interreligious Cooperation." *Journal of Ecumenical Studies* 40, no. 3 (Summer 2003): 267–95.

Glaser, John W. "Conscience and Superego: A Key Distinction." In *Conscience: Theological and Psychological Perspectives,* edited by C. Ellis Nelson, 167–88. New York: Newman, 1973.

Glasson, Barbara. *A Spirituality of Survival*. New York: Continuum, 2009.

Good Will Hunting. DVD. Directed by Gus Van Sant. 1997. Burbank, CA: Buena Vista Home Entertainment, 2000.

Gordon, Mary. *Roots of Empathy: Changing the World Child by Child*. Toronto: Thomas Allen, 2005.

Grant, Robert. *The Way of the Wound: A Spirituality of Trauma and Transformation*. Oakland, CA: Robert Grant, 1996.

Greenson, Ralph R. "Empathy and its Vicissitudes." *The International Journal of Psychoanalysis* 41 (1960): 418–24.

Griffith, James L., and Melissa E. Griffith. *Encountering the Sacred in Psychotherapy: How to Talk with People about Their Spiritual Lives*. New York: Guilford, 2002.

Grosz, Elizabeth A. *Volatile Bodies: Toward a Corporeal Feminism*. Bloomington: Indiana University Press, 1994.

Grudin, Robert. *The Grace of Great Things: Creativity and Innovation*. New York: Ticknor & Fields, 1990.

Guisinger, Shan, and Sidney J. Blatt. "Individuality and Relatedness: Evolution of a Fundamental Dialectic." *American Psychologist* 49, no. 2 (February 1994): 104–11.

Gula, Richard M. *Moral Discernment*. New York: Paulist Press, 1997.

Hamington, Maurice. *Embodied Care: Jane Addams, Maurice Merleau-Ponty, and Feminist Ethics*. Chicago: University of Illinois Press, 2004.

Hannush, Mufid J. *Becoming Good Parents: An Existential Journey*. Albany: State University of New York Press, 2002.

Hart, H. L. A. *Essays of Bentham: Studies in Jurisprudence and Political Theory*. New York: Oxford University Press, 1982.

Hart, Hendrik. "Conceptual Understanding and Knowing *Other*-wise: Reflections on Rationality and Spirituality in Philosophy." In *Knowing Other-Wise: Philosophy at the Threshold of Spirituality*, edited by James H. Olthuis, 19–53. New York: Fordham University Press, 1997.

Hart, Tobin. "From Category to Contact: Epistolary and the Enlivening and Deadening of Spirit in Education." *Journal of Humanistic Education and Development* 36, no. 1 (September 1997): 23–34.

Heidegger, Martin. *Being and Time*. Translated by John Macquarrie and Edward Robinson. New York: Harper & Row, 1962.

Hekman, Susan J. *Moral Voices, Moral Selves: Carol Gilligan and Feminist Moral Theory*. University Park: Pennsylvania State University Press, 1995.

Held, Virginia, ed. *Justice and Care: Essential Readings in Feminist Ethics*. Boulder, CO: Westview Press, 1995.

———. "Liberalism and the Ethics of Care." In *On Feminist Ethics and Politics*, edited by Claudia Card, 288–309. Lawrence: University Press of Kansas, 1999.

———. *The Ethics of Care: Personal, Political, and Global*. Oxford: Oxford University Press, 2006.

Herman, Judith L. *Trauma and Recovery*. New York: Basic Books, 1992.

Heron, John. *Feeling and Personhood: Psychology in Another Key*. London: Sage, 1992.

Higgins-D'Alessandro, Ann, and F. Clark Power. "Character, Responsibility, and the Moral Self." In *Character Psychology and Character Education*, edited by Daniel K. Lapsley and F. Clark Power, 101–20. Notre Dame: IN: University of Notre Dame Press, 2005.

Hillman, James. *The Thought of the Heart*. Dallas, TX: Spring, 1984.

Hinterkopf, Elfie. *Integrating Spirituality in Counseling: A Manual for Using the Experiential Focusing Method*. Alexandria, VA: American Counseling Association, 1998.

Hollway, Wendy. *The Capacity to Care: Gender and Ethical Subjectivity*. London: Routledge, 2006.

Huff, Margaret C. "The Interdependent Self: An Integrated Concept from Feminist Theology and Feminist Psychology." *Philosophy and Theology* 2, no. 2 (Winter 1987): 160–72.

Iacoboni, Marco. *Mirroring People: The New Science of How We Connect with Others*. New York: Farrar, Straus and Giroux, 2008.

Ignatieff, Michael. *The Warrior's Honour: Ethnic War and the Modern Conscience*. New York: Henry Holt, 1997.

The International Focusing Institute. http://www.focusing.org/.

Iyer, Raghavan N. *The Moral and Political Thought of Mahatma Gandhi*. New York: Oxford University Press, 2000.

Jacobi, Mario. *The Analytic Encounter: Transference and Human Relationship*. Toronto: Inner City Books, 1984.

James, William. *The Varieties of Religious Experience*. Cambridge, MA: Harvard University Press, 1985 (Orig. 1902).

Jernigan, Homer L. "Spirituality in Older Adults: A Cross-Cultural and Interfaith Perspective." *Pastoral Psychology* 49 (2001): 413–37.

Johnson, Mark. *Moral Imagination: Implications of Cognitive Science for Ethics*. Chicago: University of Chicago Press, 1993.

Jordan, Judith V. "The Meaning of Mutuality." In *Women's Growth in Connection: Writings From the Stone Center*, edited by Judith V. Jordan, Alexandra G. Kaplan, Jean Baker Miller, Irene P. Stiver, and Janet L. Surrey, 81–96. New York: Guilford, 1991.

———. "Empathy and Self-Boundaries." In *Women's Growth in Connection: Writings From the Stone Center*, edited by Judith V. Jordan, Alexandra G. Kaplan, Jean Baker Miller, Irene P. Stiver, and Janet L. Surrey, 67–80. New York: Guilford, 1991.

———. "Relational Development Through Mutual Empathy." In *Empathy Reconsidered: New Directions in Psychotherapy*, edited by Arthur C. Bohart and Leslie S. Greenberg, 343–51. Washington, DC: American Psychological Association, 1997.

———. "Personality Disorder or Relational Disconnection? In *Handbook of Personality Disorders: Theory and Practice*, edited by Jeffrey J. Magnavita, 120–34. Hoboken, NJ: John Wiley & Sons, 2004.

Jorna, Ton. "The Longing for Human Contact: Why it is Crucial That We Foster Awareness for the Inner Self in Ourselves and in Others." *Journal of Spirituality in Mental Health* 14 (2012): 23–37.

Josselson, Ruthellen. "The Embedded Self: I and Thou Revisited." In *Self, Ego, and Identity: Integrative Approaches*, edited by Daniel K. Lapsley and F. Clark Power, 91–106. New York: Springer-Verlag, 1988.

———. "Relationship as a Path to Integrity, Wisdom, and Meaning." In *The Psychology of Mature Spirituality: Integrity, Wisdom, Transcendence*, edited by Polly Young-Eisendrath and Melvin E. Miller, 87–102. London: Routledge, 2000.

Kalsched, Donald. *The Inner World of Trauma: Archetypal Defenses of the Personal Spirit*. London: Routledge, 1996.

———. *Trauma and the Soul: A Psycho-Spiritual Approach to Human Development and its Interruption*. New York: Routledge, 2013.

Kass, Jared D., and Susan Lennox. "Emerging Models of Spiritual Development: A Foundation for Mature, Moral, and Health-Promoting Behavior." In *Judeo-Christian Perspectives on Psychology: Human Nature, Motivation, and Change*, edited by William R. Miller and Harold D. Delaney, 185–204. Washington, DC: American Psychological Association, 2005.

Katz, Michael S., Nel Noddings, and Kenneth A. Strike, eds. *Justice and Caring: The Search for Common Ground in Education*. New York: Teachers College Press, 1999.

Kegan, Robert. *The Evolving Self: Problem and Process in Human Development*. Cambridge, MA: Harvard University Press, 1982.

Kekes, John. *The Roots of Evil*. Ithaca, NY: Cornell University Press, 2005.

———. *The Human Condition*. Oxford: Clarendon Press, 2010.

Kellenberger, J. *Relationship Morality*. University Park: The Pennsylvania State University Press, 1995.

Kelly, Eugene W., Jr. *Spirituality and Religion in Counseling and Psychotherapy: Diversity in Theory and Practice*. Alexandria, VA: American Counseling Association, 1995.

Kelly, Matthew. *The Seven Levels of Intimacy: The Art of Loving and the Joy of Being Loved*. New York: Simon & Schuster, 2005.

King, Martin L., Jr. *A Testament of Hope: The Essential Writings of Martin Luther King, Jr.*, edited by James Melvin. San Francisco: Harper & Row, 1986.

———. "The Ethical Demands for Integration." In *Testament of Hope*, 117–25.

———. "An Experiment in Love." In *Testament of Hope*, 16–20.

———. "The Most Durable Power." In *Testament of Hope*, 10–11.

———. "Nonviolence and Radical Justice." In *Testament of Hope*, 5–9.

———. "The Power of Nonviolence." In *Testament of Hope*, 12–15.

———. *Where Do We Go From Here: Chaos or Community?* New York: Harper & Row, 1967.

King, Ursula. *The Search for Spirituality: Our Global Quest for a Spiritual Life*. New York: BlueBridge, 2008.

Kitwood, Tom. *Concern for Others: A New Psychology of Conscience and Morality*. London: Routledge, 1990.

Kleingeld, Pauline. "Just Love? Marriage and the Question of Justice." In *Mutuality Matters: Family, Faith, and Just Love*, edited by Herbert Anderson, Edward Foley, Bonnie Miller-McLemore, and Robert Schreiter, 23–41. Lanham, MD: Rowman & Littlefield, 2004.

Knight, Carolyn. "Indirect Trauma: Implications for Self-Care, Supervision, the Organization, and the Academic Institution." *The Clinical Supervisor* 32 (2013): 224–43.

Koehn, Daryl. "Integrity as a Business Asset." *Journal of Business Ethics* 58 (2005): 125–36.

Kohut, Heinz. *How Does Analysis Cure?* Chicago: University of Chicago Press, 1984.

Kornfield, Jack. *A Path with Heart: A Guide through the Perils and Promises of Spiritual Life*. New York: Bantam, 1993.

Kottler, Jeffrey A., and Sally V. Hunter. "Clients as Teachers: Reciprocal Influences in Therapy Relationships." *The Australian and New Zealand Journal of Family Therapy* 31, no. 1 (2010): 4–12.

Krieger, Jonathan. "The Concept of the Object Scale and Cognitive Styles: Measures of Differentiation and Their Relationship to Empathy." PhD diss., Fordham University, 1988.

Krugman, Steven. "Male Development and the Transformation of Shame." In *A New Psychology of Men*, edited by Ronald F. Levant and William S. Pollack, 91–126. New York: Basic Books, 1995.

Krystal, Henry. *Integration and Self-Healing*. Hillsdale, NJ: Analytic Press, 1988.

Kuiper, N. A., and M. R. MacDonald. "Reason, Emotion and Cognitive Therapy." *Clinical Psychology Review* 3, no. 3 (1983): 297–316.

Labacqz, Karen, and Ronald G. Barton. "Boundaries, Mutuality, and Professional Ethics." In *Boundary Wars: Intimacy and Distance in Healing Relationships*, edited by Katherine H. Ragsdale, 96–110. Cleveland, OH: Pilgrim Press, 1996.

Labouvie-Vief, Gisela. "Cognitive-Emotional Integration in Adulthood." In *Annual Review of Gerontology and Geriatrics* 17, edited by K. Warner Schaie and M. Powell Lawton, 206–37. New York: Springer, 1998.

———. "Affect Complexity and Views of the Transcendent." In *The Psychology of Mature Spirituality: Integrity, Wisdom, Transcendence*, edited by Polly Young-Eisendrath and Melvin E. Miller, 103–19. London: Routledge, 2000.

———. "Reason and Emotion across the Life Span: A Personal View." In *A History of Geropsychology in Autobiography*, edited by James E. Birren and Johannes J. F. Schroots, 173–84. Washington, DC: American Psychological Association, 2000.

———. *Integrating Emotions and Cognition throughout the Life Span*. New York: Springer, 2015.

Lakoff, George. “Empathy, Sotomayor, and Democracy: The Conservative Stealth Strategy.” May 31, 2009. In http://www.truth-out.org/, archive item 84347.

Lamm, Zvi. *Conflicting Theories of Instruction: Conceptual Dimensions*. New York: McCutchan, 1976.

Lane, Julia. “Toward a Model of Embodied Environmental Education: Perspectives From Theatre and Indigenous Knowledges.” *Journal of Experiential Education* 35, no. 3 (2012): 395–411.

Langwith, Jacqueline, ed. *Human Rights*. New York: Greenhaven Press, 2008.

Leder, Drew. *The Absent Body*. Chicago: University of Chicago Press, 1990.

Lee, Mo Y., Siu-man Ng, Pamela P. Leung, Cecilia L. Chan. *Integrative Body-Mind-Spirit Social Work: An Empirically Based Approach to Assessment and Treatment*. New York: Oxford University Press, 2009.

Leean, Constance. “Spiritual and Psychological Life Cycle Tapestry.” *Religious Education* 83, no. 1 (Winter 1988): 45–51.

Leech, Kenneth. *Experiencing God: Theology as Spirituality*. San Francisco: Harper & Row, 1985.

Lerner, Rokelle. *Living in the Comfort Zone: The Gift of Boundaries in Relationships*. Deerfield Beach, FL: Health Communications, Inc., 1995.

Lewis, Helen B. *Shame and Guilt in Neurosis*. New York: International Universities Press, 1971.

———. “Introduction: Shame—the ‘Sleeper’ in Psychopathology.” In *The Role of Shame in Symptom Formation*, edited by Helen B. Lewis, 1–28. Hillsdale, NJ: Lawrence Erlbaum Associates, 1987.

Linehan, Marsha. *Cognitive-Behavioral Treatment of Borderline Personality Disorder*. New York: Guilford, 1993.

Litz, Brett T., Nathan Stein, Eileen Delaney, Leslie Lebowitz, William P. Nash, and Caroline Silva. “Moral Injury and Moral Repair in War Veterans: A Preliminary Model and Intervention Strategy.” *Clinical Psychology Review* 29, no. 8 (2009): 695–706.

Loewy, Roberta S. *Integrity and Personhood: Looking at Patients from a Bio/Psycho/Social Perspective*. Boston: Kluwer Academic, 2000.

Lonergan, Bernard. *A Second Collection*, edited by William F. Ryan and Bernard J. Terrell. Philadelphia: Westminster, 1974.

Loreman, Tim. “Kindness and Empathy in Pedagogy.” In *Love as Pedagogy*, 15–31. Rotterdam, The Netherlands: Sense Publishers, 2011.

MacIntyre, Alasdair. *Whose Justice? Which Rationality?* Notre Dame, IN: University of Notre Dame Press, 1988.

Maclagan, W. G. “Respect for Persons as a Moral Principle—I.” *Philosophy: The Journal of the Royal Institute of Philosophy* 35, no. 134 (July 1960): 193–217.

———. “Respect for Persons as a Moral Principle—II.” *Philosophy: The Journal of the Royal Institute of Philosophy* 35, no. 135 (October 1960): 289–305.

Mahedy, William P. *Out of the Night*. New York: Ballantine Books, 1986.

Mahon, Rianne, and Fiona Robinson, eds. *Feminist Ethics and Social Policy: Towards a New Global Political Economy of Care*. Vancouver: University of British Columbia Press, 2011.

Mahoney, Michael J. "Suffering, Philosophy, and Psychotherapy." *Journal of Psychotherapy Integration* 15, no. 3 (2005): 327–52.

Marcel, Gabriel. *Homo Viator: Introduction to a Metaphysic of Hope.* Translated by Emma Caufurd. Chicago: Henry Regnery, 1951.

———. *Metaphysical Journal.* Translated by Bernard Wall. Chicago: Henry Regnery, 1952.

Marcus, George E. *The Sentimental Citizen: Emotion in Democratic Politics.* University Park: Pennsylvania State University Press, 2002.

Marin, Peter. *Freedom and Its Discontents: Reflections on Four Decades of American Moral Experience*. South Royalton, VT: Steerforth Press, 1995.

Marks, Susan C. "Ubuntu, the Spirit of Africa: Example for the World." In *Watching the Wind: Conflict Resolution during South Africa's Transition to Democracy*, 181–90. Washington, DC: United States Institute for Peace, 2000.

Maslow, Abraham H. "A Theory of Human Motivation." In *Motivation and Personality*, 2nd ed., 35–58. New York: Harper & Row, 1970.

———. *The Farther Reaches of Human Nature*. New York: Viking, 1972.

May, Gerald G. *Will and Spirit: A Contemplative Psychology*. San Francisco: Harper & Row, 1982.

Mayeroff, Milton. *On Caring*. New York: HarperPerennial, 1972.

McCoy, Marina B. *Wounded Heroes: Vulnerability as a Virtue in Ancient Greek Literature and Philosophy*. New York: Oxford University Press, 2013. doi:10.1093/acprof:oso/9780199672783.001.0001.

McGee, Teresa R. *Transforming Trauma: A Path toward Wholeness*. Maryknoll, NY: Orbis, 2005.

Means, J. Jeffrey. *Trauma and Evil: Healing the Wounded Soul*. Minneapolis, MN: Fortress, 2000.

Meier, Deborah. "Supposing That . . ." *Phi Delta Kappan* 78, no. 4 (December 1996): 271–76.

Meissner, W. W. "The Self and the Body: IV. The Body on the Couch." *Psychoanalysis and Contemporary Thought* 21, no. 2 (Spring 1998): 277–300.

Merleau-Ponty, Maurice. *The Primacy of Perception, and Other Essays on Phenomenological Psychology, the Psychology of Art, History and Politics*, edited by James Edie. Evanston, IL: Northwestern University Press, 1964.

Metcalfe, Andrew W. "Solitude as a Community of Difference." *Journal of Spirituality in Mental Health* 15, no. 1 (2013): 3–18.

Miller, David. *Principles of Social Justice.* Cambridge, MA: Harvard University Press, 1999.

Miller, John P. *Educating for Wisdom and Compassion: Creating Conditions for Timeless Learning*. Thousand Oaks, CA: Corwin Press, 2006.

———. *The Holistic Curriculum*, 2nd ed. Toronto: University of Toronto Press, 2007.

Miller, Ronald B. "Deny No Evil, Ignore No Evil, Reframe No Evil: Psychology's Moral Dilemma." In *Humanity's Dark Side: Evil, Destructive Experience, and Psychotherapy,* edited by Arthur C. Bohart, Barbara S. Held, Edward Schneider, and J. Kirk, 213–36. Washington, DC: American Psychological Association, 2013.

Miller, William I. *Humiliation: And Other Essays on Honor, Social Discomfort, and Violence*. Ithaca, NY: Cornell University Press, 1993.

Mitchell, Stephen A. *Influence and Autonomy in Psychoanalysis*. Hillsdale, NJ: The Analytic Press, 1997.

Moore, Thomas. *Care of the Soul: A Guide for Cultivating Depth and Sacredness in Everyday Life*. New York: HarperCollins, 1992.

Morrison, Brenda E., and Dorothy Vaandering. "Restorative Justice: Pedagogy, Praxis, and Discipline." *Journal of School Violence* 11, no. 2 (2012): 138–55.

Murphy, David, Duncan Cramer, and Stephen Joseph. "Mutuality in Person-Centered Therapy: A New Agenda for Research and Practice." *Person-Centered and Experiential Psychotherapies* 11, no. 2 (June 2012): 109–23.

Musgrave, Beverly A. "Empathy: The Caregiver Looks Both Ways." In *Partners in Healing: Bringing Compassion to People with Illness or Loss—A Handbook*, edited by Beverly A. Musgrave and John R. Bickle, 31–44. New York: Paulist Press, 2003.

———. "The Ontogenesis of Empathy." In *In Search of Healing: Collected Papers from the Annual Conference of the Society for Pastoral Counselling Research*, edited by Augustine Meier, 43–60. Ottawa, ON: The Society for Pastoral Counselling Research, 2003.

Myers, Barbara K. *Young Children and Spirituality*. London: Routledge, 1997.

Nakken, Craig. *The Addictive Personality: Understanding the Addictive Process and Compulsive Behavior*, 2nd ed. Center City, MN: Hazelden, 1996.

Narvaez, Darcia, and Daniel K. Lapsley. "Teaching Moral Character: Two Alternatives for Teacher Education." *The Teacher Educator* 43 (2008): 156–72.

Noam, Gil G. "'Normative Vulnerabilities' of Self and Their Transformations." In *The Moral Self*, edited by Gil G. Noam and Thomas E. Wren, 209–38. Cambridge, MA: MIT Press, 1993.

Noddings, Nel. "Learning to Care and to Be Cared For." In *Schools, Violence, and Society*, edited by Allan M. Hoffman, 185–98. Westport, CT: Praeger, 1996.

———. *Starting at Home: Caring and Social Policy*. Berkeley, CA: University of California Press, 2002.

———. *Caring: A Feminine Approach to Ethics and Moral Education*, 2nd ed. Berkeley, CA: University of California Press, 2003.

———. *The Challenge to Care in Schools: An Alternative Approach to Education*, 2nd ed. New York: Teachers College Press, 2005.

———. "Identifying and Responding to Needs in Education." *Cambridge Journal of Education* 35, no. 2 (June 2005): 147–59.

———. "The Caring Relation in Teaching." *Oxford Review of Education* 38, no. 6 (December 2012): 771–81.

Nothwehr, Dawn M. *Mutuality: A Formal Norm for Christian Ethics*. San Francisco, Catholic Scholars Press, 1998.

———. "Mutuality and Mission: A No 'Other' Way." in *Mission Studies* 21, no. 2 (2004): 249–70.

Nussbaum, Martha. *Upheavals of Thought: The Intelligence of Emotions*, New York: Cambridge University Press, 2001.

Olinick, Stanley I. "A Critique of Empathy and Sympathy." In *Empathy I*, edited by Joseph Lichtenberg, Melvin Bornstein, and Donald Silver, 137–66. Hillsdale, NJ: The Analytic Press, 1984.

Oliver, Harold H. *Relatedness: Essays in Metaphysics and Theology*. Macon, GA: Mercer University Press, 1984.

———. *Metaphysics, Theology, and Self: Relational Essays*. Macon, GA: Mercer University Press, 2006.

Olthuis, James H., ed. *Knowing Other-wise: Philosophy at the Threshold of Spirituality*. New York: Fordham University Press, 1997.

———. "Introduction: Love/Knowledge: Sojourning with Others, Meeting with Differences." In *Knowing Other-wise: Philosophy at the Threshold of Spirituality*, 1–15. New York: Fordham University Press, 1997.

———. "Face-to-Face: Ethical Asymmetry of the Symmetry of Mutuality." In *Knowing Other-wise: Philosophy at the Threshold of Spirituality*, 131–58. New York: Fordham University Press, 1997.

Ots, Thomas. "The Silenced Body—The Expressive *Leib*: On the Dialectic of Mind and Life in Chinese Cathartic Healing." In *Embodiment and Experience: The Existential Ground of Culture and Self*, edited by Thomas J. Csordas, 116–36. New York: Cambridge University Press, 1994.

Paine, L. S. "Integrity." *The Blackwell Encyclopedia of Management: Business Ethics*, 2nd ed., edited by P. H. Werhane and R. E. Freeman, 247–49. Malden, MA: Blackwell Publishing, 2005.

Päiväsalo, Ville. "Taking Viewpoints of Fairness and Care." *Studia Theologica* 58 (2004): 123–39.

Palanski, Michael, and Francis J. Yammarino. "Integrity and Leadership: Clearing the Conceptual Confusion." *European Management Journal* 25, no. 3 (2007): 171–84.

Palmer, Parker J. *The Active Life: A Spirituality of Work, Creativity, and Caring*. San Francisco: Jossey-Bass, 1990.

———. *A Hidden Wholeness: The Journey toward an Undivided Life*. San Francisco: Jossey-Bass, 2004.

———. "Toward a Philosophy of Integrative Education." In *The Heart of Higher Education: A Call to Renewal: Transforming the Academy through Collegial Conversations*, edited by Parker J. Palmer and Arthur Zajonc with Megan Scribner, 19–33. San Francisco: Jossey-Bass, 2010.

———. Interview with Parker J. Palmer and Arthur Zajonc in *Inside Higher Ed*. February 8, 2011. https://www.insidehighered.com/news/2011/02/08/interview_with_authors_of_the_heart_of_higher_education, 2.

Pargament, Kenneth. *Spiritually Integrated Psychotherapy: Understanding and Addressing the Sacred*. New York: Guilford Press, 2007.

Parizeau, Marie-Hélène. "Scientific Integrity." In *Integrity in the Public and Private Domains*, edited by Alan Montefiore and David Vines, 152–65. New York: Routledge, 1999.

Parks, Sharon D. *Big Questions, Worthy Dreams*. San Francisco: Jossey-Bass, 2000.

Pattison, E. Mansell. "Ego Morality: An Emerging Psychotherapeutic Concept." *The Psychoanalytic Review* 55 (1968): 187–222.

Pearlman, Laurie A. "Trauma and the Self: A Theoretical and Clinical Perspective." *Journal of Emotional Abuse* 1, no. 1 (1998): 7–25.

———. "Moral Dimensions of Trauma Therapies." In *The Social Psychology of Morality: Exploring the Causes of Good and Evil*, edited by Mario Mikulincer and Phillip Shaver, 311–26. Washington, DC: American Psychological Association, 2012.

——— and Karen W. Saakvitne. *Trauma and the Therapist: Countertransference and Vicarious Traumatization in Psychotherapy with Incest Survivors*. New York: Norton, 1995.

Penn, Michael L., and Aditi Malik. "The Protection and Development of the Human Spirit: An Expanded Focus for Human Rights Discourse." *Human Rights Quarterly* 32 (2010): 666–90.

Pert, Candace B. *Molecules of Emotion: Why You Feel the Way You Feel*. New York: Scribner, 1997.

Piaget, Jean. *The Moral Judgment of the Child*. Translated by Marjorie Gabain. New York: Free Press, 1965.

Plato. *Phaedo*. In *The Collected Dialogues of Plato, Including the Letters*, edited by Edith Hamilton and Huntington Cairns, 40–98. Princeton,NJ: Princeton University Press, 1982.

Power, F. Clark. "The Just Community Approach to Moral Education." *Journal of Moral Education* 17, no. 3 (October 1988): 195–208.

——— and Ann Marie Power. "A Raft of Hope: Democratic Education and the Challenge of Pluralism." *Journal of Moral Education* 21, no. 3 (1992): 193–205.

Rawls, John. "The Sense of Justice." *Philosophical Review* 72 (1963): 281–303.

———. *A Theory of Justice*, rev. ed. Cambridge, MA: Harvard University Press, 1999.

Rayner, Colin. "Integrity in Surgical Life: What Happens If It Is Missing?" In *Integrity in the Public and Private Domains*, edited by Alan Montefiore and David Vines, 179–88. New York: Routledge, 1999.

Rhodes, Lynn. *Co-Creating: A Feminist Vision of Ministry*. Philadelphia: Westminster, 1987.

Ricoeur, Paul. *Oneself as Another*. Chicago: University of Chicago Press, 1992.

Roberts, Peter. *Paulo Freire in the 21st Century: Education, Dialogue and Transformation*. London: Paradigm Publishers, 2010.

Roberts, Rodney C. "Justice and Rectification: A Taxonomy of Justice." In *Injustice and Rectification*, edited by Rodney C. Roberts, 7–28. New York: Peter Lang, 2005.

Rogers, Carl. "A Theory of Therapy, Personality, and Interpersonal Relationships as Developed in the Client-Centered Framework." In *Psychology: A Study of a Science*, Vol. III, edited by Sigmund Koch, 184–256. New York: McGraw-Hill, 1959.

———. "The Interpersonal Relationship: The Core of Guidance." *Harvard Educational Review* 32, no. 4 (Fall 1962): 416–29.

———. "Empathic: An Unappreciated Way of Being." In *A Way of Being*. 137–63. Boston: Houghton Mifflin, 1980.

Rorty, Amelie O. "Integrity: Political, Not Psychological." In *Integrity in the Public and Private Domains*, edited by Alan Montefiore and David Vines, 126–57. New York: Routledge, 1999.

Rosen, David H. "Foreword." In John Beebe. *Integrity in Depth,* xi–xvii. College Station: Texas A&M University Press, 1992.

Ross, Susan A. "Evil and Hope: Foundational Moral Perspectives." In *Proceedings of the Catholic Theological Society of America*, edited by Paul Crowley, 46–63. Santa Clara: CA: Santa Clara University, 1995.

Sadurski, Wojciech. "Social Justice and Legal Justice." *Law and Philosophy* 3 (1984): 239–354.

Sarason, Seymour. *Caring and Compassion in Clinical Practice: Issues in the Selection, Training, and Behavior of Helping Professionals*. Northvale, NJ: Jason Aronson, 1995.

Sartre, Jean-Paul, and David Pellauer. *Notebooks for an Ethics*. Chicago: University of Chicago Press, 1992.

Schachter, Elli P., and Yisrael Rich. "Identity Education: A Conceptual Framework for Educational Researchers and Practitioners." *Educational Psychologist* 46, no. 4 (2011): 223–38.

Schaef, Anne W. *Co-Dependence: Misunderstood—Mistreated.* San Francisco: Harper & Row, 1986.

Schaeffer, Zachary. "Transference, Countertransference, and Mutuality in Relational Social Work with College Students." *Clinical Social Work Journal* 42 (2014): 13–21.

Scheff, Thomas J. "The Shame-Rage Spiral: A Case Study of an Interminable Quarrel." In *The Role of Shame in Symptom Formation*, edited by Helen B. Lewis, 109–49. Hillsdale, NJ: Lawrence Erlbaum Associates, 1987.

———. *Emotions and Violence: Shame and Rage in Destructive Conflicts*. Lexington, MA: Lexington Books, 1991.

Scheler, Max. *Man's Place in Nature*. New York: Noonday, 1962.

Schmidt, William S. *The Development of the Notion of Self: Understanding the Complexity of Human Interiority*. Lewiston, NY: Edwin Mellen Press, 1994.

Selman, Robert. *The Growth of Interpersonal Understanding: Developmental and Clinical Analyses*. New York: Academic Press, 1980.

Shea, John J. "The Adult Self: Process and Paradox." *Journal of Adult Development* 10, no. 1 (January 2003): 23–30.

———. *Finding God Again: Spirituality for Adults*. Lanham, MD: Rowman & Littlefield, 2005.

———. "The Development of Empathy: Adulthood, Morality and Religion," In *In Search of Healing: Collected Papers from the Annual Conference of the Society for Pastoral Counselling Research*, edited by Augustine Meier, 61–76. Ottawa, ON: The Society for Pastoral Counselling Research, 2003.

Sheldrake, Philip. *Spirituality: A Guide for the Perplexed*. London: Bloomsbury, 2014.

Sherman, Nancy. "The Moral Perspective and the Psychoanalytic Quest." *Journal of the American Academy of Psychoanalysis* 23, no. 2 (1995): 223–41.

Sloan, Tod. *Life Choices: Understanding Dilemmas and Decisions*. Boulder, CO: Westview Press, 1996.

Solomon, Robert C., and Mark C. Murphy, eds. *What is Justice? Classic and Contemporary Readings*. New York: Oxford University Press, 1990.

Spence, Rebecca, and Jonathan Makuwira. "Do We Make a Difference? Teaching and Researching Peace at Tertiary Level." *Journal of Peace Education* 2, no. 1 (March 2005): 17–3 1.

Starratt, Robert J. *Ethical Leadership*. San Francisco: Jossey-Bass, 2004.

———. "The Moral Character of Academic Learning: Challenging the Exclusivity of the Reigning Paradigm of School Learning." *Second International Handbook of Educational Change*, edited by Andy Hargreaves, Ann Lieberman, Michael Fullan, and David Hopkins, 631–45. New York: Springer, 2010.

Staub, Ervin. "Notes on Cultures of Violence, Cultures of Caring and Peace, and the Fulfillment of Basic Human Needs." *Political Psychology* 24, no. 1 (2003): 1–21.

Stigliano, Tony. "The Moral Construction of the Self." *Journal of Theoretical and Philosophical Psychology* 13, no. 1 (1993): 48–61.

Sullivan, Dennis, and Larry Tifft, eds. *Handbook of Restorative Justice: A Global Perspective*. London: Routledge, 2008.

Suzuki, D. T. *Zen Buddhism*. New York: Doubleday, 1956.

Taylor, Charles. *Sources of the Self: The Making of the Modern Identity*. Cambridge, MA: Harvard University Press, 1989.

Taylor, Gabrielle. "Integrity." *Proceedings of the Aristotelian Society*. Supplementary Volumes 55 (1981): 143–59.

Thandeka. *The Embodied Self: Friedrich Schleiermacher's Solution to Kant's Problem of the Empirical Self*. Albany: State University of New York Press, 1995.

The Bourne Identity. DVD. Directed by Paul Greengrass. 2002. Universal City, CA: Universal Pictures Home Entertainment, 2016.

Thompson, Linda. "Contextual and Relational Morality: Intergenerational Responsibility in Later Life." In *Aging Parents and Adult Children*, edited by Jay A. Mancini, 259–82. Lexington, MA: Lexington Books, 1989.

Tick, Edward. *War and the Soul: Healing Our Nation's Veterans from Post-traumatic Stress Disorder*. Wheaton, IL: Quest Books, 2005.

Tiemann, Johanna M. "The Survivor-Analyst as Analysand: An Autobiographical Account of An Analytic Treatment of Complex Trauma." *International Journal of Psychoanalytic Self Psychology* 7 (2012): 533–58.

Tjeltveit, Alan C. *Ethics and Values in Psychotherapy*. New York: Routledge, 1999.

To Kill a Mockingbird. DVD. Directed by Robert Mulligan. 1962. Universal City, CA: Universal Pictures Home Entertainment, 2012.

To Sir, with Love. DVD. Directed by James Clavell. 1967. Culver City, CA: Columbia Tri-Star Home Video, 1999.

Toulis, Jessica. "Teaching Children Empathy." In *Educating from the Heart: Theoretical and Practical Approaches to Transforming Education*, edited by Aostre N. Johnson and Marilyn Webb Neagley, 27–35. Lanham, MD: Rowman & Littlefield, 2011.

Turner, Victor. "Dramatic Ritual/Ritual Drama: Performative and Reflexive Anthropology." *The Kenyon Review*. New Series 1, no. 3 (July 1979): 80–93.

Tutu, Desmond M. *No Future without Forgiveness*. New York: Doubleday, 1999.

United Nations General Assembly. *Universal Declaration of Human Rights*. New York: United Nations, 1948.

United Nations General Assembly. *Declaration on a Culture of Peace*. Fifty-Third Session. Resolution 53/243. New York: September 13, 1999.

Vaillant, George E. *Triumphs of Experience: The Men of the Harvard Grant Study*. Cambridge, MA: Harvard University Press, 2012.

Van Manen, Max, and Bas Levering. *Childhood's Secrets: Intimacy, Privacy, and the Self Reconsidered*. New York: Teachers College Press, 1996.

Vettesen, Anne J. *Perception, Empathy, and Judgment: An Inquiry into the Preconditions of Moral Performance*. University Park: Pennsylvania State University Press, 1994.

Wadell, Paul J. "The Family as a Crucible of Grace: Finding God in the Mutuality of Love." In *Mutuality Matters*, edited by Herbert Anderson, Edward Foley, Bonnie Miller-McLemore, and Robert Schreiter, 11–21. Lanham, MD: Rowman & Littlefield, 2004.

Walker, Julian, and Victoria Knauer. "Humiliation, Self-esteem and Violence." *Journal of Forensic Psychiatry and Psychology* 22, no. 5 (2011): 724–41.

Walker, Lawrence J., and Russell C. Pitts. "Naturalistic Conceptions of Moral Maturity." *Developmental Psychology* 34, no. 3 (1998): 403–19.

Walker, Lawrence J., and Karl H. Hennig. "Differing Conceptions of Moral Exemplarity: Just, Brave, and Caring." *Journal of Personality and Social Psychology* 86, no. 4 (2004): 629–47.

Walker, Margaret U. "Moral Understandings: Alternative 'Epistemology' for a Feminist Ethics." *Hypatia* 4, no 2 (Summer 1989): 15–28.

Wallace, Edwin R, IV. "Freud as Ethicist." In *Freud, Appraisals and Reappraisals*, edited by Paul E. Stepansky, 83–141. Hillsdale, NJ: The Analytic Press, 1985.

Walsh, Froma. "Spirituality, Healing and Resilience." In *Re-Visioning Family Therapy: Race, Culture, and Gender in Clinical Practice*, 2nd ed., edited by Monica McGoldrick and Kenneth V. Hardy, 61–75. New York: Guilford, 2008.

Watson, John B. "Psychology as the Behaviorist Views It." *Psychological Review* 20 (1913): 158–77.

———. "What is Behaviorism?' *Harper's Magazine* 152 (1926): 723–29.

———. "The Myth of the Unconscious." *Harper's Magazine* 155 (1927): 502–8.

———. *Behaviorism*. New Brunswick, NJ: Transaction Publishers, 1998 (Orig. 1925).

Werhane, Patricia H. "Competing with Integrity: Richard De George and the Ethics of Global Business. *Journal of Business Ethics* 127, no. 4 (April 2015): 737–42.

West, Cornel. "The Moral Obligations of Living in a Democratic Society" in *The Good Citizen*, edited by David B. Batstone and Eduardo Mendieta, 5–12. New York: Routledge, 1999.

West, Robin. *Caring for Justice*. New York: New York University Press, 1997.

Wheeler, Evangeline A., Lena M. Ampadu, and Ester Wangari. " Lifespan Development Revisited: African-Centered Spirituality Throughout the Life Cycle." *Journal of Adult Development* 9, no. 1 (January 2002): 71–78.

Whitfield, Charles L. *Boundaries and Relationships: Knowing, Protecting and Enjoying the Self.* Deerfield Beach, FL: Health Communications, 1993.

Wieser, Martin. "From the Eel to the Ego: Psychoanalysis and the Remnants of Freud's Early Scientific Practice." *Journal of the History of the Behavioral Sciences* 49, no. 3 (Summer 2013): 259–80.

Winnicott, D. W. *Through Paediatrics to Psycho-Analysis*. New York: Basic Books, 1975.

Wittgenstein, Ludwig. *Philosophical Investigations,* Translated by G. E. M. Anscombe. Oxford: Blackwell, 1968.

Young-Eisendrath, Polly, and Melvin Miller, eds. *The Psychology of Mature Spirituality: Integrity, Wisdom, Transcendence*. London: Routledge, 2000.

Zaki, Jamil, and Kevin Ochsner. "The Neuroscience of Empathy: Progress, Pitfalls and Promise." *Nature Neuroscience* 15, no. 5 (May 2012): 675–80.

Zehr, Howard. *The Little Book of Restorative Justice*. Intercourse, PA: Good Books, 2002.

———. *Changing Lenses: A New Focus for Crime and Justice*, 3rd ed. Scottsdale, PA: Herald Press, 2005.

———. "The Offender" in *Changing Lenses: A New Focus for Crime and Justice*, 3rd ed., 33–44. Scottsdale, PA: Herald Press, 2005.

———. "A Restorative Lens" in *Changing Lenses: A New Focus for Crime and Justice*, 3rd ed., 177–214. Scottsdale, PA: Herald Press, 2005.

———. "The Victim" in *Changing Lenses: A New Focus for Crime and Justice*, 3rd ed., 19–32. Scottsdale, PA: Herald Press, 2005.

Zembylas, Michalinos. "The Politics of Trauma: Empathy, Reconciliation and Peace Education." *Journal of Peace Education* 4, no. 2 (September 2007): 207–24.

———. *The Politics of Trauma in Education*. New York: Palgrave Macmillan, 2008.

———. "Critical Emotional Praxis for Reconciliation Education: Emerging Evidence and Pedagogical Implications." *Irish Educational Studies* 31, no. 1 (March 2012): 19–33.

———. "Pedagogies of Strategic Empathy: Navigating through the Emotional Complexities of Anti-racism in Higher Education." *Teaching in Higher Education* 17, no. 2 (April 2012): 113–25.

———. "The Emotional Complexities of "Our" and "Their" Loss: The Vicissitudes of Teaching about/for Empathy in a Conflicting Society." *Anthropology and Education Quarterly* 44, no. 1 (2013): 19–37.

Index

academia, 81
addiction, 56–57
affective empathy, 157–158, 163
agape (love), 130–131
ahiṃsā (nonviolence), 130
American Nonviolence (Chernus), 140n60
Anderson, Frances S., 67n8
Anderson, Herbert, 19
Angyal, Andras, xiii, 29n10; on autonomy and homonomy, 204, 205, 208; holistic thought of, 203, 204; on neurosis, 204–205; in organismic tradition, 203–205, 205, 207, 208; on time gestalt, self as, 12, 246n9
Armstrong, Karen, 239, 240
Aron, Lewis, 29n4, 67n8
atomistic self, 5, 152, 176–177, 177n6
at-oneness, 124, 125, 135, 252. *See also* oneness
autonomy, 4, 29n4; homonomy and, 29n10, 204, 205, 208; mutual, 90; shame and doubt vs., 116
Axial Age, 239

Babette's Feast, 219–220
Baier, Annette, 88
Basseches, Michael, 28n2
Becker, Christina, 9
Beebe, John, 7, 31n28
behaviorism, 195, 196, 197
Bickhard, Mark H., 200
Big Questions, Worthy Dreams (Parks), 247n18
Bigwood, Carol, 67n15
Blasi, Augusto, 48, 104n67
Blatt, Sidney J., 188, 192
Blum, Lawrence A., 103n33
body-self: care and justice relation to, 82–83; in education, 158, 178n16; embodiment and, 38–39, 67n15; Gendlin on, 38; integral self-in-mutuality as, 36, 37–42; in morality, 39–41; in psychotherapy, 189–190; as relational, 38, 67n8, 67n19; spirituality and, 230–231; subject-object dichotomy and, 42. *See also* relational body
Boff, Leonardo, 88
Bone, Jane, 246n11
Bosnia and Herzegovina, 170
boundaries, 160
The Bourne Identity, 3
Bragan, Kenneth, 192, 246n11
British Psychological Society, 188
Brown, Brené, 59
Brown, David R., 246n13
Bubeck, Diemut E., 83
Buchbinder, Eli, 121
Butler, Judith, 39, 67n10

Calhoun, Cheshire, 30n22, 31n34
Canda, Edward R., 228, 230

The Capacity to Care (Hollway), 89
Caputo, John D., 83
Card, Claudia, 113–114
care: as concrete, 87; in culture, 86–92; defining, 103n24; as developmental, 89; embodiment of, 83, 103n24; as emotional, 87, 103n33; Erikson on, 91–92; ethic of, 88, 90; Held on, 90–91; Hollway on, 88–90; money, sex, power substituting for, 122; mutuality as loving, 21–22, 91; needs and, 79, 88–89; Noddings on, 88, 173–174; as personal, 87–88; as subjective, 86–87; subject-object dichotomy and, 88
care and justice, ix, xii, 254; in academia, 81; of adult and moral self, 76, 99, 101, 101n2, 121; at-oneness in, 125; body-self and, 82–83; clear boundaries with, 84–85; connection of, 77, 79, 80, 81, 98, 99; cultural disconnection of, 81, 81–82, 86–88, 92, 97–98, 100–101; defining, 76–77, 77–79, 80, 103n24; disembodied rationality with, 78; distributive, 124–126, 127; in education, 146–147, 148, 149, 150–151, 180n64; embodiment of, 82–83, 103n24; empathy, self-empathy with, 85, 94–95, 252; Erikson on, 82, 114, 138n18; of feeling self, 83; gender and, 81–82, 86–87, 87; inner and relational, 101; of integral self-in-mutuality, xi, xii, 76, 80–82, 85–86, 101, 108, 127, 252; of intimate self, 85; nonviolence as, 133; peace and violence understood with, 108, 109, 110, 121–123; peace as restorative, 126–128; in pedagogy of connection, 168–170, 173–174, 252; of responsible self, 85; restorative, 126–129, 139n46; in self of inner depth, 83–84; spirituality with, 148, 220, 236; teaching of, 168–170; violence and lack of, 123; violence annihilating, 111–112; vulnerabilities of the self and, 84; wisdom and, 218n76. *See also* distributive care and justice; restorative care and justice
Carney, Jamie S., 246n13
Cartesian dualism, 42
Casey, Edward S., 43
Cavanagh, Michael, 249n56
Chernus, Ira, 140n60
Ciaramicoli, Arthur P., 162, 165
clear boundaries, 54, 72n82, 73n85; addiction and, 56–57; care and justice with, 84–85; codependency and, 57; developmental difficulties and, 57–58; dialogue and, 55–56; in education, 156; of empathy, 159–160, 161; of integral self-in-mutuality, 36, 53–54, 55; lack of, 56; in morality, 55–56; permeable and expandable, 54; in psychotherapy, 191–192; spirituality of, 232. *See also* boundaries
Code, Lorraine, 40
Code of Ethics and Conduct (British Psychological Society), 188
codependency, 57
cognition: embodiment of, 68n36; empathy and, 44, 157–158, 163; Kohlberg and, 46
compassion: Elkins on, 240; practice of, 239; spirituality of, 238–240, 244, 245, 249n56; trauma and, 244; in world religions, 238–240, 240, 244, 249n56
conceptual knowing, 40, 68n27
conflict, ethnic and national, 170; identity-based worldview and, 172; trauma narratives of, 171
connection, ix, 251; of care and justice, 77, 79, 80, 81, 98, 99; of spirituality, 223, 224, 226, 230, 231–232, 236, 242, 243, 246n11, 246n13, 247n22; trauma and, 242, 243
conscientização (conscientization), 175
Corbin, Juliet M., 39
Csordas, Thomas J., 67n19
culture: care and justice disconnected in, 81, 81–82, 86–88, 92, 97–98, 100–101; care in, 86–92; disconnections in, 41–42, 50, 51–53, 65, 81, 81–82, 86–88, 92, 97–98, 100–101, 254; disembodied rationality in, 52, 65; integral self-in-mutuality and, 36–37; intimacy in, 61–62; intimate self disconnected in, 61–62; justice in, 92–98, 100; logics of, 37, 46; mind-body dichotomy in, 41–42, 68n31,

68n34; responsible self in, 64–66; superego of, 51–52, 65, 65–66, 96, 149, 198; violence of, 112. *See also* enculturation
culture-in-us: education and, 149; moralism as, 150
Cyprus, 170–171, 181n80

Dalal, Farhad, 71n69, 122
Damasio, Antonio, 46, 68n31
Danesh, H. B., 170, 171–172
Dead Man Walking, 107, 119, 135
Declaration on a Culture of Peace (United Nations General Assembly), 22
dehumanization: humanization and, 175, 176; spirituality and, 237–238, 249n51
Delaney, Harold D., 247n20
Deming, Barbara, 129, 131–132
depth: empathy and, 159, 161, 164, 165, 252; morality of, 50, 51, 52, 133, 200–202, 202, 253; nonviolence and, 133
Desmond, William, 104n67
development, 180n56; care in, 89; clear boundaries and difficulties of, 57–58; early, xiv–xv; in education, human and moral, 148–149; Erikson on, 14–15, 114–119, 138n20–138n21, 210; evil and, xv–xvi; moral, 14–15, 197–199; peace and violence in, 114–119, 138n20–138n21; peace as epitome of, 124; of spirituality, 220–221, 236, 246n5, 247n20; of superego, 117, 119. *See also* preadulthood
dialectic: definition of, 28n2; of integral self-in-mutuality, 4, 5
Dialectical Thinking and Adult Development (Basseches), 28n2
dialogue: adult morality and, 60–61; clear boundaries and, 55–56; psychotherapy and, 194
difference, 113
differentiation, 164
disconnection: of care and justice, 81, 81–82, 86–88, 92, 97–98, 100–101; in culture, 41–42, 50, 51–53, 65, 81, 81–82, 86–88, 92, 97–98, 100–101, 254; difference contrasted with, 113; in empathy, 157, 157–158; feeling self negating, 44–45; of intimate self, 61–62; mistrust and, 115; pedagogy of connection and, 151–153; in preadult spirituality, 234, 235, 236; of reason and emotion, 46–47, 71n60, 71n65, 251–252; self-other dichotomy and, 113, 251; of trauma, 211; violence and, 112–113, 123, 135, 252
disembodied rationality: care and justice with, 78; in culture, 52, 65; empathy contrasted with, 161–162; justice and, 78, 93, 94–95, 95; law and, 95; responsible self undermined by, 65; self of inner depth contrasted with, 52, 72n81; superego and, 65, 65–66
distributive care and justice: at-oneness in, 125; peace as, 124–126; restorative justice and violation of, 127
distributive justice. *See* justice
divided self, 13–14
Doherty, William J., 194
Dolby, Nadine, 158
Dominian, Jack, 23
doubt. *See* shame
Dowrick, Stephanie, 49, 62

early development. *See* development
education, 145–146; of adult and moral self, 148–149; banking method of, 175–176; body-self in, 158, 178n16; care and justice in, 146–147, 148, 149, 150–151, 180n64; clear boundaries in, 156; culture-in-us, us-in-the-culture and, 149; embodied, 155, 178n16; empathy in, 155, 157–168; enculturation in, 153–154; feeling self in, 155; Freire on, 175–176; goals of, 146–147; human and moral development in, 148–149; identity, 153–154; individuation in, 153–154; integral self-in-mutuality in, 146–147, 150–151, 153–154; intimate self in, 156; moralism and morality in, 149–150; Noddings on, 173–174; Palmer on, 176–177; peace and violence in, 147–148, 150–151, 175–176; peace as goal in, 147; problem-posing method of, 176; questions of, 147–151; responsible self

in, 156–157; self of inner depth in, 155–156; socialization in, 153–154; spirituality and, 148; Starratt on, 174–175. *See also* embodied pedagogy; integrative pedagogy; pedagogy of connection; pedagogy of control; teaching
Education for Peace, 170
Eisikovits, Zvi, 121
Elkins, David N.: on compassion, 240; on soul, 72n81, 231; on spirituality, 231, 233, 240, 246n6, 246n10
embodied pedagogy, 178n16
embodiment: body-self and, 38–39, 67n15; of care and justice, 82–83, 103n24; of cognition, 68n36; in education, 155, 178n16; Noddings on, 155; of nonviolence, 133; in organismic tradition, 203; peace and violence in, 110; of reason, 40, 41–42, 65, 68n34; subject-object dichotomy and, 67n18
emotions: care and, 87, 103n33; disconnection of reason and, 46–47, 71n60, 71n65, 251–252; in preadult spirituality, 234, 235, 236
empathy, ix, xiii; affective, 157–158, 163; care and justice with, 85, 94–95, 252; Ciaramicoli on, 162, 165; clear boundaries of, 159–160, 161; cognitive, 44, 157–158, 163; conceptual knowing and, 40, 68n27; definition of, 158–159; depth, intimacy of, 159, 161, 164, 165, 252; disconnection in, 157, 157–158; disembodied rationality contrasted with, 161–162; in education, 155, 157–168; feeling self and, 43–45; feminism and, 163; history of, 157–158; informed, 166–167; intimate self realized in, 59; Jordan on, 59, 162, 163; Lakoff on, 162, 165–166; misunderstood notion of, 157; of morality, 45, 49, 70n51, 150; Musgrave on, 162, 164; in mutuality, 25–26; neuroscience and, 158, 178n19; nonjudgmental, 160, 161; peace and, 134–135, 252; in pedagogy of connection, 146, 157, 162, 166–168, 168; in psychotherapy, 193–194, 215n17; reason and, 165–166; relational, 161; Rogers on, 43, 59, 162–163, 206; self of inner depth and, 49; sympathy conflated with, 157, 158–161; sympathy distinguished from, 158–161; teaching of, 166–168, 180n58; in *To Kill a Mockingbird*, 35; trauma narratives and, 171; West, C., on, 162, 164. *See also* self-empathy
enculturation, 153–154
Erikson, Erik H., 29n10, 114, 214n7; on care, 91–92; on care and justice, 82, 114, 138n18; development stages of, 14, 114–119, 138n20–138n21, 210; on identity vs. identity diffusion stage, 14, 118–119; on integral self, 6; on integrity, 14–15; on intimacy, 60; on moral development, 14–15
Evans, Donald, 49
Evans, Richard I., 115, 138n20
evil, xiv; as developmental issue, xv–xvi; nonviolence responding to, 133; violence as, 113–114
evolutionary self, 5
external standard, 65–66

The Farther Reaches of Human Nature (Maslow), 247n17
feeling: Gendlin on, 190, 207–208; Rogers on, 69n40, 205, 206, 207
feeling self: care and justice together in, 83; disconnections negated by, 44–45; in education, 155; empathy and, 43–45; inner and relational, 42–43; integral self-in-mutuality as, 36, 37, 42–47; in morality, 45, 150; in psychotherapy, 190; self-empathy of, 44–45; spirituality and, 231
Feldman, Ruth, 192
felt sensing, 44, 69n41. *See also* feeling self
feminists: on care, 90–91; on empathy, 163; on mutuality, 25–27
A Few Good Men, 75, 85
Fischer, Kathleen R., 49
Fitterer, Robert J., 46
focusing. *See* psychotherapy
Ford, Donald H., 188
Ford, Richard, 188
formal norms, 26–27

Frank, Arthur W., 246n5
Frankl, Viktor E., 29n4, 54, 242
Freire, Paulo, xiii; on humanization and dehumanization, 175, 176; on integrity and mutuality, 5; pedagogy of connection and, 173, 175–176
Freud, Sigmund: on love and work, 118, 189, 214n7; morality and, xiii, 195–196, 197, 199; psychoanalysis as science and, 195; on superego, 48, 195–196

Galtung, Johan, 112, 114, 126
Gandhi, Mahatma, 12, 51; King and, 130; nonviolence of, 129–130, 140n60; on truth, 129–130
Gardner, Howard, 63
Garvin, Lucius, 96
gender: in care and justice, 81–82, 86–87, 87; violence and, 112–113, 119–121, 238
Gendlin, Eugene T., xiii; on body-self, 38; on feeling, 190, 207–208; on felt sensing, felt knowing, 69n41; focusing and, 208–210, 217n61; in organismic tradition, 203, 207–210
Gilligan, Carol, 88
Gilligan, James, 119–120
Glasson, Barbara, 73n85
Good Will Hunting, 185, 193–194
Gordon, Mary, 167–168
The Grace of Great Things (Grudin), 9
Grant, Robert, 241
Greek Cypriots, 181n80
Grudin, Robert, 12; integrity defined by, 9–10, 13, 49; on sharing, 24
guilt, 116–117
Gula, Richard M., 45

Hamington, Maurice, 103n24
Hanfmann, Eugenia, 246n9
Hart, Hendrik, 46
Hart, H. L. A., 102n11
Hart, Tobin, 152
heart, 48, 71n68
The Heart of Higher Education (Palmer and Zajonc), 176
Hedstrom, L. James, 246n10
Heidegger, Martin, 88
Hekman, Susan J., 79
Held, Virginia: on care, 90–91; on mutual autonomy, 90
Herman, Judith L., 137n2, 138n21, 210, 242
Heron, John, 190
A Hidden Wholeness (Palmer), 13–14
Hollway, Wendy, 88–90
homonomy, 29n10, 204, 205, 208
Huff, Margaret C., 17
Hughes, Lori L., 246n10
humanization, 175, 176
human rights. *See* rights

identity: diffusion of, 14, 118–119; in education, 153–154; negative, 118; violence and, 118; worldview based on, 172
identity-in-mutuality, 118
Ignatieff, Michael, 113
imagination, 225, 247n18
individuation, 153–154
industry, 117–118
inferiority, 117–118
informed skepticism, 166, 167
initiative, 116–117
instinctoid needs. *See* needs
integral self, 6
integral self-in-mutuality, xii, 6–7, 251; adulthood, morality in emerging, 4; as body-self, 36, 37–42; care and justice of, xi, xii, 76, 80–82, 85–86, 101, 108, 127, 252; clear boundaries of, 36, 53–54, 55; culture and, 36–37; defining integrity and, 16; dialectic of, 4, 5; difficulty of realizing, 10–11; as educational goal, 146–147, 150–151, 153–154; as feeling self, 36, 37, 42–47; imperfection of, 5–6; industry precursor to, 117; inner psychological harmony or wholeness of, 10–11, 13; as intimate self, 36; mosaic of, 35–36, 36–37; nonviolence for, 132, 133, 134; notion of, influences on, 29n10; as paradox, 3–4, 7–8, 30n14; as peaceful self, xi, xii, 124, 134, 135; in pedagogy of connection, 151, 152, 252; as personal and social, 101; as practical ontology, 29n3; psychotherapy role in, 185,

187–194, 200, 200–202, 202, 253; as responsible self, 36, 62–63; restorative care and justice addressing, 127; as self of inner depth, 36, 37, 49; spirituality and, 220, 224, 228, 229–230, 235–236; therapist as, 188–189, 193; trauma and, 210, 212; violence annihilating, 111, 135. *See also* mutuality
integrative pedagogy, 176–177
integrity, xiii; of adult and moral self, 4–5; Beebe on, 7, 31n28; Calhoun on, 30n22, 31n34; conforming of, 9, 11–12; continuity of, 9, 12, 13; defining, 8–9, 16, 30n15, 30n22; Erikson on, 14–15; Freire on, 5; of fully human self, xi, xii; Grudin defining, 9–10, 13, 49; inner psychological harmony, wholeness of, 9, 10–11, 13; integral self-in-mutuality and, 16; morality characterized by, xi; mutuality and, 8, 28; Noam on, 15–16; Palmer on, 13–14, 39; as practical ontology, 29n3; in spirituality, 245n2; violence annihilating, 111; as work in progress, 12–13
intersubjectivity. *See* mutuality
intimate self, 58–59; in care and justice, 85; cultural disconnections of, 61–62; in education, 156; empathy realizing, 59; Erikson on, 60; integral self-in-mutuality as, 36; in morality, 59–61, 61; in psychotherapy, 192; sex and, 61–62; spirituality of, 232–233
Iyer, Raghavan N., 12

Jacobi, Mario, 54
James, William, 246n8
Jason Bourne (fictional character), 3
Jones, Richard M., 246n9
Jordan, Judith V.: on empathy, 59, 162, 163; on mutuality, 19, 25–26; on shame, 120–121
Josselson, Ruthellen, 103n33, 188
Judeo-Christian Perspectives on Psychology (Miller, W., and Delaney, H.), 247n20
just community, 168, 169–170
justice: as abstract, 92, 94, 95; actual needs and, 97; adult notion of, 99; in culture, 92–98, 100; defining, 80, 102n18; disembodied rationality and, 78, 93, 94–95, 95; distributive, 98–99, 100–101, 105n72, 124–126, 127; embodied, 83; equality foundational to, 100; as impersonal, 92, 94–95; law and, 22–23, 95–96; mutuality and, 22–23, 26; as objective, 92–93, 95, 104n67; as punishment, 96–98, 98, 100; reason defining, 92, 93, 95; rectificatory, 98, 99–100, 100–101, 126; restorative, 98, 100, 126–128, 168–169; retributive, 96, 98, 100–101; social, 98, 105n72; subject-object dichotomy and, 93, 94, 95

Kalsched, Donald, 71n67, 242–243
Kass, Jared D., 247n20
Kegan, Robert, 220
Kekes, John, 113
Kellenberger, J., 67n22
Kelly, Matthew, 42, 58, 61
King, Martin Luther, Jr.: on love, 130–131; nonviolence of, 129, 130–131, 132
Klem, John L., 246n13
Kohlberg, Lawrence, 88; cognitive theory of, 46; just community approach of, 168, 169–170
Kornfield, Jack, 232
Krieger, Jonathan, 216n39

Labouvie-Vief, Gisela, 70n51, 71n65, 180n56
Lakoff, George, 162, 165–166
Lamm, Zvi, 153
law: adult and moral self not above, 6; cultural superego and, 96; disembodied rationality and, 95; justice and, 22–23, 95–96; mutuality and, 22–23
Leaf, J. Andrew, 246n10
Leder, Drew, 38
Leech, Kenneth, 232
Lennox, Susan, 247n20
Linehan, Marsha, 56
Loewy, Roberta S., 177n6
Lonergan, Bernard, 37
love: as *agape*, 130–131; Freud on work and, 118, 189, 214n7; King on, 130–131; in mutuality, 26

loving care: money, sex, and power substituting for, 122; mutuality as, 21–22, 91
loving care and justice: of nonviolence, 133; violence annihilating, 111–112

MacIntyre, Alasdair, 71n60
Mahoney, Michael J., 41
Mandela, Nelson, 51
Man's Search for Meaning (Frankl), 242
Marcel, Gabriel, 24, 39
Marin, Peter, 212
Maslow, Abraham H., 20–21, 247n17
McCoy, Marina B., 31n28
meaning: spirituality and, 223; trauma and, 242, 243
Meier, Deborah, 166–167
Meissner, William, 39
Merleau-Ponty, Maurice, 38
Meyeroff, Milton, 22
Miller, David, 105n72
Miller, Melvin E., 245n2, 246n14
Miller, Ronald B., 113
Miller, William R., 247n20
mind-body dichotomy, 41–42, 68n31, 68n34
mirror neurons, 158
Mitchell, Stephen A., 29n4
money, sex, and power: as loving care substitute, 122; self of inner depth and, 52–53
Moore, Thomas, 71n69
moralism: as culture-in-me, 150; in education, morality and, 149–150; limits of, 149–150
moral pain, 212
Morrison, Brenda E., 168–169
Mother Teresa, 51
motivation, xiv, xv
Murphy, Mark, 78
Musgrave, Beverly A.: on differentiation, 164; on empathy, 162, 164
mutual autonomy, 90
mutuality: adulthood, morality and, xi, xii, xiii, 5; defining, 16–24; empathy in, 25–26; feminism and, 25–27; Freire on, 5; of fully human self, xi, xii; Huff on, 17–18; identity in, 118; integrity and, 8, 28; intersubjectivity of, 25–26; Jordan on, 19, 25–26; justice and, 22–23, 26; law and, 22–23; learning and, 174; love essential to, 26; as loving care, 21–22, 91; mutuality not demanded by, 24; needs and, 20–21; Nothwehr on, 17–18, 26–27, 64; Oliver on, 27–28; Olthuis on, 17; relational self and, 27–28; in religious ethics, 26–27; rights and freedoms appreciated in, 20, 21; self-in-relation and, 17; of spirituality, 224, 246n14; Starratt on learning and, 174; theologians on, 26–28; violence annihilating, 111; Walker and Pitts on, 17; wholeness of other and, 18–19
mutual self-in-integrity, 28
Myers, Barbara Kimes, 229–230

needs: care and, 79, 88–89; instinctoid, 20; justice and actual, 97; mutuality and, 20–21; rights based on, 102n11
negative identity, 118
neuroscience, 158, 178n19
neurosis, 204–205
Neurosis and Treatment (Hanfmann and Jones), 246n9
Noam, Gil G.: on acting morally, 12; on integrity, 15–16; on vulnerabilities of the self, 73n100, 84
Noddings, Nel, xiii; on caring, 88, 173–174; on education, 173–174; on embodiment, 155; pedagogy of connection and, 173–174
nonviolence: of adult and moral self, 133; as *ahiṃsā*, 130; of Deming, 129, 131–132; embodied, 133; evil and, 133; of Gandhi, 129–130, 140n60; inner depth of, 133; for integral self-in-mutuality, 132, 133, 134; of King, 129, 130–131, 132; loving care and justice of, 133; peace as, 129–134
Nothwehr, Dawn M.: on formal norms, 26–27; on mutuality, 17–18, 26–27, 64

Oliver, Harold H., 27–28, 207
Olthuis, James H., 17, 68n27, 233
oneness, 230, 244
organismic tradition: Angyal in, 203–205, 205, 207, 208; embodied self in, 203; Gendlin in, 203, 207–210; in

psychotherapy, 203–210; Rogers in, 203, 205–207, 207, 208, 216n57
other: justice for, mutuality and, 22–23; needs of, 20–21; rights and freedoms of, mutuality and, 20, 21; wholeness of, mutuality and, 18–19
Ots, Thomas, 67n18

Palmer, Parker J., xiii; on divided self, 13–14; on heart, 71n68; integrative pedagogy of, 176–177; on integrity, 13–14, 39; pedagogy of connection and, 173, 176–177; on wholeness, 13–14
paradigm, of fully human, ix–x
paradigm shift, fully human as, 254
paradox: adulthood as, 7, 30n14; integral self-in-mutuality as, 3–4, 7–8, 30n14
Pargament, Kenneth, 247n19
Parizeau, Marie-Hélène, 12
Parks, Sharon Daloz, 247n18
Parrish, Mark S., 246n13
peace: as at-oneness, x, 124, 125, 135, 252; as distributive care and justice, 124–126; as educational goal, 147; empathy and, 134–135, 252; as human, 123–124, 135–137; as human development epitome, 124; inner and relational, 124; for integral self-in-mutuality, xi, xii, 124, 134, 135; as nonviolence, 129–134; in pedagogy of connection, 170–172; as restorative care and justice, 126–128; spirituality and, 220, 236; teaching of, 170–172, 183n143
peace and violence, xiii, 108, 252, 254; care and justice for understanding, 108, 109, 110, 121–123; as developmental, 114–119, 138n20–138n21; education and, 147–148, 150–151, 175–176; as human, 109–110, 110–111, 123–124, 135–137; inner, embodied, 110; in pedagogy of connection, 151, 170–172, 252–253; trust, mistrust and, 115; worldviews and, 172
peacemaking circles, 129
Pearlman, Laurie Anne, 213
pedagogy of connection, xiii, 151; atomistic self and, 152, 176–177, 177n6; care and justice in, 168–170, 173–174, 252; components of, 151–152; disconnection and, 151–153; educators contributing to, 173–177; empathy in, 146, 157, 162, 166–168, 168; Freire and, 173, 175–176; within and without inseparable in, 152; integral self-in-mutuality in, 151, 152, 252; Noddings and, 173–174; Palmer and, 173, 176–177; peace and violence in, 151, 170–172, 252–253; pedagogy of control and, 168–169; self and other together in, 152; Starratt and, 173, 174–175
pedagogy of control, 168–169
perspective taking. *See* empathy
phenomenology, xi–xii
Piaget, Jean, 80, 82, 104n67, 180n56, 216n39
Pitts, Russell C., 17
Plato, 68n34
power. *See* money, sex, and power
Power, F. Clark, 170
practical ontology, 29n3
preadulthood: morality of, xiii, 253; spirituality of, 234–237, 236, 240, 253
The Psychology of Mature Spirituality (Young-Eisendrath and Miller, M.), 245n2, 246n14
psychotherapy, xiii, 186; body-self in, 189–190; clear boundaries found in, 191–192; dialogue and, 194; empathy in, 193–194, 215n17; ethics code of, 188; feeling self in, 190; focusing in, 208–210, 217n61; for integral self-in-mutuality, 185, 187–194, 200, 200–202, 202, 253; intimate self in, 192; morality and, 186, 187, 188, 189, 194–203, 200–202, 214n7, 216n40, 253; moral pain in, 212; organismic tradition in, 203–210; paying attention in, 199–200; responsible self in, 192–193; self of inner depth and, 191; therapeutic process of, 199–200; trauma in, 210–213, 217n65; voice in, 200–202, 202. *See also* superego

Rawls, John, 102n18
Rayner, Colin, 11

reason: disconnection of emotion and, 46–47, 71n60, 71n65, 251–252; disembodied, 52, 65–66, 72n81, 78, 93, 94–95, 95, 161–162; embodiment of, 40, 41–42, 65, 68n34; empathy and, 165–166; inner and relational, 40; justice defined by, 92, 93, 95; in preadult spirituality, emotion and, 234, 235, 236; self of inner depth and, 52, 72n81. *See also* disembodied rationality; mind-body dichotomy
rectificatory justice. *See* justice
relatedness, 231, 236
relational body, 67n8
relational fullness, 39–40, 67n22
relationality: of body-self, 38, 67n8, 67n19; of care and justice, 101; of empathy, 161; of feeling self, 42–43; mutuality and, 27–28; of peace, 124; of reason, 40. *See also* self-in-relation
religion: morality and, xiv, xv; spirituality and, 222
religious ethics, 26–27
responsible self, 62; care and justice defining, 85; cultural disconnections and, 64–66; disembodied rationality undermining, 65; in education, 156–157; integral self-in-mutuality as, 36, 62–63; in morality, 63–64; in psychotherapy, 192–193; spirituality of, 233–234, 236; subject-object dichotomy and, 66
restorative care and justice: appropriate process for, 128–129; community in, 128–129; distributive justice and, 127; integral self-in-mutuality addressed by, 127; offender or perpetrator in, 127–128, 128; peace as, 126–128; peacemaking circles in, 129; questions asked by, 127; rectificatory justice and, 126; *ubuntu* and, 126, 139n46; victim or survivor in, 127, 128
restorative justice. *See* justice
Rethinking Multicultural Education for the Next Generation (Dolby), 158
Rich, Yisrael, 153–154
rights, 33n77; in mutuality, 20, 21; needs as core notion of, 102n11
Rogers, Carl, xiii; on empathy, 43, 59, 162–163, 206; on feeling, 69n40, 205, 206, 207; in organismic tradition, 203, 205–207, 207, 208, 216n57
Roots of Empathy (Gordon), 167
Ross, Susan A., 22
Rwandan genocide, 113

Saakvitne, Karen W., 213
Sartre, Jean-Paul, 112
satya (truth), 129–130
satyagraha (truth force), 130
Saunders, Cheryl, 246n10
Schachter, Elli P., 153–154
Schaef, Anne Wilson, 57
Schaeffer, Zachary, 69n38
Schmidt, William S., 72n82
Self and Spirit in the Therapeutic Relationship (Bragan), 246n11
self-empathy, 163; care and justice with, 85, 94; of feeling self, 44–45; in morality, 49
self-in-relation, 17
self of inner depth, 48; care and justice in, 83–84; disembodied rationality contrasted with, 52, 72n81; in education, 155–156; empathy and, 49; integral self-in-mutuality as, 36, 37, 49; money, sex, power and, 52–53; in morality, 49–51, 50, 52, 55; nonviolence and, 133; psychotherapy and, 191; reason and, 52, 72n81; spirituality of, 231–232, 236. *See also* depth; heart; soul; spirit
self-other dichotomy: adult and moral self without, 101; disconnection and, 113, 251; pedagogy of connection and, 152; violence and, 113
Selman, Robert L., 44, 69n45
Sevenhuijsen, Selma, 79, 88
sex: intimacy understood as, 61–62; money, power, and, 52–53, 122
sexuality, 233
shame: autonomy vs., 116; Gilligan, J., on, 119–120; Jordan on, 120–121; violence and, 116, 117, 119–121
sharing, 24
Shea, John J., 30n14, 69n45
Sheldrake, Philip, 247n27

Sherman, Nancy, 192
socialization, 153–154
Solomon, Robert C., 78
soul, 48, 52, 71n69, 72n81, 231
spirit, 48, 52, 71n67
spirituality, xiii; as beyond, 228, 232, 236, 243, 244–245, 247n22; body-self and, 230–231; care and justice with, 148, 220, 236; of clear boundaries, 232; of compassion, 238–240, 244, 245, 249n56; connectedness of, 223, 224, 226, 230, 231–232, 236, 242, 243, 246n11, 246n13, 247n22; dehumanizing, 237–238, 249n51; development of, 220–221, 236, 246n5, 247n20; disconnection and, 234, 235, 236; education and, 148; Elkins on, 231, 233, 240, 246n6, 246n10; examples of mature, 226–228; feeling self and, 231; as human, 222–223, 223–225, 226, 228–229, 236, 237, 246n6, 246n8, 246n10, 247n22; imagination of, 225, 247n18; of inner depth, 231–232, 236; integral self-in-mutuality and, 220, 224, 228, 229–230, 235–236; integrated, 247n19; integrity in, 245n2; of intimacy, 232–233; less-than-human, 237–238; mature, 220–221, 223–228, 228–229, 229–230, 231–234, 236, 237, 238, 240, 241–245, 247n17, 247n20, 253–254; mutuality of, 224, 246n14; notion of, 221–222; as oneness, 230, 244; peace and, 220, 236; personally meaningful, 223; preadult, 234–237, 236, 240, 253; reason-emotion dichotomy and, 234, 235, 236; relatedness of, 231, 236; religious or not religious, 222; of responsibility, 233–234, 236; sexuality and, 233; subject-object dichotomy and, 234, 236; transforming power of, 225, 226, 241, 254; trauma and, 241–245; us vs. them thinking and, 234, 235, 236; violence and, xiv; vulnerability in, 241; wholeness in, 223, 225, 226, 228, 229–230, 230–231, 231, 231–232, 242, 243, 246n11, 247n27. *See also* religion; religious ethics; world religions
Spirituality (Sheldrake), 247n27
Spiritually Integrated Psychotherapy (Pargament), 247n19
Starratt, Robert J. (Jerry), xiii; foundational virtues of, 174–175; on mutuality, learning and, 174; pedagogy of connection and, 173, 174–175
Stigliano, Tony, 177n2
subject-object dichotomy, ix, 167, 216n39, 251, 254; body-self and, 42; care liberated from, 88; embodiment and, 67n18; justice and, 93, 94, 95; morality and, x–xi, 45, 51, 61, 198–199, 202; in preadult morality, 253; in preadult spirituality, 234, 236; responsible self and, 66. *See also* self-other dichotomy
superego: cultural, 51–52, 65, 65–66, 96, 149, 198; development of, 117, 119; disembodied rationality and, 65, 65–66; Freud on, 48, 195–196; law and, 96; morality of, 50, 55, 149, 198–199, 200, 200–202, 202
survivor-based worldview, 172
sympathy: as being with, 159; boundaries shared by, 160; comforting, affirming, 160; definition of, 159; empathy conflated with, 157, 158–161; empathy distinguished from, 158–161
Syria, 227

Taylor, Charles, 48
Taylor, Gabrielle, 49
teaching: of care and justice, 168–170; of empathy, 166–168, 180n58; of peace, 170–172, 183n143
Thandeka, 41
theology, 26–28
time gestalt, self as, 12, 13, 223, 246n9
Tjeltveit, Alan C., 194
To Kill a Mockingbird, 35
To Sir, with Love, 145
trauma, 137n2, 138n21; compassion and, 244; connection and, 242, 243; disconnection of, 211; empathy for, 171; integral self-in-mutuality and, 210, 212; meaning and, 242, 243; moral pain in, 212; narratives of, 171; politics of, 171; in psychotherapy, 210–213, 217n65; spirituality and, 241–245; therapist and, 211, 213; vulnerability

and, 241; wholeness and, 242–243
Trauma and Recovery (Herman), 137n2, 138n21, 242
Trauma and the Soul (Kalsched), 242–243
Triumphs of Experience (Vaillant), 218n76
Tronto, Joan, 88
trust vs. mistrust, 115
truth, 129–130
Turner, Victor, 42
Tutu, Desmond M., 139n46

ubuntu, 126, 139n46
UNICEF, 170
United Nations: *Declaration on a Culture of Peace* by, 22; *Universal Declaration of Human Rights* of, 21
unity-based worldview, 172
Universal Declaration of Human Rights (United Nations General Assembly), 21
Urban, Hugh B., 188
us-in-the-culture: education for, 149; morality as, 150
us vs. them thinking, 234, 235, 236

Vaandering, Dorothy, 168–169
Vaillant, George E., 82, 218n76
The Varieties of Religious Experience (James), 246n8
violence: care and justice lacking and, 123; cultural, 112; disconnection and, 112–113, 123, 135, 252; domestic, 112–113, 121; Erikson development stages and, 114–119, 138n20–138n21; as evil, 113–114; gender and, 112–113, 119–121, 238; Gilligan, J., on, 119–120; guilt and, 117; as human, 110–114, 135–137; inferiority and, 117–118; integral self-in-mutuality annihilated by, 111, 135; loving care and justice annihilated by, 111–112; in men, 119–120; negative identity and, 118; of oppressors, 175; personal, xiv, 112; self-other dichotomy and, 113; shame and, 116, 117, 119–121; spirituality and, xiv; structural, 112; women and, 120–121
voice, 29n5; morality as, 50, 60, 85; in psychotherapy, 200–202, 202
vulnerabilities of the self, 58, 73n100, 84
vulnerability, 241

Wadell, Paul J., 21–22
Walker, Lawrence J., 17
Walsh, Froma, 230
Watson, J. B., xiii; behaviorism of, 195, 196, 197; morality and, 195, 196–197, 197, 199
The Way of the Wound (Grant), 241
West, Cornel, 162, 164
West, Robin, 101n2
Whitfield, Charles L., 54
wholeness: of integrity, 9, 10–11, 13; of other, mutuality and, 18–19; Palmer on, 13–14; spirituality and, 223, 225, 226, 228, 229–230, 230–231, 231, 231–232, 242, 243, 246n11, 247n27; trauma and, 242–243
Winnicott, D. W., 6
wisdom, 213, 218n76
Wittgenstein, Ludwig, 231
world religions: compassion in, 238–240, 240, 244, 249n56; institutional egoism in, 240; preadult morality in, 253

Young-Eisendrath, Polly, 245n2, 246n14

Zajonc, Arthur, 176
Zehr, Howard, 127
Zembylas, Michalinos, 170–171
Zen, 232, 244

About the Author

John J. Shea has been a professor of psychology and religion, human development, pastoral counseling, and pastoral care for many years, first at Fordham University and then at Boston College. He has authored *Religious Experiencing: William James and Eugene Gendlin* (University Press of America, 1987) and *Finding God Again: Spirituality for Adults* (Rowman & Littlefield, 2005). He studied at Villanova University (BA, philosophy, 1964), Augustinian College (MA, theology, 1968), the Catholic University of America (MA, philosophy, 1970), St. Paul University (MPS, pastoral counseling, 1974), the University of Ottawa (PhD, psychology of religion, 1980), and Fordham University (MSW, clinical social work, 1998).